ADVANCED MACHINE VISION PARADIGMS FOR MEDICAL IMAGE ANALYSIS

Hybrid Computational
Intelligence for Pattern Analysis
and Understanding Series

ADVANCED MACHINE VISION PARADIGMS FOR MEDICAL IMAGE ANALYSIS

Series Editors

SIDDHARTHA BHATTACHARYYA

NILANJAN DEY

Edited by

TAPAN GANDHI

SIDDHARTHA BHATTACHARYYA

SOURAV DE

DEBANJAN KONAR

SANDIP DEY

ELSEVIER

ACADEMIC PRESS
An imprint of Elsevier

Academic Press is an imprint of Elsevier
125 London Wall, London EC2Y 5AS, United Kingdom
525 B Street, Suite 1650, San Diego, CA 92101, United States
50 Hampshire Street, 5th Floor, Cambridge, MA 02139, United States
The Boulevard, Langford Lane, Kidlington, Oxford OX5 1GB, United Kingdom

Notices
Knowledge and best practice in this field are constantly changing. As new research and experience broaden our understanding, changes in research methods, professional practices, or medical treatment may become necessary.

Practitioners and researchers must always rely on their own experience and knowledge in evaluating and using any information, methods, compounds, or experiments described herein. In using such information or methods they should be mindful of their own safety and the safety of others, including parties for whom they have a professional responsibility.

To the fullest extent of the law, neither the Publisher nor the authors, contributors, or editors, assume any liability for any injury and/or damage to persons or property as a matter of products liability, negligence or otherwise, or from any use or operation of any methods, products, instructions, or ideas contained in the material herein.

Library of Congress Cataloging-in-Publication Data
A catalog record for this book is available from the Library of Congress

British Library Cataloguing-in-Publication Data
A catalogue record for this book is available from the British Library

ISBN: 978-0-12-819295-5

For information on all Academic Press publications visit our website at https://www.elsevier.com/books-and-journals

Publisher: Mara Conner
Editorial Project Manager: Gabriela Capille
Production Project Manager: Sruthi Satheesh
Cover Designer: Victoria Pearson

Typeset by TNQ Technologies

Working together
to grow libraries in
developing countries

www.elsevier.com • www.bookaid.org

Dedication

Tapan Gandhi would like to dedicate this book with love and affection to his parents, teachers, and the Almighty God.

Siddhartha Bhattacharyya would like to dedicate this book to His Eminence Saint Kuriakose Elias Chavara; founder of CMI congregation; a great educationist and a social reformer of the 19th century.

Sourav De would like to dedicate this book to his respected parents Satya Narayan De and Tapasi De, loving wife Debolina Ghosh, beloved son Aishik De, sister Soumi De, grandfather Late Habal Chandra De, grand-mother Late Kamala Bala De, maternal grandfather Sahadeb Mallick, and maternal grandmother Late Debjani Mallick.

Debanjan Konar would like to dedicate this book to his grandparents Late Narayan Konar, Late Katyayani Konar, his parents Mr. Debidas Konar and Mrs. Smritikana Konar who have encouraged him all the way, and his beloved daughter Sanvi.

Sandip Dey would like to dedicate this book to the loving memory of his father, Late Dhananjoy Dey, his dearly loved mother Smt. Gita Dey, his wife Swagata Dey Sarkar, his children Sunishka and Shriaan, his siblings Kakali, Tanusree, Sanjoy, and his nephews Shreyash and Adrishaan.

Contents

Contributors

J. Anitha
Department of Computer Science and Engineering, Karunya Institute of Technology and Sciences, Coimbatore, Tamilnadu, India

Maíra Araújo de Santana
Department of Biomedical Engineering, Universidade Federal de Pernambuco, Recife, Pernambuco, Brazil

Washington Wagner Azevedo da Silva
Department of Biomedical Engineering, Universidade Federal de Pernambuco, Recife, Pernambuco, Brazil

Siddhartha Bhattacharyya
Christ University, Department of Computer Science and Engineering, Bangalore, Karnataka, India

R. Bhavani
Department of CSE, Annamalai University, Chidambaram, Tamilnadu, India

P. Malin Bruntha
Department of ECE, Karunya Institute of Technology and Sciences, Coimbatore, Tamil Nadu, India

Fernando Cervantes-Sanchez
Centro de Investigación en Matemáticas (CIMAT), Guanajuato, Gto, Mexico

Santanu Chaudhury
Department of Electrical Engineering, Indian Institute of Technology, Delhi, New Delhi, India

Ivan Cruz-Aceves
CONACYT − Centro de Investigación en Matemáticas (CIMAT), Guanajuato, Gto, Mexico

Sourav De
Cooch Behar Government Engineering College, Department of Computer Science and Engineering, Cooch Behar, West Bengal, India

Omer Deperlioglu
Department of Computer Programming, Afyon Kocatepe University, Afyonkarahisar, Merkez, Turkey

Sandip Dey
Sukanta Mahavidyalaya, Department of Computer Science, Dhupguri, Jalpaiguri, West Bengal, India

Tapan Kumar Gandhi
Department of Electrical Engineering, Indian Institute of Technology, Delhi, New Delhi, India

E. Grace Mary Kanaga
Department of Computer Science and Engineering, Karunya Institute of Technology and Sciences, Coimbatore, Tamilnadu, India

Abel Guilhermino da Silva Filho
Informatics Center, Universidade Federal de Pernambuco, Recife, Pernambuco, Brazil

Arturo Hernandez-Aguirre
Centro de Investigación en Matemáticas (CIMAT), Guanajuato, Gto, Mexico

Martha A. Hernández-González
Unidad de Investigación, UMAE 1 Bajio, IMSS, León, Gto, Mexico

Dibya Jyoti Bora
SCS, The Assam Kaziranga University, Jorhat, Assam, India

D. Kavitha
Assistant Professor, MVJ College of Engineering, Bangaluru, Karnataka, India

Debanjan Konar
Sikkim Manipal Institute of Technology, Department of Computer Science and Engineering, Sikkim Manipal University, Majitar, Sikkim, India

Utku Kose
Department of Computer Engineering, Suleyman Demirel University, Isparta, Merkez, Turkey

Sidney Marlon Lopes de Lima
Department of Electronic and Systems, Universidade Federal de Pernambuco, Recife, Pernambuco, Brazil

Shipra Madan
Department of Electrical Engineering, Indian Institute of Technology, Delhi, New Delhi, India

Shanmugakumar Murugesan
Senior Assistant Professor, Department of Electronics and Communication Engineering, Madanapalle Institute of Technology and Science, Chittor, Andhra Pradesh, India

Wellington Pinheiro dos Santos
Department of Biomedical Engineering, Universidade Federal de Pernambuco, Recife, Pernambuco, Brazil

V. Pooja
Easwari Engineering College, Chennai, India

Sneham Priya
Easwari Engineering College, Chennai, India

R. Priya
Department of CSE, Annamalai University, Chidambaram, Tamilnadu, India

R. Priyatharshini
Easwari Engineering College, Chennai, India

B. Rajalingam
Department of CSE, Priyadarshini College of Engineering & Technology, Nellore, Andhra Pradesh, India

M. Renith Sam
Department of ECE, Karunya Institute of Technology and Sciences, Coimbatore, Tamil Nadu, India

K. Martin Sagayam
Department of ECE, Karunya Institute of Technology and Sciences, Coimbatore, Tamil Nadu, India

V. Sakthivel
Associate Professor, Ramaiah Institute of Technology, Bangaluru, Karnataka, India

Rudraraju Shruthi
Easwari Engineering College, Chennai, India

Sergio Solorio-Meza
Unidad de Investigación, UMAE 1 Bajio, IMSS, León, Gto, Mexico

S. Sridevi
Assistant Professor, Department of Electronics and Communication Engineering, Veltech Rangarajan Dr. Sagunthala R & D Institute of Science and Technology, Chennai, Tamilnadu, India

M. Sridevi
Department of Computer Science and Engineering, National Institute of Technology, Trichy, Tamil Nadu, India

D. Sujitha Juliet
Department of Computer Science and Engineering, Karunya Institute of Technology and Sciences, Coimbatore, Tamilnadu, India

R. Sai Swarna
Easwari Engineering College, Chennai, India

Preface

Computer vision and machine intelligence (known as machine vision) paradigms are always promoted in the domain of medical image applications including computer-assisted diagnosis, image-guided radiation therapy, landmark detection, imaging genomics, and brain connectomics. The complex real-life problems prevalent in medical image analysis and understanding are daunting tasks owing to the massive influx of multimodal medical image data during routine clinal practice. In the field of medical science and technology, the objective of such advanced computational paradigms is to provide robust and cost-effective solutions for the emerging problems faced by humanity. Medical image analysis includes the fields of medical image enhancement, segmentation, classification, and object detection. Advanced computer vision and machine intelligence approaches have been employed in the field of image processing and computer vision. However, because of unstructured medical image data, and considering the volume of data produced during routine clinical processes, the applicability of these metaheuristic algorithms remains to be investigated.

This publication presents major emerging trends in technology that support current advances in medical image analysis with the help of computational intelligence. It also aims to highlight advances in conventional approaches to the field of medical image processing. The scope of this publication involves proposing novel techniques and reviewing the state of the art in the area of machine learning, computer vision, soft computing techniques, and so on, and relates them to their applications in medical image analysis. The motivation of this publication is to put forward new ideas in technology innovation and also to analyze their effect in the current context of medical image analysis.

The book is organized into eleven well-integrated chapters on different aspects of medical image analysis.

Chapter 1 identifies existing challenges in the management of information security in the 21st century. The chapter sets the scene for discussions presented by various authors. In particular, the chapter identifies the global orientation of businesses and related problems with managing information security. It also identifies the importance of establishing security policies, structures of responsibility, and disaster recovery plans.

A sizable proportion of infant mortality exists due to congenital heart disease (CHD). Fetal heart asymmetry is the potential sonographic marker in clinical ultrasound (US) CHD diagnosis. Chapter 2 presents a computer-aided decision support system (CADSS) to diagnose prenatal CHD from two-dimensional (2D) US fetal heart images by the synergism of three functional modules of fuzzy inference rule-based image despeckling with adaptive maximum likelihood estimation, followed by several morpho-logical operations, to quantify and extract the pathological features, and finally, an adaptive neuro–fuzzy inference system classifier, which classifies the fetal heart as either normal or abnormal with CHDs associated with an asymmetric heart appearance, such as hypoplastic left heart syndrome, hypoplastic right heart syndrome, or tetralogy of Fallot CHD. Because this proposed CADSS is the pioneering system for diagnosing prenatal CHDs, performance analysis was carried out by comparing the results of each module of CADSS with state-of-the-art techniques.

According to the World Health Organization, breast cancer is one of the deadliest types of cancer, affecting adult women around the world. Early diagnosis can contribute to reducing mortality rates and increasing treatment options. In Chapter 3, the authors propose morphological extreme learning machines (mELMs), in which neurons of hidden layers employ kernels based on morphological erosions and dilations. The authors validated their method using 2796 mammographies from the Image Re-covery in Medical Applications database. mELMs of erosion and dilation may present equivalent or even superior classification performance compared with classic and cutting-edge classifiers.

Four-dimensional medical imaging symbolizes the next step in imaging. This advanced imaging method makes image analysis much faster and more accurate than before. Four-dimensional medical imaging is a technique that combines 3D images with time such that movement and variation can be observed and analyzed more accurately. Four-dimensional medical imaging includes time-resolved volumetric computed tomography (CT), magnetic resonance imaging (MRI), positron emission tomography, and single-photon emission CT and US imaging. Chapter 4 offers current improve-ments in 4D medical imaging and diagnosis.

Feature-based fusion of multimodality images can be used to diagnosis symptomatic patients affected with tumors and abnormal characteristics (structural issues) of the brain. The advantage is that a fused image displays more information than the source images. Chapter 5 presents the proce-dural steps for different hybrid fusion algorithms for dealing with patients with neurocysticercosis, neoplastic, Alzheimer's, and astrocytoma diseases. The performance of the proposed system on several datasets for different diseases is also tested and compared with other algorithms, and the results prove that the proposed technique is a promising technique in clinical disease analysis.

Designing automatic binary descriptors for vessel enhancement using morphological operators is a computationally intensive problem. Consequently, this problem has been mainly addressed by an empirical process and the high-dimensional search space has not been properly explored. In Chapter 6, the design of automatic binary descriptors is addressed by comparing three different metaheuristics for the coronary artery segmentation problem in x-ray angiograms. The main advantage of such a design is that the search space is explored properly, avoiding empirical process or a priori knowledge by an expert to design deterministic descriptors.

The most prominent research area in the field of the advanced machine vision paradigm for medical imaging applications is in content-based image retrieval. With the help of emerging medical imaging systems, a patient's medical background can easily be obtained in the form of digitized data such as x-rays, MRI, CT, US, nuclear imaging, and so forth. In the past, radiologists manually analyzed patients' health conditions. Now, the medical imaging process provides better information and a depiction of different cases. However, conventional techniques have created some controversy in the literature regarding an insufficient feature set, high semantic gap, and computational time complexity. Chapter 7 uses a gray-level co-occurrence matrix, local binary pattern, color co-occurrence matrix, and support vector machine on MRI data for content retrieval.

Parkinson's disease (PD) is the second most common age-related neurological disorder after Alzheimer's disease. Diagnosis is usually based on a voice dataset or spiral drawings. The proposed framework is composed of a multimodular arrangement consolidating the static and dynamic spiral test and voice datasets for the early discovery of Parkinson's disease. Notwithstanding vocal informational indexes, spiral test illustrations from the University of California Irvine Artificial Intelligence archive are used to develop the proposed framework. Individuals experience different side effects at the furthest point of PD. Thus, the authors propose a multimodal approach in Chapter 8 that improves the reliability of characteristics of PD-tolerant people. A voice and spiral imaging dataset is trained with standard classifier models. Finally, an ensemble-based method is used for disease classification.

Hard-based techniques as applied for the contrast improvement of MRI images or hematoxylin—eosin stain images are unsatisfactory due to the high level of fuzziness involved in medical images. Traditional techniques are unable to deal with this level of fuzziness. Therefore, an advanced fuzzy logic—based technique is introduced in Chapter 9 to improve the contrast of different medical images such as HE stain and MRI. Also, because noise has a bad effect on the overall quality of medical images, before attempting to improve contrast in the proposed approach, noise removal using an improved median filter is first implemented. This has a good impact on the final result of the enhancement process. The experimental analysis shows the efficiency of the proposed technique.

Bone age is an effective indicator for diagnosing various diseases and determining the time of treatment. These radiological procedures are performed routinely by pediatricians and endocrinologists to investigate developmental abnormalities, genetic disorders, and metabolic complications. However, one of the biggest challenges in radiodiagnosis is estimating bone age because it is time-consuming and requires domain expertise. In Chapter 10, the authors propose a metric learning technique for a small sized dataset. The model performs efficient multiclass classification to predict bone age by learning latent representation of images using an end-to-end structure. The authors offer compelling evidence that the use of metric learning can yield state-of-the-art classification accuracy and reduce training data requirements to just a tenth of those employed by current approaches. The proposed model holds promise for assisting radiologists in estimating bone age with speed and accuracy.

Chapter 11 presents concluding remarks and highlights the achievements of the book.

This book aims to benefit researchers and several categories of students for some part of their curriculum. The editors hope that the academic and scientific communities will benefit from this novel venture.

January, 2020

New Delhi, India   Tapan K. Gandhi
Bangalore, India   Siddhartha Bhattacharyya
Cooch Behar, India   Sourav De
Sikkim, India   Debanjan Konar
Jalpaiguri, India   Sandip Dey

CHAPTER 1

An introductory illustration of medical image analysis

Sandip Dey[1], Debanjan Konar[2], Sourav De[3], Siddhartha Bhattacharyya[4]

[1]Sukanta Mahavidyalaya, Department of Computer Science, Dhupguri, Jalpaiguri, West Bengal, India; [2]Sikkim Manipal Institute of Technology, Department of Computer Science and Engineering, Sikkim Manipal University, Majitar, Sikkim, India; [3]Cooch Behar Government Engineering College, Department of Computer Science and Engineering, Cooch Behar, West Bengal, India; [4]Christ University, Department of Computer Science and Engineering, Bangalore, Karnataka, India

Contents

1. Introduction

Computer vision and machine intelligence (known as machine vision) paradigms are always promoted in the domain of medical image applications, including computer-assisted diagnosis, image-guided radiation therapy, landmark detection, imaging genomics, and brain connectomics. The complex real-life problems prevalent in medical image analysis and its understanding are daunting tasks owing to the massive influx of multimodal medical image data during routine clinical practice. In the field of medical science and technology, the objective of such advanced computational paradigms is to provide robust and cost-effective solutions for the emerging problems faced by humanity. Medical image analysis includes the fields of medical image enhancement, segmentation, classification, and object detection, to name a few. Advanced computer vision and machine intelligence approaches have been employed in the field of image processing and computer vision. However, because of unstructured medical image data, and considering the volume of data produced during routine clinical

Advanced Machine Vision Paradigms for Medical Image Analysis
ISBN 978-0-12-819295-5
https://doi.org/10.1016/B978-0-12-819295-5.00001-9

processes, the applicability of the metaheuristic algorithms remains to be investigated. Classical computer vision and machine learning techniques often fall short in offering a strong solution in the field of medical image analysis. To overcome this problem, different components of the computer vision and machine intelligence paradigms are conjoined; the resultant hybrid machine intelligence techniques are more efficient and robust by design and performance. At the same time, some technologies in the field of soft computing have evolved, such as rough sets, fuzzy sets, and evolutionary computing. These advanced computer vision and machine intelligence techniques are efficient enough to handle different aspects of medical image processing. This book aims to provide an in-depth analysis of advanced computer vision and machine intelligence techniques using contemporary algorithms in the field of medical image processing and analysis. The exploration of shape, contour, texture and prior contextual information prevalent in medical image slices is the key in the field of computer vision research. It also exploits the volumetric information of medical image sequences by processing voxels (three-dimensional [3D] and 4D information) for accurate and efficient segmentation. There are plethora of machine learning and computer vision paradigms (image reconstruction, image classification, image segmentation, tracking, etc.) that enable experts to analyze disease better using the required relevant information of medical images with minimal human intervention.

2. Medical image analysis: issues and challenges

Medical image analysis has a significant role in human society. Medical analysis generally analyzes various medical problems and rectifies them by considering several imaging modalities. Apart from this, various digital image analysis methods are used on several occasions to achieve a good outcome from these analyses. Medical imaging systems may generate a gigantic amount of images with a huge quantity of information. However, the information is essentially concealed in the data. To deal with this situation, image analyses techniques are required to extract the information, which needs to be easily available for make correct medical decisions. Medical image analysis has been exceedingly well-studied. As a consequence, researchers have successfully developed several algorithms and approaches to address medical image issues. The success of image analysis has also been commercially employed on several occasions with regard to accuracy, trustworthiness, and speed [1,2].

There is growing exigency to standardize the reciprocity of medical image data because of the needs of education, practice, and research. The necessity of shared access of medical image databases has become of the utmost urgency for proper use by multiple agents. Specialists using incompatible computer platforms and possessing incompatible software systems thus may interact with one another to exchange views and share colossal reference digital image data sets. Rapid technological advancements can be found in the field of medical imaging technology.

In addition, several novel clinical applications have been introduced by a pool of scientists. These facts encouraged a number of researchers to participate actively in the field of research in medical image analysis. Several factors have a direct influence on medical image analysis, including changes in clinical demands, improvements in the quality of images, the introduction of new and advanced versions of computer hardware, and so on. Current medical images are usually multidimensional. Their range may vary widely from 2D to nD (n-dimensional). This, in turn, produces various imaging modalities, especially in the hospital, and creates a high and demand for software for human—computer interconnection and visualization. Hence, automation of the analysis of medical images is extremely essential for accurate diagnosis. This automation should deal with several challenging research problems efficiently.

Medical image segmentation is an important and significant term in medical image analysis. It can be defined as the process of detecting boundaries within an image (2D or 3D). Several automatic or semi-automatic approaches can be applied for this purpose. Different variants in medical images may exist that create difficulty in image segmentation. For example, the human anatomy possesses extensive modes of variation. In addition, a large number of different modalities, such as x-ray, magnetic resonance imaging, endoscopy, and microscopy, are used to form medical images. Results obtained from medical image segmentation can be used further for detailed diagnostics.

Validation is a vital issue with regard to medical image analysis [3]. Traditionally, validation is done by researchers in line with the merit of assessment. People associated with this task typically analyze and interpret a lot of data. Validation typically designates the accuracy of a specific technique, which can be obtained with a certain segmentation method. It may be difficult to judge accuracy in few cases for obvious reason, especially when the results need to be firmly controlled by user interactions or specific choices with regard to several parameters of an automatic method.

Validation is basically done for automatic segmentation. If the results from segmentation rely on a user-selected threshold, such as a gradient threshold, validation is performed to assess the sensitivity of the parameter [3].

Image registration is another appealing feature in which various sets of data are transformed into a single coordinate system. In this process, data may be presented in different formats collected from multiple sources, such as multiple photographs. Also, data can be taken from different viewpoints, depths, sensors, and so on [4]. They can be used for various purposes such as medical imaging and computer vision [5]. They can also be used to compile and analyze satellite data and their corresponding images. Registration is an important process capable of comparing or integrating data acquired from dissimilar measurements. In medical imaging, this process enables data to be integrated from different modalities such as computed tomography (CT), mitral regurgitation or single-photon emission CT (SPECT) to acquire complete information with relevance to the patient. It can be very effective for medical practitioner to use to monitor tumor growth, facilitate treatment verification, and improve interventions, for example [6].

Image understanding (IU) is another appealing characteristic in medical imaging, in which actual interpretation of relevant regions and objects is figured out to signify what literally happens in the image. This process may encompass figuring out objects with a spatial relationship to one another, and so forth. Computer vision is used with IU as a single unit. IU may include eventually making few relevant decisions for further action, as well. Several artificial intelligence methods can also be used with this process. These hybrid kinds of techniques will help to explain images by identifying, characterizing, and acknowledging objects and other related properties in the scene. IU is a popular and widely accepted research area with regard to the design and extensive experimentation of different computer systems [7].

A large number of applications need visualization and analysis of 3D objects in medical imaging. Visualization can be defined as the process of exploring, transforming, and viewing data as images to acquire a detailed and deep understanding. Visualization can effectually be used to characterize the quality of medical images, especially for biological images. The best results can be obtained by acquiring fast and accessible simulation steps of visualization of 3D objects. On different occasions, visualization has become a crucial part of the simulation process, considered for possible future development.

Over the past few decades, there have been intense technological advancements in the field of medical image analysis. At the same time, several challenges have become known from an industrial viewpoint. Hence, this has encouraged many researchers to develop a number of image analysis methods in line with different commercial problems. Thus, new sorts of challenges have come to light. First, there is the need for more generic image analysis methods that can be adapted to performing a particular clinical task. Furthermore, methodical approaches to deal with ground truth generation are required that can efficiently handle increasing demands with regard to machine learning and validation. Versatile image analysis techniques empowering efficient growth are the foremost challenge. Moreover, image data in heterogeneous form sometimes become crucial for analysis. Hence, efficient algorithms that can handle heterogeneous image data need to be developed. Finally, in certain situations, organ and anatomical models can have a significant role in several applications. In addition, patient-specific models dealing with image data with almost no interaction from users can be effective. Hence, appropriate algorithms needed to be developed to serve this purpose [2]. In line with the ongoing demand, these challenges are vital. Therefore, more efficient and dedicated algorithms in terms of correctness, reliability, and operational time are needed to be introduced.

3. Summary of all contributory chapters (challenges and findings)

Congenital heart defects (CHDs) [8] are one of the most significant intrinsic problems in babies. In the clinical ultrasound (US) CHD diagnosis, fetal heart asymmetry is the potential sonographic marker. The ordinary fetal heart is described as having a symmetric appearance through anomalous fetal hearts with hypoplastic left heart syndrome (HLHS) [9], hypoplastic right heart syndrome (HRHS) [10] and tetralogy of Fallot (TOF) [11]. CHDs are portrayed with anti-symmetric or asymmetric appearance. In Chapter 2, a computer-aided decision support system is applied to diagnose prenatal CHD from 2D US fetal heart images. It is performed with three functional modules of fuzzy inference rule-based adaptive maximum likelihood estimation. Several morphological operations are applied on previously obtained processed images to evaluate and extricate the pathological features. In the final step, an adaptive neuro-fuzzy inference system classifier is employed to distinguish the fetal heart from the normal or abnormal fetal heart with CHDs according to asymmetric heart appearances such as HLHS, HRHS, or TOF CHD.

As indicated by the World Health Organization, breast cancer is perhaps the deadliest type of disease in adult women around the globe. Early determination can decrease death rates and expand treatment choices. In recent years, different types of computer-aided diagnosis have evolved to detect cancer cells. Mathematical morphology, a set of techniques for the nonlinear processing of digital images, is a well-known technique in this area. In Chapter 3, extreme learning machines (ELMs) [12] are emphasized. ELMs are consist of at least one hidden layer with random-weight neurons and an output layer made of nodes with linear kernels. The Moore–Penrose pseudoinverse is employed to determine the weights of the output. This network is efficient for handling complex classification problems by means of decision boundaries of greater complexity. To execute this, researchers use different kernels in the neurons of the hidden layers. The authors present a modified version of ELM, morphological ELMs. In this approach, the neurons of the hidden layers use kernel-based morphological erosions and dilations. The method is applied to 2796 mammography images from the Image Recovery in Medical Applications database.

The next generation in imaging technology, 4D medical imaging, will make image analysis much faster and more exact than at any other time in memory. 4D medical imaging is a system that joins 3D images with time so that the development and variety can be watched and broke down in a progressively precise manner. The different types of medical imaging techniques are time-resolved volumetric CT, magnetic resonance imaging (MRI), positron emission tomography, and SPECT and US imaging [13,14]. The motion artifact of 3D medical imaging, which evolved for voluntary or involuntary patient motion such as digestive, cardiac, respiratory, and muscular motion, can be taken care of proficiently by 4D image analysis. In Chapter 4, the authors tried to determine the proper use of 4D imaging to achieve a proper diagnosis so that doctors and specialists will be empowered to determine the best treatment for patients by limiting dangers and boosting precision and security.

Neurocysticercosis, the contamination brought about by the larval type of the tapeworm *Taenia solium* is the most widely recognized parasitic disease of the central nervous system and the most well-known reason for acquired epilepsy in the world [15,16]. A neoplasm is an unusual development of tissue, called neoplasia. The development of a neoplasm is clumsy compared with that of the typical encompassing tissue, and it develops unusually, regardless of whether the first trigger is evacuated. This unusual development for the most part creates a mass known as a tumor.

Alzheimer's disease is an irreversible, dynamic brain disorder that gradually annihilates memory and thinking aptitudes, and, in the end, the capacity to complete the easiest assignments. Astrocytomas are the most widely recognized sort of primary brain tumor inside the gathering of mind tumors called gliomas. The word "primary" signifies that they have started from the brain instead of spreading from somewhere else. Symptomatic patients who are influenced by tumors and anomalous qualities (auxiliary issues) of the brain can be treated using the feature-based fusion of multimodality images. In Chapter 5, different hybrid fusion algorithms are described with their procedural steps. The methods are tested on different types of data sets of patients infected with neurocysticercosis, neoplastic, Alzheimer's and astrocytoma diseases.

The empirical process and the high-dimensional search space can be applied to handle the problem of automatic binary descriptors design for vessel enhancement using morphological operators that have O(2n) computational complexity. In Chapter 6, automatic binary descriptors are presented and compared with three different metaheuristics for the coronary artery segmentation problem in x-ray angiograms. This method is advantageous because the search space can be examined thoroughly without the help of an expert to design deterministic descriptors. Chapter 7 deals with the advanced machine vision paradigm for medical imaging applications by content-based image retrieval (CBIR). In the earlier days, a patient's health condition was examined and analyzed by radiologists, but nowadays medical imaging processes such as x-rays, MRI, CT, US, and nuclear imaging not only can provide an analysis but also give better information and a depiction of different cases. Common methods applied for content retrieval are gray-level co-occurrence matrix, local binary pattern, color co-occurrence matrix, and support vector machine. A semantic image retrieval-based CBIR is proposed in this chapter by combining 3D features.

The detection of Parkinson's disease (PD) is not easy because it is the second most common neurological disorder. A nervous system specialist considers the patient's therapeutic history, an review of signs and manifestations, and a neurological and physical examination for detection. In Chapter 8, a framework consisting of multimodular arrangement consolidating the static and dynamic spiral test, and voice data sets for the early discovery of PD is presented. The vocal informational indexes and spiral test illustrations from the University of California–Irvine Artificial Intelligence archive are also considered in that framework.

In the field of automatic medical diagnosis processes, medical images such as MRI and hematoxylin—eosin (HE) stain accelerate the diagnosis process by improving the accuracy over the manual process. For medical image analysis, a precise result cannot be obtained because the contrast of medical images is low. Traditional contrast enhancement techniques do not contribute satisfactory results because of the high level of fuzziness in the test image. In Chapter 9, an advanced fuzzy logic—based technique is presented to improve the contrast of different types of medical images such as HE stain and MRI. The proposed methods also handle noise removal efficiently.

4. Discussion and conclusion with future trends

This chapter is intended to examine several facets of medical image analysis. The authors attempted to throw light on current issues and probable challenges in this field. Several related works in connection with medical image analysis are briefly presented throughout the chapter. Furthermore, the contributory chapters are analyzed separately to find the challenges and findings of each. Finally, the chapter comes to a conclusion that is aligned with the theme of the topic. To cope with increasing needs in the field of medical imaging, a lot of researchers have engaged in introducing several algorithms in this direction.

References

[1] J. Duncan, Medical image analysis: progress over two decades and the challenges ahead, IEFE Transactions on Pattern Analysis and Machine Intelligence 22 (1) (2000) 85—106.
[2] T. McInerney, D. Terzopoulos, Deformable models in medical in qc analysis: a survey, Medical Image Analysis 1 (2) (1996) 91—108.
[3] J.P.W. Pluim, S.E.A. Muenzing, K.A.J. Eppenhof, K. Murphy, The truth is hard to make: validation of medical image registration, cancun, Mexico, in: Proceedings of 23rd International Conference on Pattern Recognition, ICPR), 2016.
[4] L.G. Brown, A survey of image registration techniques, ACM Computing Surveys archive 24 (4) (1992) 325—376.
[5] A.A. Goshtasby, 2-D and 3-D Image Registration: For Medical, Remote Sensing, and Industrial Applications, Wiley Press, 2005.
[6] P. Besl, N.D. McKay, A method for registration of 3-d shapes, IEFE Transactions on Pattern Analysis and Machine Intelligence 14 (2) (1992) 239—256.
[7] S.C. Shapiro, Encyclopedia of Artificial Intelligence, John Wiley & Sons, New York, NY, United States, 1992.
[8] J. Hoffman, S. Kaplan, The incidence of congenital heart disease, Journal of the American College of Cardiology 39 (12) (2002) 1890—1900.
[9] D. Barron, M. Kilby, B. Davies, J. Wright, T. Jones, W. Brawn, Hypoplastic left heart syndrome, The Lancet 374 (9689) (2009) 551—564.

[10] A. Macedo, M. Ferreira, A. Borges, A. Sampaio, F. Ferraz, F. Sampayo, Fetal echo-cardiography. the results of a 3-year study, Acta Medica Portuguesa 6 (1993) 9—13.

[11] R. Kapoor, S. Gupta, Prevalence of congenital heart disease, kanpur, India, Indian Pediatrics 45 (4) (2008) 309.

[12] G. Huang, H. Zhou, X. Ding, R. Zhang, Extreme learning machine for regression and multiclass classification, IEEE Transactions on Systems, Man, and Cybernetics, Part B (Cybernetics) 42 (2) (2012) 513—529.

[13] P.X. Shajan, N.J.R. Muniraj, J.T. Abraham, 3d/4d image registration and fusion techniques: a survey, International Journal of Computer Science and Information Technologies 3 (4) (2012) 4829—4839.

[14] G. Li, D. Citrin, K. Camphausen, B. Mueller, C. Burman, B. Mychalczak, et al., Advances in 4d medical imaging and 4d radiation therapy, technol cancer res treat, International Journal of Computer Science and Information Technologies 7 (1) (2008) 67—81.

[15] A.D.M. Bryceson, Neurocysticercosis, A clinical handbook. Brain 122 (2) (1999) 372—373.

[16] O.H.D. Brutto, Neurocysticercosis, Eminars in Neurology 25 (3) (2005) 243—251.

CHAPTER 2

Computer-aided decision support system for symmetry-based prenatal congenital heart defects

S. Sridevi[1], Shanmugakumar Murugesan[2], V. Sakthivel[3], D. Kavitha[4]

[1]Assistant Professor, Department of Electronics and Communication Engineering, Veltech Rangarajan Dr. Sagunthala R & D Institute of Science and Technology, Chennai, Tamilnadu, India; [2]Senior Assistant Professor, Department of Electronics and Communication Engineering, Madanapalle Institute of Technology and Science, Chittor, Andhra Pradesh, India; [3]Associate Professor, Ramaiah Institute of Technology, Bangaluru, Karnataka, India; [4]Assistant Professor, MVJ College of Engineering, Bangaluru, Karnataka, India

Contents

1. Introduction

Congenital heart defects (CHDs) are one of the most important congenital malformations in a fetus. Around 33%—50% of CHDs are the basic cause of life-threatening problems among neonates [1] and hence sonographologists provide more emphasis on prenatal CHD screening. Among various types of asymmetric heart appearance—oriented CHDs, hypoplastic left heart syndrome (HLHS) is a rare and critical CHD, with an apparent underdeveloped left heart chamber of the fetus [2]. This defect can be prenatally diagnosed from 18 to 22 weeks of gestational age [3]. According to

Advanced Machine Vision Paradigms for Medical Image Analysis
ISBN 978-0-12-819295-5
https://doi.org/10.1016/B978-0-12-819295-5.00002-0

a three-year study reported by Macedo et al. [4], the prevalence of HLHS was around 13.5% among a group of 875 growing fetus clinical details. In addition, the presence of hypoplastic right heart syndrome (HRHS) is very critical and is responsible for around 25% of infant mortality. Moreover the occurrence of tetralogy of fallot (TOF) is around 3%–10% among all CHDs [5]. Hence it is obvious that earlier diagnosis of prenatal CHD can help save the life of newborn neonates. In India, sonographologists use sonography, 2D echocardiography, and color Doppler as standard modalities to diagnose CHD [5]. Ultrasonography modality is used in obstetrics owing to the harmless nature of ultrasound radiation [6]. High accuracy in extraction of major cardiac anomalies associated with prenatal CHD from 2D ultrasound (US) images demands sonographologists with a high skill set and expertise [7].

Fetal ultrasonography is the potential clinical modality where highly developed image processing can better enhance the rate of earlier disease diagnosis and detection of congenital defects. Many research works ponder development of a computational algorithm to automate the US clinical disease diagnosis. The inherent speckle noise distribution of the US image obscures the clinical diagnosis. Due to its irregular boundary information, it becomes difficult to localize various biological structures of the fetus. In this context, the first step is to appropriately choose the preprocessing procedure with effective speckle reduction and edge preservation of anatomical structures. This paved the way for the researchers to develop many scientific approaches for preprocessing the US images. Literature investigates a plethora of despeckling algorithms both in spatial and frequency domain. Among statistical filters, empirical- and modeling-based approaches are quite familiar. Initially, Lee modeled a statistical feature-based equivalent number of looks to envisage the smoothing process in the image region [8]. Though the Lee filter aims at despeckling the image, it does not provide adaptability for the process. Then Frost et al. [9] used an exponential-shaped kernel for the modeling of statistical adaptive weighted mean filter to achieve a trade-off between mean filtering and all pass filtering. This method concentrates more on removing the speckle noise only in the smooth region but not in the edge region. The Bayesian nonlocal mean (BNLM) filter [10] proposed by Coupe et al. imparts optimized filtering by using an adaptive distance measure of the Bayesian approach to suppress speckle noise and to preserve edge features. Many despeckling filters were contrived based on statistical modeling of the speckle pattern. The inherent speckle noises present in US images are better modeled with the Nakagami-Rayleigh joint probability density function. Probabilistic patch-based weighted maximum likelihood estimation (PPBMLE) proposed by Charles et al. [11] was contrived based on modeling the speckle pattern with the Nakagami-Rayleigh probability function and hence it removes the speckle noise and mean while preserving the edges. The only demerit upon the BNLM filter and PPBMLE filter is that they consume a lot of time to perform the denoising process.

The second step in computer-aided decision support system (CADSS) is morphological processing, which facilitates extraction of desired diagnostic features. This morphological analysis helps in accurate measurements even for less experienced sonographologists, thereby ensuring the reduction in variability of intra- and interobserver diagnosis [12]. In literature, very little automated segmentation and morphological analysis has been reported for clinical practice of fetal US image analysis. Among them, AutoOB [13] was the only commercial fetal biometry system. Semiautomatic quantitative analysis of segmented fetal brain fossa structures was developed by Claude et al. [14]. Followed by Claude, Ciurte et al. [15] proposed a semiautomated segmentation approach to enable fetal biometry measurements of the abdominal circumference. Then Rueda et al. [16] presented an automated segmentation schema to aid various fetal morphometric measurements of a growing fetus with various gestational ages. They faced a problem of varying image quality and the appearance of fetal position that in turn complicated the diagnosis.

Though the researchers developed various morphodiagnostic analyses for fetus anatomical examination, presently viability of such work is much less, particularly for fetal heart examination. Instead literature greatly supports various other image processing algorithms like image denoising, segmentation, and classification schemes implemented for US fetal heart disease diagnosis. For instance, Dindoyal et al. [17] made use of an improved level set segmentation approach to quantify the blood volumes from the fetal heart chambers. Sriraam et al. [18] proposed an automated scheme for scanning the fetal heart chambers from 2D US sequences. They also proposed a computer-aided automated procedure based on fetal heart biometry to automatically extract the fetal heart chambers in another study. The main problem was that it does not help in earlier disease diagnosis. Eso [19] presented a system to diagnose HLHS CHD from 4D fetal US heart images.

The rest of this chapter is organized in the following order: Section 2 explains the design of the database and collection of clinical data set used to conduct this experimental study. Moreover it describes in detail the clinical context of CHD disease diagnosis and methodology involved in the design of proposed CADSS. Sections 3 and 4 discuss in detail the obtained results and conclusion.

2. Clinical dataset, clinical perspectives of CHD screening and methodology

This section describes in detail the dataset collection, clinical context, and perspectives of screening CHD from US images and methodology involved in contriving the proposed CADSS. In order to clearly describe the methodology adopted to implement the proposed CADSS system for prenatal CHDs, it is essential to know the fundamental clinical perspectives involved in the diagnosis of prenatal CHDs.

2.1 Dataset collection and database development

Owing to the availability of many standard databases with a wide range of a clinical dataset with ground truth, plenty of research innovations and generalizations have been extensively increased substantially in the area of medical image processing over the past years, and this has been made possible. Those databases were the main source of knowledge base to support the researchers. In fact, there are no standard databases available for 2D US fetal heart images to validate the algorithms involved in automated analysis of prenatal screening of CHD. Hence, a database has been constructed with a dataset comprising 513 numbers of 2D US fetal heart images that were collected over a period of 4 years (2012–15) from few private scan centers and government hospitals in Tamilnadu. Those images were collected from the pregnant mothers with growing fetus of varying gestational ages ranging from 0 to 30 weeks of gestation. The dataset is a collection of US images with two different visualization planes, namely 3-vessel view (3VV) plane, which shows three blood vessels (aorta, superior vena cava, and pulmonary artery), and 4-chamber view (4CV) plane, which shows four chambers of the heart. In the future this database would be iteratively extended with the collection of various other US visualization planes to support the research enhancement in this field.

The images of this dataset were acquired with two different types of imagers, GE Logic 400 equipment with specifications of curvilinear transducer producing two US beaming frequencies around 3—5 MHz, and GE Voluson E6 equipment with multiple transducers ranging up to 11 MHz frequency. The image resolution relies on the imaging parameter specifications such as depth and gain of the transducers. The image resolution ranges from 500×500 pixels to 1000×1000 pixels with pixel depth of 24bits/pixel. With respect to the ethical principles of World Medical Association and Helsinki Declaration, the patient's name and hospital name were cropped out from the images available in this database. In addition to that the validations carried out for the designed CADSS system was based on the ethical standards mentioned by Helsinki declaration. The images were collected from the pregnant mothers, each of them signing in a written consent form requesting that their fetal heart images can be used for the purpose of validation of research. These images were utilized to validate the performance of our previous works involved in CADSS design to diagnose prenatal CHDs [19—21]. A dataset with 513 images has been broken down as follows: among 289 images, 264 were normal 4CV image planes and 25 were abnormal 4CV image planes. Among 224 images, 185 were normal 3VV image planes and 39 were abnormal 3VV image planes. Table 2.1 illustrates the consolidated numerals of dataset collection and Table 2.2 shows the details of dataset collection according to the gestational age of the fetus.

Table 2.1 Consolidated numerals of dataset collection.

S.No	Image planes/ count	Normal images	Abnormal images	Total images
1.	4CV	264	25	289
2.	3VV	185	39	224
3.	Total count	449	64	513

Table 2.2 Dataset collection according to gestational age.

S.No	Type of image plane	Gestational ages in weeks					Total images
		0—22	22—24	24—26	26—28	28—30	
1.	4CV	24	49	58	92	66	289
2.	3VV	13	76	92	25	18	224
3.	Total count	37	125	150	117	84	513

2.2 Clinical background of ultrasonography in asymmetric heart-oriented CHD screening

Few of the types of prenatal CHDs such as HRHS, HLHS, and TOF are associated with the malformations of heart chamber structures and are considered cardiac defects with respect to asymmetry between the two sides of the heart chambers. This proposed CADSS system is implemented to detect those asymmetry-oriented heart defects and hence this experimental study involves only the analysis of 4CV US fetal heart images. Moreover, visualization of the 4CV US image plane has become an essential part of fetal echocardiography among various visualization plans in clinical radiology to investigate the structural and functional malformations of fetal heart. This 4CV alone is sufficient to identify 60% of CHDs [22]. Various structural information that a radiologist can see from a 4CV US image plane are spine, four chambers of the fetal heart, aorta, and moderator band in the right ventricle. Fig. 2.1A shows the schematic view of a 4CV US image plane highlighted with anatomical parts of a fetal heart. Fig. 2.1B shows the real-time clinical normal US 4CV image plane of a fetal heart. Fig. 2.1C and D show the abnormal US 4CV image planes of HLHS and HRHS CHD, respectively.

Fetal heart asymmetry is considered the main sonographic marker [22] in heart abnormality diagnosis. In routine CHD screening, the sonographologist primarily measures cardiothoracic ratio (CTR), right ventricle–to–left ventricle width ratio (RVLVWR), and right ventricle–to–left ventricle diameter ratio (RVLVDR) to identify the fetal heart asymmetric appearance and its associated types of CHDs, namely HLHS, HRHS, and TOF. In the context of clinical radiology, CTR is an important index in the detection of abnormalities of the cardiac defect or heart failure [22–26] and the size of normal heart should occupy one-third of the chest region or 50% of the circumference of chest region [26]. Generally sonographologists measure either perimeter or area of the heart and chest region to quantify CTR pathological feature. Fig. 2.2 illustrates the quantification made by the sonographologists in terms of perimeter measurement to measure CTR from the 4CV US image plane. In this experimental study, CTR features are computed in terms of two measurements, CTR area and CTR perimeter. With reference to sonographologists' experience [26], the normal range of CTR perimeter feature is assigned as 35%–50% and the range for CTR area feature is assigned based on experimental results.

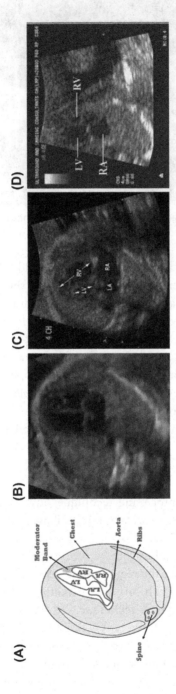

Figure 2.1 (A) Schematic diagram of US 4CV (B) US 4CV of normal image (C) US 4CV of abnormal image with HLHS (D) US 4CV of abnormal image with HRHS.

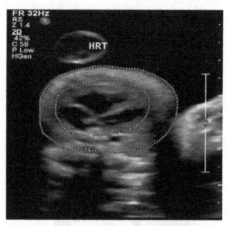

Figure 2.2 Quantification made by Sonographologist to measure CTR from 4CV US image plane.

The normal reference range of RVLVWR should be around 1.0389 to 1.263 and the normal reference range of RVLVDR should be around 0.93 to 0.962 [27]. In order to avoid complexity in the feature extraction process in this experimental study, the features of RVLVDR and RVLVWR are combined into a single index, right ventricle to left ventricle ratio (RVLVR). This RVLVR feature is measured in terms of RVLVR area and RVLVR perimeter. With reference to the sonographologists' experience [28,29], and as there were no reference values available for RVLVR feature values, the normal range for RVLVR feature values are assigned as 0.6 to 11 and the abnormal range is assigned as 0.4 to 0.58 based on obtained experimental results.

2.3 Methodology

The sequence of image processing techniques involved in the design of CADSS system to diagnose prenatal CHDs is illustrated in the architecture diagram shown in Fig. 2.3.

The clinical 2D US fetal heart image is first preprocessed by combining the steps such as carving out the region of interest and fuzzy inference rule-based image despeckling with adaptive maximum likelihood estimation (FIRAMLE) [20] despeckling technique. As CHD diagnosis requires quantification of diagnostic features (CTR and RVLVR) to characterize the cardiac asymmetric appearance of the fetal heart, it is essential to follow two levels of morphological processing tasks in the input fetal heart 2D US images, which facilitate extraction of diagnostically important features to

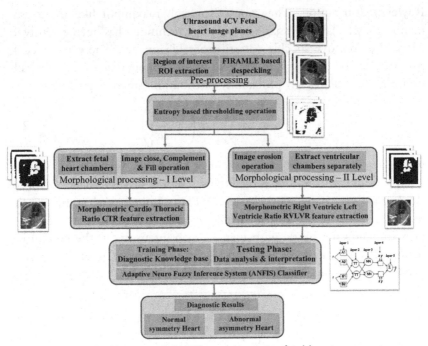

Figure 2.3 Architecture of CADSS to characterize fetal heart asymmetry.

provide computerized decision support. Thus after preprocessing, the process is followed by Level-I and Level-II morphological processing modules. Measured CTR and RVLVR values are then compared with the reference normal range to diagnose the prenatal CHD. If the CTR of the test image is not lying within the normal reference range, then it is diagnosed as abnormal heart with asymmetric appearance. The diagnostic features are then used to train and test the adaptive neurofuzzy inference system (ANFIS)-based classifier, which actually provides the computer-aided decision about the input test image.

The following sections elaborate the techniques involved in various modules composed in the proposed CADSS system for diagnosis of prenatal CHD.

2.3.1 Fuzzy inference rule-based adaptive maximum likelihood estimation–based preprocessing

The presence of a speckle pattern in clinical US images degrades the captured biological appearance with missing boundaries. The behavior of speckle pattern in 2D US images can be modeled exactly by

Rayleigh distribution. The robust Rayleigh maximum likelihood estimation (RMLE)-based image despeckling technique has been exclusively adopted to remove speckle pattern from US images. The noisy speckle pattern can be well approximated by independently and identically distributed the Rayleigh probability distribution function given by

$$p(x, \sigma_\eta) = \frac{x}{\sigma_\eta^2} \exp\left(-\frac{x^2}{2\sigma_\eta^2}\right) \tag{2.1}$$

where x is the quadrature component of US waves, which gets backscattered randomly from US modality. σ_η^2 represents the shape factor of Rayleigh distribution. The classic RMLE technique [30] computes the noise-free pixel values $\widehat{O}(u, v)$ from noisy image $N(u, v)$. Let ω be a set of pixel intensities inside with u and v span intensities in the computing region. RMLE used for estimating noise-free pixel intensity from a Rayleigh distributed statistical model is given by

$$\widehat{O}(u, v) = \sqrt{\left(\frac{1}{2\|\omega\|\sigma_\eta^2} \sum_{(u,v)\in\omega} N^2(u, v)\right)} \tag{2.2}$$

where ω represents 3×3 kernel neighborhood, $\|\omega\|$ denotes the cardinality, $\widehat{O}(u, v)$ represents the despeckled image, and $2\sigma_\eta^2$ represents the tuning parameter assigned as α. The RMLE despeckling approach adaptively switches between two different tuning parameters, α_E edge tuning parameter and α_S smooth tuning parameter. The RMLE method has been generalized as modified Rayleigh maximum likelihood despeckling with fuzzy rules [31] by incorporating inference rules to distinguish edge and smooth region. The RMLE method has been further improvised as FIRAMLE by harnessing the fuzzy rules with image connectivity measure to avoid ambiguous image region discrimination and adapt an appropriate tuning parameter. This FIRAMLE method involves three steps of computation to impart optimized trade-off between speckle reduction and edge structure preservation.

Step 1. Fuzzy inference

This step intends to frame fuzzy inference rules in order to categorize image region as edge and background. Image intensities are converted into fuzzy spels and various fuzzy relations such as fuzzy adjacency, fuzzy affinity, path strength, and degree of fuzzy connectedness have been computed in this step in order to frame fuzzy rules and make inference about the type of image region.

Step 2. Adaptive tuning

This step intends to provide spatial adaptive tuning of the filter parameter in order to enhance the appearance of the biological structures clearly. This adaptive tuning acts as a decisive element to operate the filter in either of the two different modes, maximum filter mode or minimum filter mode.

Step 3. Maximum likelihood estimation–based filtering

This step intends to remove the speckle pattern from noisy US images. Estimating noise-free pixel intensities requires appropriate inputs from steps 1 2.

2.3.2 Morphological operations

Morphological processing deals with processing the binary image. It provides the advantage of performing a variety of object analysis in order to enhance automated image processing. This experimental study involves two levels of morphological operations, Level-I processing and Level-II processing, in order to aid the process of extracting two significant diagnostic features, CTR and RVLVR, from the 4CV US fetal heart image planes. The techniques explained in the following subsections were sequentially involved in the progression of contriving this CADSS for prenatal CHD diagnosis.

2.3.2.1 Entropy thresholding

The segmentation process plays a significant role in the task of automated image analysis. In this experimental study, segmentation is needed to segment the fetal heart (region of interest) from the thoracic region (background). The thresholding operation is one of the automatic segmentation processes carried out in several image processing applications. One of the most trivial tasks in this process is optimal selection of threshold value, owing to the nature of threshold selection, which relies on the contrast enhancement process. Literature supports a multitude of thresholding methodologies [32] applicable in diverse image types. It was found that the entropy thresholding method works well for all types of images and is best suited for segmenting US images [33–35]. US echogenicity pattern resembles the probability distributions and the entropy measure of gray shades with these distributions maximizes the differences in intercluster regions capable of forming the foreground and background regions. This fact tends to aid in the process of segmentation of clinical US images. Albuquerque et al. [36] proposed the Tsallis entropy-based image thresholding technique to process clinical US images. Moreover many generalizations have been contrived to improve the Tsallis entropy image thresholding operation; for example, El-Sayed et al. [37] extended the Tsallis entropy formalism from 2D histogram to perform an automatic global thresholding operation. Sadek et al. and Qi [38,39] generalized the maximum entropy method by synergizing the fuzzy logic approach and particle swarm optimization method. On the other hand, Rodrigues et al. [40] generalized the Tsallis entropy method by utilizing the ratio of background and foreground area estimation from image histogram in order to segment the clinical US images. Barbieri et al. [41] proposed entropy-based automatic image segmentation methodology to segment different regions of interest areas from satellite color images. Marsico et al. [42] presented an extended version of the image entropy-based thresholding method to aid automatic extraction of tumor regions from MRI brain images. Thus the entropy-based thresholding operation yields the best results in the case of US images. Fig. 2.4 shows the results of various thresholding operations performed in clinical US images. It is obvious from Fig. 2.4E that the entropy measure-based thresholding operation segments the clinical US images appropriately into foreground and background.

Entropy-based thresholding works based on the principle of local entropy measurement and linear arrangement of pixel intensities. According to Shannon theory [35] the average information emitted from a source outcome is defined as entropy. In this context, the image itself is assumed as a source of information. Let L be the maximum number of gray level intensities; the probability distribution of normalized gray level is given by $p(i) = p\_\{1\}, p\_\{2\} \dots p\_\{L\}$. The histogram of the information source (image) is given by

$$\sum_{i=0}^{L} p(i) = 1 \tag{2.3}$$

The principle of entropic thresholding relies on the belief of characterizing the image information in terms of entropy and it is given by

$$H(i) = - \sum_{i=0}^{L} \frac{p_i}{\sum_{j=0}^{L} p_i} \ln \frac{p_i}{\sum_{j=0}^{L} p_i} \tag{2.4}$$

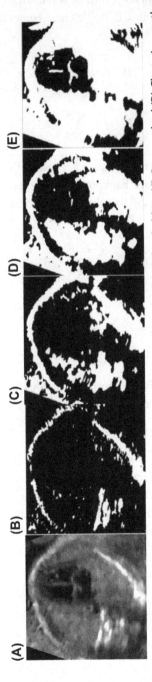

Figure 2.4 Thresholded images with (A) Pre-processed US image (B) Multiple global thresholding (C) Otsu method (D) Clustering method (E) Entropy method.

An image can be decomposed into two statistically independent classes, object O and the background B, with their respective probability distributions mentioned by P_O and P_B

$$P_O(i) = \sum_{i=0}^{t} p_i \tag{2.5}$$

$$P_B(i) = \sum_{i=t+1}^{t} p_i \tag{2.6}$$

In Eq. (2.6), t represents the selected threshold value, which optimally segregates the object and the background. The entropy measure for the object is represented by $H_O(i)$ and the entropy measure for background is represented by $H_B(i)$.

$$H_O(i) = -\sum_{i=0}^{t} \frac{p_i}{\sum_{j=0}^{t} p_i} \ln \frac{p_i}{\sum_{j=0}^{t} p_i} \tag{2.7}$$

$$H_B(i) = -\sum_{i=t+1}^{L} \frac{p_i}{\sum_{j=t+1}^{L} p_i} \ln \frac{p_i}{\sum_{j=t+1}^{L} p_i} \tag{2.8}$$

With reference to the additive property of the Shannon entropy theorem, it is optimal to obtain the second-order transition entropy measure of the object and the background regions.

$$H(O + B) = H_O(i) + H_B(i) \tag{2.9}$$

Now it is possible to select an appropriate value, which maximizes the information measure from the histogram with between class variance of object and background. This optimal threshold value T is used to segment the image object and background. The mathematical representation for T is given by

$$T = \max_{t=0...L} [H_O(t) + H_B(t)] \tag{2.10}$$

At the end of this process, the preprocessed US image is converted into a binary image.

2.3.2.2 Morphological processing

Morphological image processing helps to perform binary object analysis [43,44] using the connected component features. Morphological processing facilitates the process of extracting the diagnostically important biological sonographic markers of the fetal heart. In clinical radiology, manual diagnosis of prenatal CHD requires measurement of two diagnostic features, CTR and RVLVR parameters. In order to help the user perform both of these diagnostic parameter measurements, two levels of morphological operations are involved in the design procedure, Level-I morphological operations and Level-II morphological operations. Fig. 2.5 illustrates the flowchart with schematic processed outputs for each block of morphological operations performed in both Level-I and Level-II processing.

Level-I morphological processing crafts the image in such a way as to separate fetal heart from chest and makes it suitable to extract the CTR feature. The sequence of processing involved in this step are an entropy-based thresholding operation followed by an image close operation, image fill operation, subtract closed and filled images to separate fetal heart,

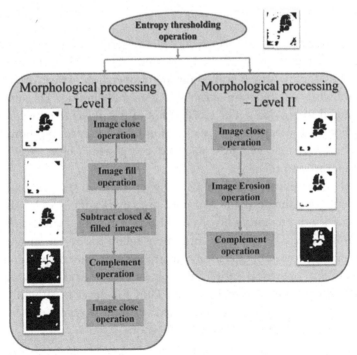

Figure 2.5 Various steps involved in Level I and Level II morphological operations.

image complement operation, image close operation, and connected component analysis.

In the previous step (thresholding operation), the image is segmented and converted into a binary image denoted by $B(m,n)$; even then it is composed of a few small unwanted patches surrounding the region of interest. Morphological image close operation plays a vital role in morphological image processing [45], which completely removes unwanted small patches from the binary image. It is the combination of image dilation followed by the image erosion operation using the structuring element denoted by S. This image closing operation can be expressed mathematically by

$$B \cdot S = (B \oplus S) \ominus S \qquad (2.11)$$

On completion of the image close operation it is optimal to perform an image filling operation, which is essential to vanish very small unwanted white patches around the region of interest. This procedure removes the regional minima values surrounding the image boundaries. The image filling operation can be mathematically expressed by

$$B_{f=}(B \cdot S) \cap \overline{B} \qquad (2.12)$$

Images that underwent close and fill operations were subtracted to segregate the fetal heart from the background region. Then the process is followed by the morphological complement operation, which reverses the black and white combination of the object and background. This operation is performed to provide better visualization of the object (fetal heart) from the background to ease the process of morphometric quantification. Then the process was followed by connected component object analysis and feature extraction process.

Level-II morphological processing greatly helps in segregation of the four chambers of the heart and hence it aids to extract the RVLVR feature. The sequence of processing involved in Level-II morphological processing are entropy-based thresholding operation followed by an image close operation, image erosion operation, and image complement operation. The image erosion operation shrinks the object region and wipes out the confined pixels from the background. Thus this level of morphological processing helps the image show detached ventricular chambers, where the user can perform morphometric quantifications.

2.3.2.3 Feature extraction

In binary image analysis, measurement of object area A_i is one of the significant features and is measured in terms of the number of pixels within the contour of the object. In this experimental study, this metric is used to infer the size of the fetal heart and chest region. The formula for computing area A_i of a binary image is given by

$$A_i = \sum_{r=0}^{height-1} \sum_{c=0}^{width-1} I_i(r, c) \tag{2.13}$$

where i represents ith object, and r and c represent the number of rows and columns in the image. Perimeter of the thresholded binary image is the significant global feature and is measured in terms of length of pixels around the boundary of a region. In this experimental study, this metric is used to infer the circumference of the fetal heart and chest region. Fig. 2.6 shows a small binary image with a boundary or chain of pixel elements. The horizontal chain element is named N_H the vertical chain element is named N_V, and diagonal chain element is named N_D.

A pixel in the chain of object boundary in horizontal or vertical direction has a length 1 and in diagonal direction has a length $\sqrt{2}$. Perimeter of a binary image is termed as the length of chain of boundary pixels. The formula for computing perimeter is given by

$$P = N_V + N_H + \sqrt{2}N_D \tag{2.14}$$

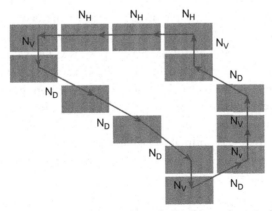

Figure 2.6 Binary image with a chain of boundary pixels.

Feature extraction of the prominent diagnostic features CTR and RVLVR were computed by using the following quantifications:
1. Area of fetal heart
2. Area of chest region
3. Area of right ventricle
4. Area of left ventricle
5. Perimeter of fetal heart
6. Perimeter of chest region
7. Perimeter of right ventricle
8. Perimeter of left ventricle

From these measurements, the following four different ratio values are calculated in order to be used as important features to do the classification process. The feature vector comprises the following four measurements:
1. CTR area = Ratio of area of fetal heart to area of chest
2. CTR perimeter = Ratio of perimeter of fetal heart to perimeter of chest
3. RVLVR area = Ratio of area of right ventricle to left ventricle
4. RVLVR perimeter = Ratio of perimeter of right ventricle to left ventricle

Among these four ratio values, the first two values represent CTR features and next two values represent RVLVR features useful in the clinical CHD screening process. Accuracy of the classification process relies on choosing the appropriate feature set. CTR and RVLVR features utilized for the proposed CADSS were the same parameters used by the radiologists in manual diagnosis. Fig. 2.7 shows the discriminative statistical details of diagnostic features for normal and abnormal class in the form of special box plot functions. Fig. 2.7A shows the distribution of the different range of CTR features measured in perimeter value for normal and abnormal classes. Normal class of images occupies the feature value in the range of 33–50 and abnormal classes possess CTR values below and above the normal range up to 63. Fig. 2.7B shows the distribution of different ranges of the RVLVR feature measured in perimeter value. Normal class of images occupies RVLVR in the range of 0.6–11 and abnormal classes possess values from 0.4 to 0.58. Hence, this shows that the feature set used was optimal to provide better classification results. The features were capable of precisely characterizing the normal image class and abnormal classes.

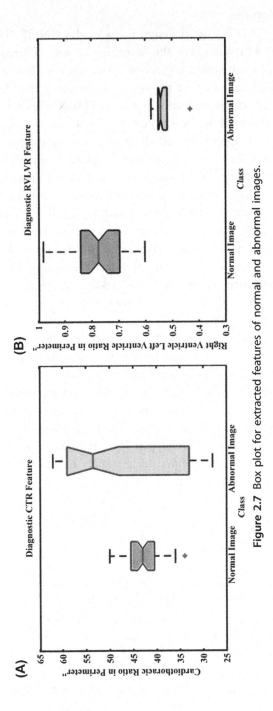

Figure 2.7 Box plot for extracted features of normal and abnormal images.

2.3.3 ANFIS classifier

The proposed CADSS system design includes the ANFIS classifier. The structure of ANFIS synergizes the learning capacity of artificial neural networks (ANNs) and basic straightforward decision-making capability of a fuzzy logic approach. One of the main advantages is that ANFIS infers the system's behavior by generating fuzzy IF-THEN rules and models the system's self-adaptation by using ANN. ANFIS is a standout among the most proficient, appealing, and effective modeling systems to actualize the expert system with self-learning and adaptation capability [46]. The prominent step involved in this module was the representation of input diagnostic feature vectors in terms of fuzzy membership functions (MFs) with the grade of low (L), medium (M), and high (H) linguistic variables. This partitions the feature vector within the range of 0 to 1. Input space of each feature vector is an overlapped function of three grades L, M, and H. This protrudes a facility of simultaneously activating several local regions of single-input feature vector. Decision-making capability of the ANFIS classifier solely depends on the resolution input grade partitioning, determined by number of MFs. The number of fuzzy rules generated in this experimental study were 81 IF-THEN rules; the number of input feature vectors were four and each input vector was partitioned into three grades of linguistic variables as L, M, and H.

Fig. 2.8 shows the ANFIS structure, which comprises five layers, with each layer performing distinct important roles in creating hybrid intelligence. The first layer performs the task of partitioning the input feature vector with several grades of overlapped MFs and hence this layer is termed the fuzzification layer. MFs defined are generally based on the generalized bell function and are mathematically defined as

$$\mu(i, m) = \cfrac{1}{1 + \left\{ \left[\dfrac{x - c}{a} \right]^2 \right\}^b} \tag{2.15}$$

where a, b, and c are called as premise parameters. These parameters are antecedent parameters capable of automatically adjusting the shape and size of MFs with respect to input feature value. The second layer performs the fuzzy AND operation in order to compute the firing strength of fuzzy rules. The number of input feature vectors and linguistic grade of each input feature determines the number of fuzzy rules created in order to model the training dataset. The third layer computes the normalized value

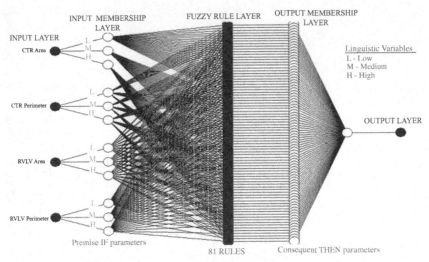

Figure 2.8 Structure of ANFIS Classifier designed for prenatal CHD diagnosis.

of the firing strength of the fuzzy rules. Parameters of the fourth layer are termed the consequent parameter, which determines the THEN part of fuzzy logic IF-THEN rules. The fifth layer consists of one single output node, the overall computation of which decides the diagnostic result.

Fuzzy inference part of the ANFIS classifier is built with the Takagi—Sugeno fuzzy inference system. The principle behind the fuzzy inference system along with fuzzy logic rules works in the following way: IF (the premise parameters) input feature vector value is known, THEN (the consequent parameters) the diagnostic result of the input test image can be recognized. The input feature (premise parameters) vector was represented by $[X_i]$, which comprises four input features, CTR area $[X_1]$, CTR perimeter $[X_2]$, RVLVR area $[X_3]$, and RVLVR perimeter $[X_4]$. Each input feature vector is partitioned into MFs with linguistic variables as $\mu(i,1) = Low, \mu(i,2) = Medium,$ and $\mu(i,3) = High$. The MFs of the input feature vector partitioned using the generalized bell curve function is illustrated in Fig. 2.9.

The output node of the fifth layer of the ANFIS classifier produces the diagnostic result upon computation of IF-THEN rules. The diagnostic result is denoted by $\omega_{out} = \omega_{normal}, \omega_{abnormal}$, with ω_{normal} as normal heart and $\omega_{abnormal}$ as abnormal heart, with heart asymmetry appearance having any one of the CHDs of HRHS, HLHS, and TOF. This proposed CADSS built with ANFIS classifier acquires the diagnostic knowledge base by creating 81 fuzzy IF-THEN rules. Based on ANFIS modeling,

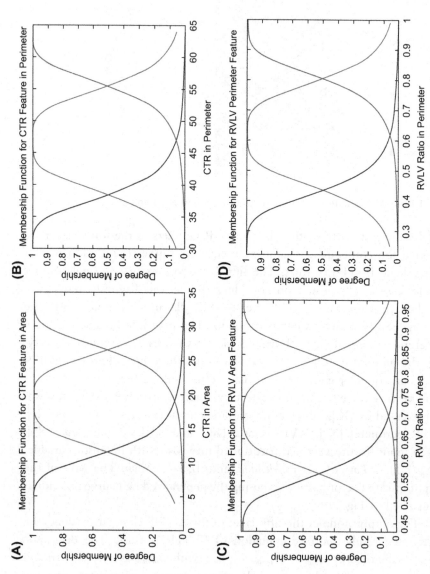

Figure 2.9 Memberships functions of input features (A)CTR area feature (B) CTR perimeter feature (C) RVLV area feature (D) RVLV perimeter feature.

mathematical expression for the nth standard rule among 81 numbers of fuzzy rules is given as

$$Rule_N = IF\ (X_1 is \mu(1,1)) AND\ (X_i is \mu(i,m)) THEN\ (\omega\ is\ \omega_{out}) \quad (2.16)$$

where Xi represents input feature vectors, $\mu(i,m)$ represents fuzzy sets, m represents number of linguistic variables, and ω_{out} represents classifier output. The ANFIS classifier is made self-learning and self-adaptive by subjecting it to a training procedure and a testing procedure. The training procedure was conveyed by a quick synergized learning method. This approach combines gradient descent strategy in the first layer and least squares technique in the fifth layer to alter the premise and consequent parameters. In order to perform training and testing process, images in the database were partitioned into two groups as training dataset and testing dataset.

3. Results and discussion

This section elucidates the demonstrated results of the proposed CADSS system implemented to diagnose prenatal CHD associated with asymmetric appearance of the fetal heart. The manual diagnosis is difficult, time consuming, and may lead to intra- and interobserver variability. This experimental study is an attempt to implement computerized diagnosis from 2D US images. Fig. 2.10 shows the graphical user interface (GUI) with many user interfaces to navigate through the diagnosis process. User interfaces were arranged with respect to various steps and operations

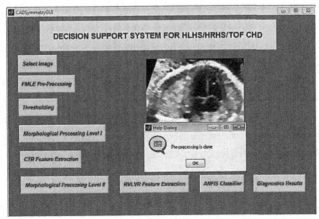

Figure 2.10 Graphical user interface based computer aided decision support system.

involved in the procedure of disease diagnosis. The user interface modules available are arranged in the order of (1) select image, (2) FIRAMLE preprocessing, (3) thresholding, (4) morphological processing Level-I for CTR analysis, (5) CTR feature extraction, (6) morphological processing Level-II for RVLVR analysis, (7) RVLVR feature extraction, (8) training and testing phase for ANFIS classifier, and (9) display diagnostic results.

The first fact of this section describes the prominent means of inherent speckle noise removal from clinical US images. The performance of the robust FIRAMLE despeckling method has been exhibited by comparing it with other existing filters. Few of the regular image quality metrics reported in various research works such as peak signal-to-noise ratio and mean square error, which compares original and despeckled images, were said to conflict with respect to visual interpretation, because visual perception of the despeckled image may not be apparently similar to the original noisy image.

Hence, the filters were evaluated with different types of performance metrics, the speckle index, entropy, and 2D plot of image intensity profile. Fig. 2.11 shows the clinical US images despeckled using different types of filters. It illustrates the original noisy image followed by despeckled images by using Lee filter, Frost filter, BNLM filter, PPBMLE filter, and FIRAMLE filter.

Image smoothness in distinct image regions is one of the important factors to be investigated in order to prove the performance of the speckle reduction technique. Hence, the graphical illustration in the form of 3D intensity profile plot for the selected edge and smooth regions of US clinical image is shown in Fig. 2.12.

Fig. 2.13 shows the series of 3D intensity profile plot for noisy image and various filtered images correspondingly. The FIRAMLE-based filter better preserves the edges of the image and at the same time removes the speckle noise efficiently whereas other filters show some unevenness of the image profile. Moreover, the PPBMLE method of speckle reduction provides comparatively more or less equal performance to the FIRAMLE filter but with very high computational time.

Quantitative evaluation of the filters was performed with the speckle index (SI) and entropy measure. SI performance metric is used to investigate the despeckling efficiency in terms of computing average contrast of the image. SI is defined as the ratio of standard deviation to mean value in a

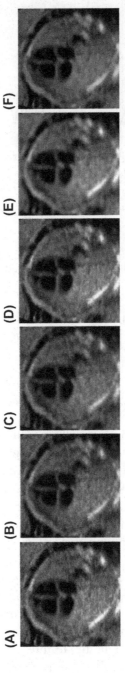

Figure 2.11 (A) Original clinical US image; Denoised images of (B) Lee filter (C) Frost filter (D) BNLM filter. (E) PPBMLE filter (F) FIRAMLE filter.

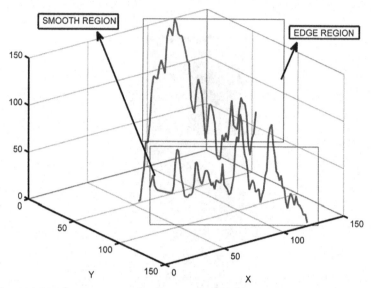

Figure 2.12 3D Intensity profile for US image with edge and smooth regions.

prescribed region of interest [47]. The smaller the value of this index, the better the performance of the filter for noise reduction. SI is mathematically denoted by

$$SI = \frac{1}{MN} \sum_{u=1}^{M} \sum_{v=1}^{N} \frac{\sigma(u,v)}{\mu(u,v)} \qquad (2.17)$$

Tsai et al. [48] used Shannon's entropy measure as a performance metric for evaluating the image quality of the radiographic image. The edge preservation capability of the despeckling procedure can be evaluated by the measurement of entropy for the despeckled image [48]. The quality of despeckling is better if the measured entropy value is high. Table 2.3 shows the quantitative results obtained to prove the competent behavior of the robust FIRAMLE-based denoising method in comparison with various existing filters.

This proposed CADSS system performs computerized diagnosis in two stages of morphological operations, Level-I and Level-II processing, in order to perform CTR and RVLVR feature extractions, respectively. In order to evaluate the performance of the proposed CADSS system, it is essential to compare the diagnostic feature quantifications performed manually by the physician and the same performed automatically by the

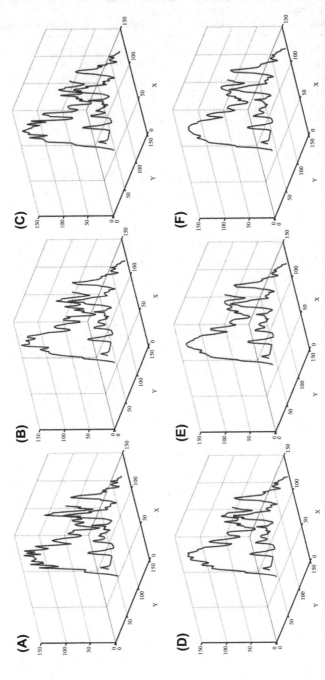

Figure 2.13 Image profile of (A) Original noisy image (B) Lee filter (C) Frost filter (D) BNLM filter (E) PPBMLE filter (F) FIRAMLE filter.

Table 2.3 Performance comparison of denoising methods.

S.No	Despeckling Methods	Speckle index	Entropy	Computation time (s)
1.	Lee method	10.4103	2.986	18.10
2.	Frost method	16.9832	3.876	23.53
3.	BNLM method	8.1295	5.782	29.99
4.	PPBMLE method	7.1871	8.364	77.61
5.	FIRAMLE method	5.2711	9.922	10.92

CADSS system. Fig. 2.14 shows the clinical diagnostic features of CTR and RVLVR quantifications performed manually by the physician.

Fig. 2.15 illustrates a sequence of responses obtained while the user navigates with several GUI interface modules to perform CTR diagnostic feature extraction through Level-I morphological processing in a normal 4CV US fetal heart image. Level-I processing is performed after the entropy-based thresholding operation, and this facilitates the extraction of CTR area and CTR perimeter features from the image. Fig. 2.15 shows the illustration of CTR area measurement alone from the normal image. Fig. 2.15A and B show the original and filtered image. Fig. 2.15C shows the thresholded image, and Fig. 2.15D shows the result of the image close operation, which removes unwanted patches. Fig. 2.15E shows the result of the image fill operation, which helps to erase the object of interest, and hence it shows the outer chest region in US 4CV. Fig. 2.15F shows the result of subtraction from image filled operation and image close operation, which helps to view only the heart region in US 4CV. Fig. 2.15G shows the result of image complement operation, which helps the user to view the bright portion as region of heart. Fig. 2.15H shows the result of image close operation, which helps to bring the heart chambers into a single region so that the measurement area and perimeter of heart region can be performed easily. Fig. 2.15I and J shows the user interaction to select the heart region for measurement and the measured area of heart region respectively. Fig. 2.15K and L shows the user interaction to select the chest region for measurement and the measured area of chest region respectively. Similarly Fig. 2.16. Shows the series of responses of the obtained for performing Level-I morphological operation in an abnormal fetal heart with HLHS CHD.

Once CTR feature extraction is performed, the process continues with Level-II morphological processing which greatly helps to extract RVLVR feature. Fig.2.17A−J and Fig. 2.17K−T illustrates the series of

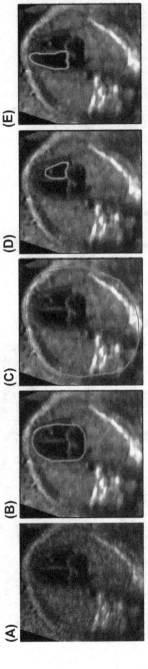

Figure 2.14 (A) Original Image ROI (B) manual quantification of fetal heart (C) Manual quantification of chest region (D) manual quantification of right ventricle (E) left ventricle.

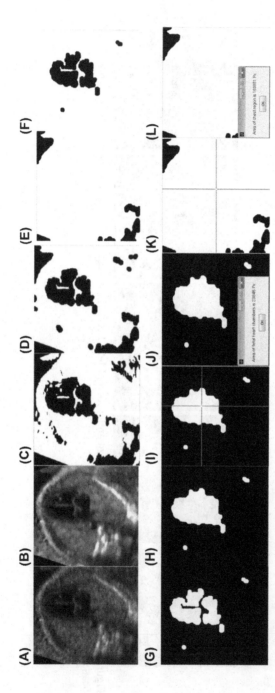

Figure 2.15 (A) 4CV US image (B) filtered image (C) threshold operation (D) image close operation (E) image fill operation (F) subtract operation (G) complement operation (H)image close operation (I) user interaction to choose heart region (J) quantification of heart region (K) user interaction to choose chest (L) quantification of chest region.

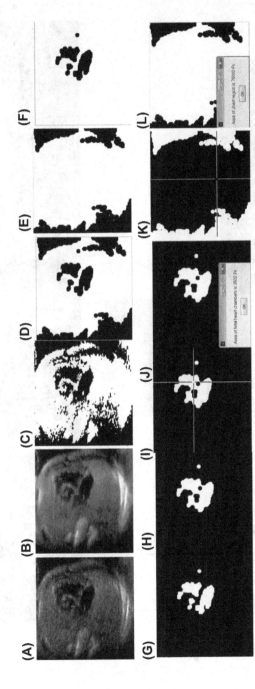

Figure 2.16 (A) 4CV US image with HLHS CHD (B) filtered image (C) threshold operation (D) image close operation (E) image fill operation (f) subtract operation (G) complement operation (H)image close operation (I) user interaction to choose heart region (J) quantification of heart region (K) user interaction to choose chest region (L)quantification of chest region.

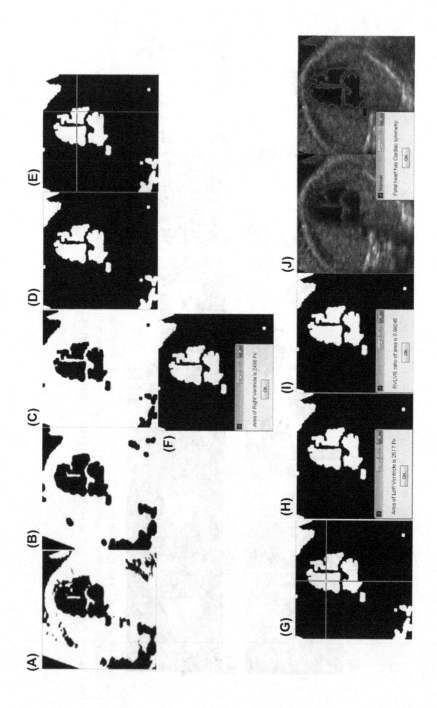

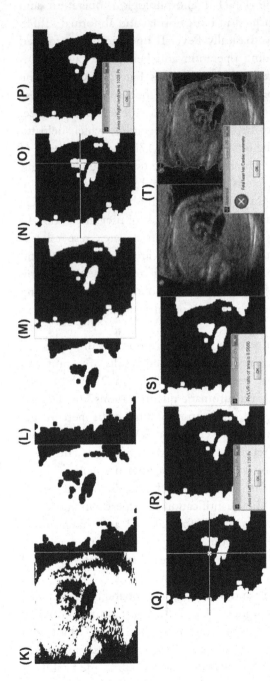

Figure 2.17 (A) Thresholded image (B) close operation (C) erosion operation (D) complement operation (E) user interaction to select right ventricle (F) quantification of right ventricle (G) user interaction to select left ventricle (H)quantification of left ventricle (I) RVLVR Area quantification (J) diagnostic result for normal image (K) thresholded HLHS abnormal image (l) close operation (m) erosion operation (n) complement operation (O) user interaction to select right ventricle (P) quantification of right ventricle (Q) user interaction to select left ventricle (r) quantification of left ventricle (s) RVLVR area quantification (t) diagnostic result for HLHS abnormal image.

demonstrated outputs of the Level-II morphological operation and RVLVR quantifications performed in both normal and abnormal HLHS fetal heart images respectively. Basically Level-II operation is performed after Entropy based thresholding operation and hence the Fig. 2.17 is started from the result of thresholding operation. Fig. 2.17A shows the result of thresholding operation. Fig. 2.17B shows the result of image close operation, which helps to remove the unwanted patches in the image. Fig. 2.17C shows the result of image erosion operation, which helps to detach the four chambers of the fetal heart. Fig. 2.17D shows the result of image complement operation, which the helps the user to view the bright portion of region of heart chambers. Fig. 2.17E and F shows the result of user interaction to measure right and quantified display of right ventricle area respectively. Fig.2.17G and H shows the result of user interaction to measure left and quantified display of left ventricle area respectively. Fig. 2.17I and J shows the display of RVLVR area measurement and diagnostic result of CADSS for normal heart image respectively. Similarly Fig. 2.17K−T shows the series of responses of the obtained for performing Level-II morphological operation in an abnormal fetal heart with HLHS CHD.

To evaluate the performance of automatic diagnosis of the proposed CADSS system, the diagnostic results of obtained results are compared with the physician's diagnostic results. Tables 2.4 and 2.5. shows the comparative results for manual and automatic quantifications of CTR and RVLVR diagnostic features and the corresponding error percentage. Tables 2.4 and 2.5 lists the comparative CTR and RVLVR feature values by counting the pixels in terms of area and perimeter. The error percentage [14] between manual and automatic measurement of diagnostic features are figured out in Tables 2.4 and 2.5. The average error percentage obtained between the quantification of expert and automatic diagnostic methods are shown as 5.76% for CTR-P and 15.08 % for CTR-A quantifications. Similarly the average error percentage for RVLVR-P and RVLVR-A quantifications are obtained as 5.5% and 4.778% respectively.

The impact of intra–observer and inter-observer variability plays a vital role in the process of disease diagnosis. Fig. 2.18. illustrates the intra and inter observer variability in clinical diagnosis in the form of 2D plot with CTR diagnostic feature values measured by different physician experts against number of times the measurements repeated for the same fetal heart image. The figure highlights the variations of the CTR feature value lying

Table 2.4 Comparison of manual and computerized CTR quantifications made by expert and CADSS.

Type of image	Diagnosis type	Perimeter of				Area of			
		Heart	Chest	CTR-P	Error %	Heart	Chest	CTR-A	Error %
Abnormal	Expert	347	1,144	30	6.66	4,742	96464	4.9	22
	Automatic	382	1,182	32		5,675	91,038	6	21.2
Normal	Expert	380	948	40	7.5	9,597	65,365	14.6	
	Automatic	365	992	37		11,043	62,084	17.7	
Normal	Expert	662	1,820	36	2.7	28,649	232,408	12.3	13.8
	Automatic	680	1,928	35		29,832	209,836	14	
Normal	Expert	444	996	45	4.44	14,400	74,244	19	10.53
	Automatic	422	898	47		11,749	69,073	17	
Abnormal	Expert	488	929	53	7.5	16,046	60,876	26	11.50
	Automatic	521	912	57		15,972	54,038	29	

Table 2.5 Comparison of manual and computerized RVLVR quantifications made by expert and CADSS.

Type of image	Diagnosis type	Perimeter of				Area of			
		RV	LV	RVLVR-P	Error %	RV	LV	RVLVR-A	Error %
Abnormal	Expert	131	194	0.675	10.66	1101	2329	0.473	2.75
	Automatic	139	186	0.747		1078	2217	0.486	
Normal	Expert	121	138	0.877	3.53	1093	1187	0.921	7.82
	Automatic	129	142	0.908		1069	1076	0.993	
Normal	Expert	121	130	0.931	4.94	1238	1292	0.958	9.08
	Automatic	129	132	0.977		1457	1394	1.045	
Normal	Expert	148	138	1.072	5.41	1178	1098	1.073	1.4
	Automatic	165	146	1.13		1200	1103	1.088	
Abnormal	Expert	195	232	0.841	3.09	1757	2374	0.740	2.84
	Automatic	189	218	0.867		1648	2165	0.761	

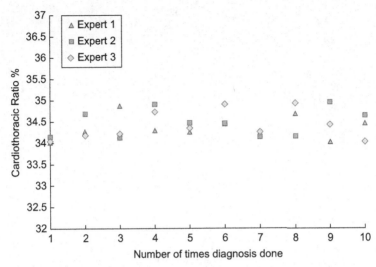

Figure 2.18 Potential analysis of intra-inter observer variability.

within the range of 34—35%, when measured by three different expert physicians. The deviation is found to be very small and this shows the close correlation between intra and inter expert observations.

The performance assessment of the proposed CADSS designed with ANFIS classifier has been compared with other existing classifiers namely radial basis function neural network (RBFNN) and modified back propagation neural network (MBPNN). Image data-set utilized for performance appraisal comprises of 289 number of 4CV US fetal heart images collected with around 0—30 weeks of varying gestational ages available in the database mentioned in Section II. In order to efficiently utilize the dataset, k-fold cross validation methodology has been used to train and test the ANFIS classifier. The number of cross folds represented to partition the dataset was K = 10. The real point of interest in using this method is that, it imparts training procedure k-1 number of times and thereby ensures efficient training. The receiver operating characteristics (ROC) curve analysis for the proposed CADSS system has been illustrated in Fig. 2.19. The area under the ROC curve obtained for this diagnosis was about 0.9134.

In order to demonstrate the classification performance of the proposed CADSS system with other classifiers, the image data-set with a total of 289 number of 4CV fetal heart images has been segregated into training data-set comprising of 176 normal with symmetric heart appearance, 13 abnormal

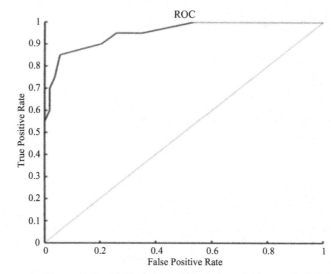

Figure 2.19 Receiver operating characteristic curve.

images with asymmetric heart appearance and testing data-set comprising of 88 normal images with symmetric heart appearance, 12 abnormal images with asymmetric heart appearance. The performance measures utilized to evaluate the classifiers were Accuracy (*Acc*), Sensitivity (*Sn*) and Matthews's correlation coefficient (*Mcc*). *Acc* is the ratio of number of correctly classified samples to total number of samples.

$$Acc = \frac{TN + TP}{TN + TP + FN + FP} \tag{2.18}$$

Sn is the measure of the classifier to identify the abnormal images as abnormal images.

$$Sn = \frac{TP}{TP + FN} \tag{2.19}$$

Mcc is the best performance measure to describe the confusion matrix and is mathematically [49,50] denoted by

$$Mcc = \frac{TP \times TN - FP \times FN}{\sqrt{(TP + FP)(TP + FN)(TN + FP)(TN + FN)}} \tag{2.20}$$

Table 2.6 shows the confusion matrix obtained for the proposed CADSS with ANFIS classifier in comparison with other classifiers.

Table 2.6 Confusion matrix of various classifiers.

Classifier Type	Sn	Acc	Mcc	Class name	Total no. of images	No. of images classified as normal class		No. of images classified as abnormal class	
ANFIS	96.4%	90%	59%	Normal class	88	TP	81	FP	7
				Abnormal class	12	FN	3	TN	9
RBFNN	93.9%	84%	38%	Normal class	88	TP	77	FP	11
				Abnormal class	12	FN	5	TN	7
MBPNN	92.4%	79%	26%	Normal class	88	TP	73	FP	15
				Abnormal class	12	FN	6	TN	6

4. Conclusion

Efficient US prenatal CHD screening process is principally experience reliant and subjective to clinical practice. Early diagnosis of prenatal CHD is a fundamental requirement in order to achieve a significant reduction in infant mortality rates. Literature has documented very few computerized system developed for US prenatal CHD diagnosis but rather supports multitude of systems developed for ultrasonography based disease diagnosis. This suggests that computerized solution for prenatal CHD screening is a major research topic. This chapter describes a pioneering novel CADSS system developed to fully characterize the asymmetric appearance oriented prenatal CHD from fetal heart US images. It also displays clinical diagnostic results while entailing nominal user interaction. The developed system was evaluated on a database comprising of 264 2D US 4CV fetal heart images segregated as 25 abnormal fetal heart images with asymmetric anomaly and 239 normal fetal heart images. In light of the results attained, it creates the impression that the proposed CADSS system genuinely provides an appropriate diagnostic decision about prenatal CHD. The proposed CADSS demonstrated with 90% diagnostic accuracy and the obtained standardized area under the ROC curve was 0.9134. Thus this proposed prenatal CHD CADSS framework can possibly empower diagnostic decision making and its accuracy by introducing a target translation of characterized diagnostic features and give second opinion to the obstetricians and gynecologists. In future by including the tele-medicine expert modules, this system can also be used to provide diagnostic decision support through distributed computing in different places of the hospital. The main drawback of this system is that it can characterize the fetal heart asymmetric appearance alone and also this proposed CADSS system is a pioneering work, it would secure a good future extension and upgrades. There exist other different types of CHDs, which can likewise in future be incorporated as separate diagnostic modules and integrated into a single CADSS system.

References

[1] J.I. Hoffman, S. Kaplan, The incidence of congenital heart disease, Journal of the American College of Cardiology 39 (12) (2002) 1890–1900.
[2] D.J. Barron, M.D. Kilby, B. Davies, J.G. Wright, T.J. Jones, W.J. Brawn, Hypoplastic left heart syndrome, The Lancet 374 (9689) (2009) 551–564.

[3] K.R. Chatura, G.V. Neethu, K.S. Mavintop, Hypoplastic left heart syndrome with parchment left ventricle: a rare perinatal autopsy case report, Journal of Medicine, Radiology, Pathology and Surgery 1 (2) (2015) 26—28.
[4] A.J. Macedo, M. Ferreira, A. Borges, A. Sampaio, F. Ferraz, F. Sampayo, Fetal echocardiography. The results of a 3-year study, Acta Medica Portuguesa 6 (1993) 9—13.
[5] R. Kapoor, S. Gupta, Prevalence of congenital heart disease, Kanpur, India, Indian Pediatrics 45 (4) (2008) 309.
[6] J.S. Carvalho, E. Mavrides, E.A. Shinebourne, S. Campbell, B. Thilaganathan, Improving the effectiveness of routine prenatal screening for major congenital heart defects, Heart 88 (4) (2002) 387—391.
[7] N.B. Mohammed, A. Chinnaiya, Evolution of foetal echocardiography as a screening tool for prenatal diagnosis of congenital heart disease, Journal of the Pakistan Medical Association 61 (9) (2011) 904.
[8] J.S. Lee, Speckle suppression and analysis for synthetic aperture radar images, Optical Engineering 25 (5) (1986) 255636.
[9] V.S. Frost, J.A. Stiles, K.S. Shanmugan, J.C. Holtzman, A model for radar images and its application to adaptive digital filtering of multiplicative noise, IEEE Transactions on pattern analysis and machine intelligence (2) (1982) 157—166.
[10] P. Coupé, P. Hellier, C. Kervrann, C. Barillot, Nonlocal means-based speckle filtering for ultrasound images, IEEE transactions on image processing 18 (10) (2009) 2221—2229.
[11] C.A. Deledalle, L. Denis, F. Tupin, Iterative weighted maximum likelihood denoising with probabilistic patch-based weights, IEEE Transactions on Image Processing 18 (12) (2009) 2661—2672.
[12] M. Pramanik, M. Gupta, K.B. Krishnan, March. Enhancing reproducibility of ultrasonic measurements by new users, in: Medical Imaging 2013: Image Perception, Observer Performance, and Technology Assessment, vol. 8673, International Society for Optics and Photonics, 2013, p. 86730Q.
[13] G. Carneiro, B. Georgescu, S. Good, Knowledge-based automated fetal biometrics using syngo auto OB measurements, Siemens Medical Solutions 67 (2008).
[14] I. Claude, J.L. Daire, G. Sebag, Fetal brain MRI: segmentation and biometric analysis of the posterior fossa, IEEE Transactions on Biomedical Engineering 51 (4) (2004) 617—626.
[15] A. Ciurte, S. Rueda, X. Bresson, S. Nedevschi, A.T. Papageorghiou, J.A. Noble, M. Bach Cuadra, Ultrasound image segmentation of the fetal abdomen: a semi-supervised patch-based approach, in: Proceedings of Challenge US: Biometric Measurements from Fetal Ultrasound Images, ISBI, 2012, pp. 13—15.
[16] S. Rueda, S. Fathima, C.L. Knight, M. Yaqub, A.T. Papageorghiou, B. Rahmatullah, A. Foi, M. Maggioni, A. Pepe, J. Tohka, R.V. Stebbing, Evaluation and comparison of current fetal ultrasound image segmentation methods for biometric measurements: a grand challenge, IEEE Transactions on medical imaging 33 (4) (2013) 797—813.
[17] I. Dindoyal, T. Lambrou, J. Deng, A. Todd-Pokropek, Level set snake algorithms on the fetal heart, in: 2007 4th IEEE International Symposium on Biomedical Imaging: From Nano to Macro, IEEE, April 2007, pp. 864—867.
[18] N. Sriraam, S. Vijayalakshmi, S. Suresh, Automated screening of fetal heart chambers from 2-D ultrasound cine-loop sequences, International Journal of Biomedical and Clinical Engineering (IJBCE) 1 (2) (2012) 24—33.
[19] O.B. Eso, Detection of Congenital Heart Defects in Fetuses using Four-Dimensional Ultrasound, The University of Utah, 2014.

[20] S. Sridevi, S. Nirmala, Fuzzy inference rule based image despeckling using adaptive maximum likelihood estimation, Journal of Intelligent and Fuzzy Systems 31 (1) (2016) 433–441.

[21] S. Sridevi, S. Nirmala, S. Nirmaladevi, Binary connectedness based ANT algorithm for ultrasound image edge detection, Indian Journal of Science and Technology 8 (12) (2015) 1.

[22] S. Sridevi, S. Nirmala, ANFIS based decision support system for prenatal detection of truncus arteriosus congenital heart defect, Applied Soft Computing 46 (2016) 577–587.

[23] S. Nirmala, S. Sridevi, Markov random field segmentation based sonographic identification of prenatal ventricular septal defect, Procedia Computer Science 79 (2016) 344–350.

[24] J.S. Kirk, C.H. Comstock, W. Lee, R.S. Smith, T.W. Riggs, E. Weinhouse, Fetal cardiac asymmetry: a marker for congenital heart disease, Obstetrics and Gynecology 93 (2) (1999) 189–192.

[25] A. Chanthasenanont, C. Somprasit, D. Pongrojpaw, Nomograms of the fetal heart between 16 and 39 weeks of gestation, Medical journal of the Medical Association of Thailand 91 (12) (2008) 1774.

[26] R.I. Abdulla, D.M. Luxenberg, Cardiac interpretation of pediatric chest X-ray, in: Heart Diseases in Children, Springer, Boston, MA, 2011, pp. 17–34.

[27] D. Paladini, S.K. Chita, L.D. Allan, Prenatal measurement of cardiothoracic ratio in evaluation of heart disease, Archives of disease in childhood 65 (1 Spec No) (1990) 20–23.

[28] T. Tongsong, C. Wanapirak, S. Sirichotiyakul, W. Piyamongkol, P. Chanprapaph, Fetal sonographic cardiothoracic ratio at midpregnancy as a predictor of Hb Bart disease, Journal of ultrasound in medicine 18 (12) (1999) 807–811.

[29] G.K. Sharland, L.D. Allan, Normal fetal cardiac measurements derived by cross-sectional echocardiography, Ultrasound in Obstetrics and Gynecology: The Official Journal of the International Society of Ultrasound in Obstetrics and Gynecology 2 (3) (1992) 175–181.

[30] T.C. Aysal, K.E. Barner, Rayleigh-maximum-likelihood filtering for speckle reduction of ultrasound images, IEEE Transactions on Medical Imaging 26 (5) (2007) 712–727.

[31] S. Nirmala, S. Sridevi, Modified Rayleigh maximum likelihood despeckling filter using fuzzy rules, in: 2013 International Conference on Information Communication and Embedded Systems (ICICES), IEEE, February 2013, pp. 755–760.

[32] P.K. Sahoo, S. Soltani, A.K.C. Wong, Y.C. Chen, A Survey of Thresholding Techniques, Computer Vision, Graphics, and Image Processing, 1988.

[33] Y. Zimmer, R. Tepper, S. Akselrod, A two-dimensional extension of minimum cross entropy thresholding for the segmentation of ultrasound images, Ultrasound in medicine and biology 22 (9) (1996) 1183–1190.

[34] Y. Zimmer, S. Akselrod, R. Tepper, The distribution of the local entropy in ultrasound images, Ultrasound in medicine and biology 22 (4) (1996) 431–439.

[35] J.N. Kapur, P.K. Sahoo, A.K. Wong, A new method for gray-level picture thresholding using the entropy of the histogram, Computer vision, graphics, and image processing 29 (3) (1985) 273–285.

[36] M.P. De Albuquerque, I.A. Esquef, A.G. Mello, Image thresholding using Tsallis entropy, Pattern Recognition Letters 25 (9) (2004) 1059–1065.

[37] M.A. El-Sayed, S. Abdel-Khalek, E. Abdel-Aziz, Study of Efficient Technique Based on 2D Tsallis entropy for Image Thresholding, 2014 arXiv preprint arXiv:1401.5098.

[38] S. Sadek, A. Al-Hamadi, Entropic image segmentation: a fuzzy approach based on Tsallis entropy, International Journal of Computer Vision and Signal Processing 5 (1) (2015) 1–7.

[39] C. Qi, Maximum entropy for image segmentation based on an adaptive particle swarm optimization, Applied Mathematics and Information Sciences 8 (6) (2014) 3129.

[40] J.S. Suri, R.F. Chang, G.A. Giraldi, P.S. Rodrigues, Non-extensive entropy for cad systems of breast cancer images, in: 2006 19th Brazilian Symposium on Computer Graphics and Image Processing, IEEE, October 2006, pp. 121−128.

[41] A.L. Barbieri, G.F. De Arruda, F.A. Rodrigues, O.M. Bruno, L. da Fontoura Costa, An entropy-based approach to automatic image segmentation of satellite images, Physica A: Statistical Mechanics and its Applications 390 (3) (2011) 512−518.

[42] M. De Marsico, M. Nappi, D. Riccio, Entropy-based automatic segmentation and extraction of tumors from brain MRI images, in: International Conference on Computer Analysis of Images and Patterns, Springer, Cham, September 2015, pp. 195−206.

[43] P. Soille, Morphological Image Analysis: Principles and Applications, Springer Science & Business Media, 2013.

[44] K. Michielsen, H. De Raedt, Integral-geometry morphological image analysis, Physics Reports 347 (6) (2001) 461−538.

[45] M.H. Wilkinson, J.B.T.M. Roerdink, Mathematical morphology and its application to signal and image processing, in: Proc. 9th International Symposium on Mathematical Morphology, Springer, 2009.

[46] A.M. Abdulshahed, A.P. Longstaff, S. Fletcher, The application of ANFIS prediction models for thermal error compensation on CNC machine tools, Applied Soft Computing 27 (2015) 158−168.

[47] C.P. Loizou, C.S. Pattichis, M. Pantziaris, T. Tyllis, A. Nicolaides, Quality evaluation of ultrasound imaging in the carotid artery based on normalization and speckle reduction filtering, Medical and Biological Engineering and Computing 44 (5) (2006) 414.

[48] D.Y. Tsai, Y. Lee, E. Matsuyama, Information entropy measure for evaluation of image quality, Journal of digital imaging 21 (3) (2008) 338−347.

[49] B.W. Matthews, Comparison of the predicted and observed secondary structure of T4 phage lysozyme, Biochimica et Biophysica Acta (BBA)-Protein Structure 405 (2) (1975) 442−451.

[50] D.M. Powers, Evaluation: From Precision, Recall and F-Measure to ROC, Informedness, Markedness and Correlation, 2011.

CHAPTER 3

Morphological extreme learning machines applied to the detection and classification of mammary lesions

Washington Wagner Azevedo da Silva[1], Maíra Araújo de Santana[1], Abel Guilhermino da Silva Filho[3], Sidney Marlon Lopes de Lima[2], Wellington Pinheiro dos Santos[1]

[1]Department of Biomedical Engineering, Universidade Federal de Pernambuco, Recife, Pernambuco, Brazil; [2]Department of Electronic and Systems, Universidade Federal de Pernambuco, Recife, Pernambuco, Brazil; [3]Informatics Center, Universidade Federal de Pernambuco, Recife, Pernambuco, Brazil

Contents

Advanced Machine Vision Paradigms for Medical Image Analysis
ISBN 978-0-12-819295-5
https://doi.org/10.1016/B978-0-12-819295-5.00003-2

1. Introduction

Breast cancer is one of the most common types of cancer in adult women worldwide. The World Health Organization estimates that there are 1.7 million new cases per year [12]. Survival rates can range from 40% to 80% in low- and high-income countries, respectively [6]. The low national survival rates are commonly associated with the lack of early detection programs. These programs have a major impact on prognosis, because treatment becomes more difficult in later stages. Mammography has become the standard image diagnosis method [33]. Yet, visual analysis of mammography can be difficult even for a specialist. Image quality, the radiologist's experience, and the tumor shape affect the accuracy of the diagnosis.

Imaging diagnosis is a complex task owing to the great variability in clinical cases. Many cases observed in clinical practice do not correspond to classical images and theoretical descriptions [28]. This is why computer-aided diagnosis has an important role in helping radiologists to improve diagnostic accuracy. It contributes to make diagnoses more robust to errors, improving the ability to identify anatomical abnormalities [9,46].

Extreme learning machines (ELMs) are learning machines based on flexible kernels. Their main characteristic is fast training. This is possible because of the use of random weights on hidden layer nodes. They also usually have good classification performance [25]. Like multilayer perceptrons (MLPs), ELMs have hidden layers, but with neurons with configurable kernels and random weights. The output layer, however, is composed of nodes with linear kernels [5,25]. The synaptic weights of the neurons in the output layer are determined through the Moore–Penrose pseudoinverse [25].

Morphological neural networks emerged from the algebra of images and their similarities with artificial neural networks [40]. In morphological neural networks, the neurons are based on operations from mathematical morphology. We use operations such as erosion and dilation, or combinations of these, as in the morphological perceptron [40].

An interesting characteristic of ELMs is their ability to build nonlinear decision boundaries. This may help solve complex classification problems [40]. On the other hand, the main limitation of these networks is the difficulty of implementing training algorithms; this leads to the use of optimization algorithms for training [40].

In this chapter, we propose morphological ELMs (mELMs), which are ELMs with hidden layer kernels based on morphological operators. We implemented the basic nonlinear erosion and dilation operators. Our main objective was to combine the ability of morphological neural networks to construct complex nonlinear decision boundaries with the simplicity of the training algorithms of the ELMs. As a case study, we applied mELMs to the task of detecting and classifying lesions in regions of interest of mammograms. We compared the results with those ones obtained using classical classifiers and assessed their performance using widely explored classification metrics.

1.1 Main goals

Based on the presented problem and the described hypothesis, this work had a main goal and some specific goals that needed to be progressively achieved. The next subsections address each of them:

(a) Main goal: Our main goal was the application and analysis of mELM performance in the detection of breast lesions in mammography images. We sought to achieve a more accurate diagnosis of breast alterations. We also aimed to speed diagnosis and provide a decision support tool for medical staff.

(b) Specific goals: The main goal can be broken down into the following specific objectives:

- To study critically the main classifiers referenced in the literature that are used in the task of mammography lesion detection;
- To raise the state of the art of using ELM as a lesion classifier in mammography images;
- To develop and analyze an mELM network architecture using dilation and erosion kernels in the intermediate layer;
- To perform experiments using the main classifiers referenced in the literature, applied to the task of classifying tumors in mammography;
- To perform experiments with an mELM network using dilation and erosion kernels, in classifying masses in mammography images;
- To analyze classical classifiers, as pointed out in the literature, and mELMs, using precision metrics regarding the classification rate;
- To analyze the improvement in the classification rate obtained by mELM networks, comparing the results obtained with those of the classic techniques indicated in the state of the art.

1.2 Chapter structure

This chapter is structured as follows:

- **Introduction:** Contextualizes this work by reporting the main motivations involved, listing the desired research goals.
- **Breast cancer:** Presents a brief description of breast cancer, the main methods used to obtain digital images of the breast, and the challenges health professionals found in the diagnosis. We also describe the different types of breast cancer, related to its contour.
- **Proposed method:** Presents the methodology used throughout the study. We also describe Image Retrieval in Medical Applications (IRMA) database in detail, because we used this database in the experiments.
- **Results:** Presents the achieved results using the proposed method (mELM). Techniques on the state of the art using the IRMA mammography database are presented.
- **Conclusions:** Presents some final considerations about the proposed method, including contributions and indications for future work.

2. Breast cancer

Cancer is a leading cause of death and one of the largest public health issues worldwide. For decades, breast cancer has been the most common type of cancer in adult women. Breast cancer is one of the top five causes of cancer death around the world [1,7].

Furthermore, the incidence of breast cancer increases every year. The best way to treat cancer is by early detection. The earlier the lesion is identified, the easier and more efficient the treatment of the disease is. Many techniques such as mammography, thermography, ultrasonography, magnetic resonance imaging, and clinical breast examination (*Exame Clínico da Mama*, ECM) are the standard indicated methods in mastology [10,37].

Mammography is an imaging technique that uses x-rays to scan the breast. It is currently considered the standard method for breast cancer image diagnosis. However, identifying breast cancer in early stages using this technique is difficult. As a consequence, there is greater dependence on imaging equipment and more efficient segmentation techniques, as well as the greater experience of the radiologist [4,15,16,21,35,39,41].

Because of the challenge of identifying and classifying breast lesions in mammograms, many groups are investing in exploring computational tools to help health professionals in this task.

2.1 Breasts and cancer classification in mammography

The Breast Imaging Reporting and Data System (BI-RADS) is a classification system proposed by the American College of Radiology [32]. It has the greatest acceptance owing to its simplicity, comprehensiveness, and ease of use [44]. This classification considers four patterns of breast tissue density:

- Type I: predominantly adipose breasts (25% of the fibroglandular component);
- Type II: partially fatty breasts (with fibroglandular tissue densities occupying 26%–50% of breast volume);
- Type III: mammaries with a dense and heterogeneous pattern (51%–75% of fibroglandular tissue, making it difficult to see nodules);
- Type IV: very dense breasts, presenting more than 75% of fibroglandular tissue, decreasing the sensitivity of mammography.

Fig. 3.1 shows mammographic images for each type of breast composition, according to the BI-RADS classification.

Young women usually have little adipose tissue and more dense breasts. The muscles of other mammary tissues (i.e., the parenchyma) occupy most regions of the breast. In predominantly dense breasts, the breast parenchyma corresponds to 50%–75% of the breast. In predominantly adipose breasts, the mammary parenchyma occupies 25%–50% of the breast volume. In adipose breasts, there is little parenchyma, less than 25%. Elderly patients usually have breasts with adipose characteristics. As women age, muscles and other mammary tissues tend to be replaced by adipose tissue.

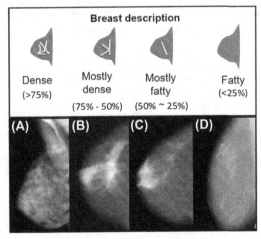

Figure 3.1 Breast classification.

The study of the shape of the lesion is extremely important in choosing appropriate treatment. The lesion can be classified as one of the following five groups according to its contour: regular, lobular, microlobular, irregular, and spiculate. Fig. 3.2 shows examples of this classification. Regular tumors have benign features. Spiculated lesions are usually malignant.

A regular tumor exhibits slightly rough borders with soft changes. A lobular tumor has a wavy outline. A microlobular tumor has a border with small undulations. A spiculated tumor has radiating lines at the edges of the tumor. Finally, an irregular tumor does not fit the definition of any other grouping.

As for density, we may classify a lesion into five groups: heterogeneous, fat density, hypodense, isodense, and hyperdense. Fig. 3.3 shows examples of each group.

A hyperdense lesion has higher density than the skin. Isodense lesions have density equal to breast tissue. Hypodense lesions have a lower density than the skin. Lesions with fat density are hypodense and surrounded by fat.

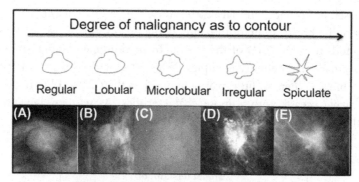

Figure 3.2 Tumor classification of contour.

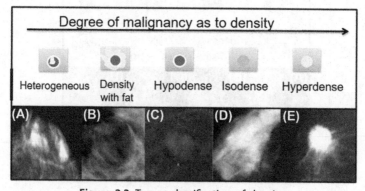

Figure 3.3 Tumor classification of density.

Finally, heterogeneous lesions are hypodense and partially occupied by mammary parenchyma.

Hypothetically, malignant lesions have higher density compared with the entire breast. Tumors with lower breast density are usually benign. BI-RADS, for example, cites that tumors of fat density are benign in most cases [3].

3. Extreme learning machines

Artificial neural networks are among the most successful techniques applied to classification problems [26]. In most neural networks, it is necessary to tune network parameters to achieve optimal performance [30]. In most neural network algorithms, the tuning process is critical to avoid local minima and reduce computational complexity (i.e., memory use and execution time). Computational complexity tends to be high in architectures such as MLPs.

ELMs are known for their ability to provide reduced training and execution time compared with other connectionist methods [25]. ELM networks usually consist of nonrecurrent intermediate layers composed of neurons with random weights [5,25]. Because we define the output weights in a noniterative way, the network is obtained from few steps, which reduces the computational cost [25]. In ELMs, it is not necessary to define the stopping criteria for the training phase [25].

The learning process of the ELM network is based on the inverse generalized Moore–Penrose function (pseudoinverse) to calculate the output weights [22,25,38]. ELMs are not based on gradient descent methods. Thus, the network is free of local minima problems. Moreover, it is not necessary to define a learning rate parameter or the maximum number of iterations, because the algorithm is not recursive [23,24,36]. The result is an output layer formed by linear kernel neurons. The final architecture is similar to MLPs and support vector machines.

Let us consider an intermediate layer of an ELM network with m_h intermediate neurons and n inputs. The output will be given by:

$$y_{h,i} = K_h(x, w_{h,i}), \tag{3.1}$$

where $y_{h,i}$ is the output and $w_{h,i} \in \mathbb{R}^n$ are the weight vectors of the i-th hidden layer neuron; $x \in \mathbb{R}^n$ is the input vectors, whereas $K_h : \mathbb{R}^h \times \mathbb{R}^h \to \mathbb{R}$ is the kernel of hidden layer neurons for $i = 1, 2, \ldots, m_h$.

As an example of the most used kernels in the hidden layer, we can mention the linear kernel:

$$K_h(x, w_{h,i}) = b_i + x \cdot w_{h,i}, \tag{3.2}$$

where b_i is the bias and $\cdot$ stands for the internal product between two vectors; and the radial base Gaussian function of the kernel is:

$$K_h(x, w_{h,i}) = exp\left(-\frac{\|x - w_i\|^2}{2\sigma_i^2}\right), \tag{3.3}$$

where σ_i controls the radius of the Gaussian function for $i = 1, 2, \ldots, m_h$.

Considering an ELM network with an intermediate layer with m exits, n inputs, and m_h neurons in the hidden layer, the output is given by:

$$y_i = \sum_{j=1}^{m_h} w_{o,i,j} K_h(x, w_{h,j}), \tag{3.4}$$

where $w_{o,i,j}$ is the j-th synaptic weight of the i-th neuron output for $i = 1, 2, \ldots, m_e$ and $j = 1, 2, \ldots, m_h$.

Let us consider the training set $\Omega = \{(x_i, y_i)\}_{i=1}^{M}$. The H matrix is given by:

$$H = \begin{pmatrix} K_h(x_1, w_{h,1}) & \cdots & K_h(x_1, w_{h,m_h}) \\ \vdots & \ddots & \vdots \\ K_h(x_M, w_{h,1}) & \cdots & K_h(x_M, w_{h,m_h}) \end{pmatrix}. \tag{3.5}$$

The ELM outputs are calculated by the basic ratio:

$$HW_o = Y, \tag{3.6}$$

where

$$W_o = \left(w_{o,1}^T, w_{o,2}^T, \ldots, w_{o,m}^T\right)^T$$

and

$$Y = \left(y_1^T, y_2^T, \ldots, y_m^T\right)^T.$$

The batch-training process consists of calculating W_o by the inverse relation:

$$W_o = \check{H}\, Y, \tag{3.7}$$

where $\check{H}$ is the general inverse of the Moore–Penrose of H.

3.1 Morphological operators

Mathematical morphology is a well-established nonlinear image processing theory widely applied in pattern recognition problems and a plethora of applications. As a constructive theory, it is based on fundamental operators. Its main operators are erosions and dilations. These operators are composed of shape transformations, in which object relations of inclusion are preserved [40,42]. Furthermore, for specific applications such as nonlinear filtering and feature extraction, mathematical morphology bases have been used to build several operators [40,42].

Basically, in mathematical morphology, we want to investigate images using fundamental elements of the structure, simply called structure elements [18,40,42]. Structure elements have the same role in mathematical morphology as convolution masks in linear image processing. Generally, structure elements are much smaller than the original images and are used to conduct image transformation according to determined neighborhood directions.

In dilatations, structure elements are used to maximize regions. Similarly, in erosions, we use structure elements to minimize regions. In case the higher pixel values are associated with larger values of brightness, dilations tend to generate brighter images, whereas erosions are related to darker ones. Minimization and maximization are related to intersection and union, respectively.

An image $f : S \rightarrow K$ is a function to map a two-dimensional array $u \in S$ in the point $f(u) \in K$, where S is the grid or image support, u is the grid's pixel S; and $f(u) \in K$ is the value of $u \in S$ pixel [40].

More strictly, the pixel is defined as the Cartesian pair $(u, f(u))$, that is, the vector built by the position u in the grid S and associated value $f(u)$. K is the set of possible values of $f(u)$. The notation K^S represents the set of all possible images of the grid S in K [40,42].

When the grid S is discrete, that is $S \subseteq \mathbb{Z}^2$, we say that $f : S \rightarrow K$ is a discrete image. K is defined by $k = V^p$, where $V \in \mathbb{R}$ is the set of grayscale and $p \in \mathbb{N}^*$ is the number of bands in image f [40].

The f image, with p bands, $f : S \rightarrow V^p$, can also be represented by the notation [40]:

$$f(u) = \{ f_1(u),\ f_2(u),\ ...,\ f_p(u) \}, \quad u \in S$$

where $f_i(u)$ is the j-th band of $f : S \rightarrow V^p$, for $f_i : S \rightarrow V$ and $1 \leq j \leq p$.

An image $f : S \to K$ is a digital image when it is discrete and quantized: in other words, when the pixel assumes only discrete values. Mathematically, $f : S \to K$ is a digital image when $K = \{0, 1, ..., K\}^p$ and $S \in \mathbb{Z}$, where $k, p \in \mathbb{N}^*$.

Using a digital image represented using N bits, $k = 2^n - 1$.

We commonly represent digital images by changing $K = \{0, 1, ..., K\}^p$ for $\overline{K} = [0, 1]^p$. Thus, we do not need to know how many bits we used to represent pixel values. Then, an image $f : S \to \{0, 1, ..., k\}^p$ could be represented by $\widetilde{f} : S \to [0, 1]^p$.

Comparison, subtraction, intersection, and union are basic operations in mathematical morphology. These operations are limited to monospectral images, (i.e., gray-scale and binary images). Working with several spectral bands demands separated monospectral operations over each band [40,42]. Given two images $f_1 : S \to [0, 1]$ and $f_2 : S \to [0, 1]$, the comparison $\leqq$ is the operation $[0, 1]^S \times [0, 1]^S$ for $[0, 1]^S$ defined as [40,42]:

$$(f_1 \leqq f_2)(u) = \begin{cases} 1, & f_1(u) \leq f_2(u) \\ 0, & c.c. \end{cases}, \quad \forall_u \in S \tag{3.8}$$

Given image $f : S \to [0, 1]$, the negative of f, is $\overline{f}$ or $\sim f$, and is the operation $[0, 1]^S$ for $[0, 1]^S$ defined as [2,40]:

$$\overline{f}(u) = 1 - f(u), \quad \forall_u \in S \tag{3.9}$$

The union between $f_1 : S \to [0, 1]$ and $f_2 : S \to [0, 1]$ is the operation $[0, 1]^S \times [0, 1]^S$ for $[0, 1]^S$, denoted by $f_1 \vee f_2$, defined in Eq. (3.10) [40,42]:

$$(f_1 \vee f_2)(u) = \max\{f_1(u), f_2(u)\}, \quad \forall_u \in S \tag{3.10}$$

The intersection between $f_1 : S \to [0, 1]$ and $f_2 : S \to [0, 1]$ is the operation of $[0, 1]^S \times [0, 1]^S$ for $[0, 1]^S$, denoted by $f_1 \wedge f_2$, defined as [40,42]:

$$(f_1 \wedge f_2)(u) = \min\{f_1(u), f_2(u)\}, \quad \forall_u \in S \tag{3.11}$$

Because unions and intersections in mathematical morphology and fuzzy logic are similar, especially when we adopt normalized image notation, we can consider normalized images to be fuzzy sets [40].

The subtraction or difference between $f_1 : S \to [0, 1]$ and $f_2 : S \to [0, 1]$ is the operation $[0, 1]^S \times [0, 1]^S$ for $[0, 1]^S$ given by [2,40]:

$$(f_1 \sim f_2)(u) = \min\{f_1(u) \wedge f_2(u)\}, \quad \forall_u \in S \tag{3.12}$$

Dilation and erosion are the base for other operators. We can build other operators by combining dilations and erosions. In fact, almost all other operators are built by combining these two basic operators [40,42].

The dilatation of $f : S \rightarrow [0, 1]$ by $g : S \rightarrow [0, 1]$, denoted by $\delta_g(f)$ or $f \oplus g$ (sum of Minkowski, in binary cases) [17,40,42], is an operator of $[0, 1]^S \times [0, 1]^S$ for $[0, 1]^S$, defined in Eq. (3.13):

$$\delta_g(f)(u) = (f \oplus g)(u): = \vee_{v \in S} f(v) \wedge g(u - v), \qquad \forall_u \in S \quad (3.13)$$

where g is the structural element. The dilation transforms the original image to make the structural element fit the original image. Thus, the original image f will be modified to make the areas similar to magnification g, in the case g.

If we associate 1's with the maximum of brightness and 0's with the peek of darkness, we notice the results of dilation in the increase in the brighter areas and the elimination of the darker areas.

The erosion of $f : S \rightarrow [0, 1]$ by $g : S \rightarrow [0, 1]$, denoted by $\varepsilon_g(f)$ or $f \ominus g$ (subtraction of Minkowski in binary cases) [17,40,42], is an operator of $[0, 1]^S \times [0, 1]^S$ for $[0, 1]^S$, defined as:

$$\varepsilon_g(f)(u) = (f \ominus g)(u) := \wedge_{v \in S} f(v) \vee \bar{g}(v - u), \qquad \forall_u \in S. \quad (3.14)$$

Erosion transforms the original image so as to make the negative of the structural element. In other words, the original image f will be modified to make the areas similar to magnification $\bar{g}$, in the case $\bar{g}$.

Similar to dilation, we notice the results of erosion in the increase in the darker areas and the elimination of the brighter areas.

Table 3.1 presents the mathematical expressions of dilation, erosion, and convolution, exhibiting important similarities among these operations.

Applying De Morgan's Theorem to Eq. (3.15), we have:

$$\delta_g(f)(u) = \overline{\wedge_{v \in S} \bar{f}(v) \vee \bar{g}(u - v)}, \qquad \forall_u \in S \quad (3.15)$$

Table 3.1 Expression for dilatation, erosion and convolution for images.

Operation	Expression
Dilatation	$(f \oplus g)(u) = \vee_{v \in S} f(v) \wedge g(u - v)$
Erosion	$(f \ominus g)(u) = \wedge_{v \in S} f(v) \vee \bar{g}(v - u)$
Convolution	$(f * g)(u) = \sum_{v \in S} f(v) g(u - v)$

If we have a symmetrical structure element g, then $g(u) = g(-u)$, $\forall_u \in S$, Eq. (3.15), becomes:

$$\overline{\delta_g(f)}(x) = \wedge_{v \in S} \overline{f}(v) \vee \overline{g}(v - u), \quad \forall_u \in S \qquad (3.16)$$

From erosion definition, changing f for $\overline{f}$, we achieve:

$$\varepsilon_g(f)(u) = \overline{\delta_g(\overline{f})(u)}, \quad \forall_u \in S \qquad (3.17)$$

An n-dilatation of $f : S \to [0, 1]$ by $g : S \to [0, 1]$, denoted by $\delta_g^n(f)$, is given by the following equation, for $n > 1$ [40]:

$$\delta_g^n(f)(u) := \underbrace{\delta_g \delta_g \dots \delta_g(f)(u)}_{n}, \quad \forall_u \in S \qquad (3.18)$$

Likewise, n-erosion of $f : S \to [0, 1]$ by $g : S \to [0, 1]$, denoted by $\varepsilon_g^n(f)$, is given as follows, for $n > 1$ [40]:

$$\varepsilon_g^n(f)(u) := \underbrace{\varepsilon_g \varepsilon_g \dots \varepsilon_g(f)(u)}_{n}, \quad \forall_u \in S \qquad (3.19)$$

Banon and Barrera [2] demonstrated that structure elements larger than 3×3 can be decomposed into various 3×3 structure elements (e.g., a dilation by a particular structure element h $m \times n$), because $m > 3$ and $n > 3$ may be performed by using a number of expansions by structural elements of b_k, with 3×3 dimensions, where b_k is a structural element composing h [36].

3.2 Image descriptors

In pattern recognition applications, it is important to represent the objects under analysis. When these objects are digital images, we are interested in representing these images by features that express properties and characteristics in a reasonable way. Image features are usually composed of numerical information derived from pixel decomposition analysis. This image representation is essential for classifying an object in the image, such as a lesion in a mammography image.

Feature extraction techniques can be applied to the entire image to extract texture information, for example. We may also apply them to regions of interest, such as the area, perimeter, and shape of a segmented region. Generally, this extraction is performed by image descriptors, which can extract features related to the shape or texture, for example. These descriptors have properties that are invariant to rotation and scaling. Thus, even if the object is on a smaller or rotated scale, the value of the descriptor will be the same.

3.2.1 Haralick features

Haralick descriptors [19] are widely used image descriptors in the literature and have also been applied to detect tumors in mammography images [27]. Haralick descriptors describe texture-based features performed from statistical calculations between neighboring pixels, which define characteristics obtained through co-occurrence matrices. These matrices map pixel gray values for a given image. These characteristics are used to differentiate textures that do not follow a certain pattern of repetition. Therefore, co-occurrence matrices express the spatial distribution and neighborhood dependence on gray levels [19,24]. Each $(i, j)^{th}$ position of a matrix is associated with the probability of changing from one pixel with gray level i to another with gray level j considering a given angle and distance. The standard angle values are: 0, 45, 90, and 135 degrees. In this work, we set distance d to be 32 texture features.

3.2.2 Wavelet series decomposition

Numerical transforms such as Fourier are commonly used to represent images in other domains than space. The Fourier transform maps spatial information images into frequence information ones. The wavelets transform combines spatial and frequency information by decomposing images into a series of images of details and approximations with different spatial resolutions. Consequently, wavelets have been successfully applied in a plethora of problems to represent images in a multiresolution way.

Mallat [34] proposed a fast algorithm to implement the discrete wavelet transform by decomposing the original information (signals or images) into high and low components using a series of discrete high-pass and low-pass filters, obtaining approximations and details components. Fig. 3.4 presents a block diagram of the discrete transform algorithm proposed by Mallat [34]. Image A_j is convolved by filters $h(n)$ and $g(n)$. These images are then downsampled by a factor of 2. This process is repeated over the subsequent approximation images until a predetermined maximum of levels is reached. In each level, we get an approximation image and three detail images. Fig. 3.5 presents two-level wavelet decomposition based on the Daubechies 88 algorithm.

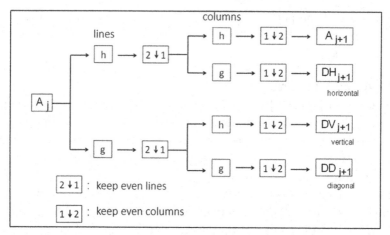

Figure 3.4 Bidimensional wavelet decomposition algorithm for one-level resolution.

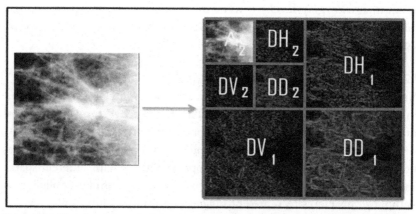

Figure 3.5 Wavelet decomposition, in two levels, based on Daubechies 8 algorithm.

The filters depend on each algorithm used by wavelets. We may also call these algorithms a family. Within each family, the filters may have different lengths. The longer the filters become, the smoother the approximation images become. Smoothness implies the reduction in image detail. The Daubechies family, for example, has several filters of different lengths. Daubechies 8 is able to soften the image with greater intensity relative to Daubechies 4. This occurs because the filters of the functions Daubechies 8 and Daubechies have lengths of 16 and 8, respectively.

3.3 Metrics

To assess classification performance, we acquired accuracy and κ statistics for each configuration. Accuracy is the percentage of correctly classified instances [31]. The κ statistic is a statistical method to assess the level of agreement or reproducibility between two sets of data [45]. κ can assume values between -1 and 1. We used Cohen's κ statistic. The interpretation of the κ statistic is shown in Table 3.2.

4. Proposed methodology

4.1 Morphological approximation in binary images

Our arithmetic approximation of morphological operators obviously employs arithmetic operations as well as Boolean algebra. The set operations, employed by our proposed morphological approximations, can be represented by Boolean algebra, seen in Table 3.3, where $f_1 : S \to [0, 1]$ and $f_2 : S \to [0, 1]$, where S is in the format of a two-dimensional matrix.

The Boolean AND operation, graphically $\wedge$, is shown in Table 3.3(A). It corresponds to the minimum operation. Eq. (3.20) shows our approximation of the operation $\wedge$ through arithmetic operators. The operator '.' means multiplication.

$$\min\{f_1(u),\, f_2(u)\} = \wedge\{f_1(u),\, f_2(u)\} = f_1(u) \cdot f_2(u), \quad \forall\, u \in S \quad (3.20)$$

When extrapolating to n-Boolean functions, our approximate operation of the theory of minimum sets occurs between the productory of these n-functions, as shown in Eq. (3.21), where $f_i : S \to [0, 1]$.

$$\min\{f_1(u), f_2(u), f_3(u), ..., f_n(u)\} = \wedge\{f_1(u), f_2(u), f_3(u), ..., f_n(u)\}$$
$$= f_1(u) \cdot f_2(u) \cdot f_3(u), ..., f_n(u), = \prod_{i=0}^{n} f_i(u), \quad \forall u \in S.$$

$$(3.21)$$

Table 3.2 Interpretation of Kappa statistic.

κ Statistic	Level of agreement
$0 < \text{kappa} \leq 0.2$	None
$0.21 < \text{kappa} \leq 0.39$	Weak
$0.4 < \text{kappa} \leq 0.59$	Moderate
$0.6 < \text{kappa} \leq 0.79$	Strong
$0.8 < \text{kappa} \leq 1.0$	Excellent

Table 3.3 Minimum and maximum operations associated with Boolean algebra properties, represented in (A) and (B), respectively.

(A)		
f_1	f_2	$\min(f_1, f_2) = \wedge(f_1, f_2)$
0	0	0
0	1	0
1	0	0
1	1	1
(B)		
f_1	f_2	$\max(f_1, f_2) = \vee(f_1, f_2)$
0	0	0
0	1	1
1	0	1
1	1	1

By observing Table 3.3(B), it is possible to notice that Boolean operation OR, graphically $\vee$, corresponds to the *maximum* operation, as shown in Eq. (3.22). The last term of the equation is in accordance with the property of the Boolean algebra named the Involution Theorem: $A = \overline{\overline{A}}$, $A \rightarrow [0, 1]$:

$$\max\{f_1(u), f_2(u)\} = \vee\{f_1(u), f_2(u)\} = \overline{\overline{f_1(u) \vee f_2(u)}}, \quad \forall u \in S.$$
$$(3.22)$$

Between Eq. (3.23) and Eq. (3.26), the operation of *maximum* set is always developed from the equations immediately preceding. Eq. (3.23) follows the De Morgan theorem, where $\overline{A \vee B} = \overline{A} \wedge \overline{B}$, $\{A, B\} \rightarrow [0, 1]$:

$$\max\{f_1(u), f_2(u)\} = \overline{\overline{f_1}(u) \wedge \overline{f_2}(u)}, \quad \forall u \in S \qquad (3.23)$$

Eq. (3.24) uses the standard fuzzy set operations: $\overline{A} = 1 - A$, $A \rightarrow [0, 1]$ [29]:

$$\max\{f_1(u), f_2(u)\} = 1 - \left(\overline{f_1}(u) \wedge \overline{f_2}(u)\right), \quad \forall u \in S \qquad (3.24)$$

Eq. (3.25) again employs the standard fuzzy set operation, this time for functions $\overline{f_1}(u)$ and $\overline{f_2}(u)$:

$$\max\{f_1(u), f_2(u)\} = 1 - (1 - f_1(u)) \wedge (1 - f_2(u)), \quad \forall u \in S \qquad (3.25)$$

Eq. (3.26) corresponds to an arithmetic approximation of Boolean operation of $\wedge$:

$$\max\{f_1(u), f_2(u)\} = 1 - (1 - f_1(u))\cdot(1 - f_2(u)), \qquad \forall\, u \in S. \qquad (3.26)$$

Therefore, when extrapolating to n-Boolean functions, the *maximum operation* is in accordance with Eq. (3.27), $f_i : S \rightarrow [0, 1]$:

$$\max\{f_1(u), f_2(u), ..., f_n(u)\} = 1 - \prod_{i=1}^{n} 1 - f_i(u), \qquad \forall\, u \in S. \qquad (3.27)$$

Then, the operations of the *maximum* and *minimum* set theory can be implemented in an approximate manner through arithmetic operators. Therefore, it is possible to create morphological approximations based on notions of sets through arithmetic operators. After the calculations of the *minimum* and *maximum* approximations implemented through arithmetic operations, the objective is to modify the classic formulations of *minimums* and *maximums* present in the erosion and dilatation operations seen in Eqs. (3.28) and (3.29), respectively:

$$\varepsilon_g(f)(u) = \bigcap_{v\,\in\,S} f(v) \vee \overline{g}(u - v) \qquad (3.28)$$

$$\delta_g(f)(u) = \bigcap_{v\,\in\,S} f(v) \wedge g(u - v), \qquad (3.29)$$

In Eq. (3.30), the approximation of erosion $\widetilde{\varepsilon}_g$ initially modifies classical erosion. The *maximum* operation of $\vee$, between f and $\overline{g}$, is now implemented, approximately, through arithmetic operators:

$$\widetilde{\varepsilon}_g(f)(u) = \bigcap_{v\in S} 1 - (1 - f(v))\cdot(1 - \overline{g}(u - v)). \qquad (3.30)$$

Eq. (3.31) employs the standard fuzzy operation for term $\overline{g}$ [29]:

$$\widetilde{\varepsilon}_g(f)(u) = \bigcap_{v\in S} 1 - (1 - f(v))\cdot(1 - (1 - g(u - v))). \qquad (3.31)$$

Eq. (3.32) simplifies the previous equation:

$$\widetilde{\varepsilon}_g(f)(u) = \bigcap_{v\in S} 1 - (1 - f(v))\cdot g(u - v) \qquad (3.32)$$

In Eq. (3.33) our erosion approximation $\widetilde{\varepsilon}_g$ employs Eq. (3.29) to approximate the *minimum* operation $\bigcap$, through arithmetic operations:

$$\widetilde{\varepsilon}_g(f)(u) = \prod_{v\,\in\,S} 1 - (1 - f(v)).\, g(u - v) \qquad (3.33)$$

Fig. 3.6A illustrates the performance of our erosion approximation, described in Eq. (3.33). Initially, there is the calculation of expression $1 - (1 - f(v)) \cdot g(u - v)$ between the region v of the original image f overlapped by g. The 1's are associated with absolute white and 0's with absolute black. After this, the calculation of the productory $\prod$ occurs between the n-results of the expression. In the example shown in Fig. 3.6A, the value $\tilde{\varepsilon}_g(f)(u)$ in the u position of the eroded image receives the value 0 associated with absolute black.

Eq. (3.34) formalizes our dilation approximation $\tilde{\delta}_g$. The *minimum* operation of $\wedge$, between f and g, is now implemented approximately through arithmetic operators:

$$\tilde{\delta}_g(f)(u) = \bigcup_{v \in S} f(v) \cdot g(u - v) \tag{3.34}$$

In Eq. (3.35), our dilation approximation $\tilde{\delta}_g$ employs Eq. (3.27) to approach the *maximum operation* $\bigcup$ with arithmetic operations:

$$\tilde{\delta}_g(f)(u) = 1 - \prod_{v \in S} 1 - f(v) \cdot g(u - v) \tag{3.35}$$

Fig. 3.6B illustrates the performance of our dilation approximation, described in Eq. (3.35). Initially, there is the calculation of expression $1 - f(v) \cdot g(u - v)$ between region v of the original image f overlapped by g. The 1's are associated with absolute white and 0's with absolute black. After that, calculation of the productory $\prod$ occurs between the n-results of the expression. Finally, the value 1 is subtracted by the result of the productory $\prod$. In the example shown in Fig. 3.6B, the value $\tilde{\delta}_g(f)(u)$, in the u position of the eroded image receives the value 0 associated with absolute black.

In binary images, our erosion approximation $\tilde{\varepsilon}_g$ and our dilation approximation $\tilde{\delta}_g$ generate the same results as classical erosion and dilation, respectively. The proposed work, however, does not use binary images. Therefore, adaptations are necessary so that our proposed morphological approximations can act on gray-scale images such as mammograms, accompanied by minimal distortion in relation to the morphological operations described in the literature.

4.2 Proposal: morphological neurons

Based on the morphological definitions of dilation and erosion, and our arithmetic approximations of the morphological operators presented in the previous section, we defined two nonlinear neurons: dilation and erosion. An ELM whose hidden nodes are based on these neurons can be considered

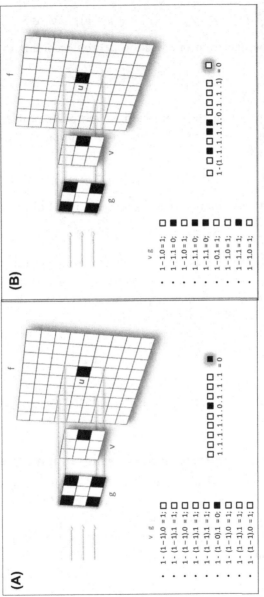

Figure 3.6 Performance of our morphological approximation in binary image. (A) Erosion approximation $\varepsilon \tilde{\ }_g$. (B) Dilation approximation $\delta \tilde{\ }_g$.

an mELM described in Eq. (3.36). Given the expression of morphological dilation for a monospectral image $S \rightarrow [0, 1]$ and a structuring element g : $S \rightarrow [0, 1]$:

$$\delta_g(f)(u) = \bigvee_{v \in S} f(v) \wedge g(u - v), \quad \forall_u \in S \qquad (3.36)$$

we can define the operation of a dilation neuron according to Eq. (3.37):

$$K_\delta(x, w) = \bigvee_{i=1}^{n} (x_i \wedge w_i). \qquad (3.37)$$

where $x, w \in [0, 1]^n$.

Similarly, considering the expression of morphological erosion for a monospectral image $f : S \rightarrow [0, 1]$ and a structuring element $g : S \rightarrow [0, 1]$ exposed in Eq. (3.38):

$$\varepsilon_g(f)(u) = (f \ominus g)(u) := \bigwedge_{v \in S} f(v) \vee \bar{g}(v - u), \quad \forall_u \in S \qquad (3.38)$$

we can define the operation of an erosion neuron as Eq. (3.39):

$$K_\varepsilon(x, w) = \bigwedge_{i=1}^{n} (x_i \vee \overline{w_i}). \qquad (3.39)$$

To obtain computationally efficient expressions, we can use the De Morgan theorem and fuzzy logic approximations for maximum and minimum operations. This results in approximate expressions (arithmetic approximations) in Eq. (3.40) and Eq. (3.41):

$$K_\delta(x, w) = \overline{\bigwedge_{i=1}^{n} \overline{x_i \wedge w_i}} = 1 - \prod_{i=1}^{n}(1 - x_i w_i). \qquad (3.40)$$

$$K_\varepsilon(x, w) = \bigwedge_{i=1}^{n} \overline{(\overline{x_i} \wedge w_i)} = \prod_{i=1}^{n}(1 - (1 - x_i) \cdot w_i). \qquad (3.41)$$

4.3 Detection and classification of lesion in mammograms

The proposed study employs the detection and classification of lesions in mammograms as a case study to validate our two mELM classifiers, dilation and erosion. Fig. 3.7 shows the proposed methodology as a block diagram. Initially, detection of the existence or absence of a lesion in the digital mammography image is performed. When detecting the presence of a lesion, we select the region of interest (ROI) of the image. Through the ROI, the phase of feature extraction begins. These data serve as input attributes for the classification phase, performed by the mELM. We defined the classes according to the criteria of the American College of Radiology, expressed in the scale [3]. Finally, the cases are classified as normal (without lesion), benign, or malignant.

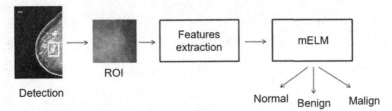

Figure 3.7 Diagram of the proposed methodology. *mELM*, morphological extreme learning machine; *ROI*, region of interest.

4.4 Image feature extraction

The ROI of a mammography image is first preprocessed. Equalization occurs based on the histogram information. The objective is to make the pixels lighter closer to absolute white and the darkest pixels closer to absolute black. In isolation, histogram-based equalization is incapable of segregating the lesion from other elements of the image. The reason is that muscles and other mammary tissues, technically named parenchyma, usually have a texture analogous to the lesion and may overlap it. Therefore, equalization based on the histogram information, acting on the image contrast, highlights not only the lesion but also the muscles and mammary parenchyma. After equalization based on the histogram information, features are extracted from the equalized image.

4.5 Classification using the proposed method (morphological extreme learning machine)

The classification employs as an input attribute vectors obtained in the feature extraction phase in concatenated form. Fig. 3.8A presents the proposed mELM method with erosion neurons in the hidden layer. Let us use input vector $x = 1, 1, 0, 1, 1$ and set of weights $w = 1, 0, 1, 0, 1$, as shown in Fig. 3.8B. First, expression $(1 - (1 - x_i) \cdot w_i)$ will be calculated using the input vector and the synaptic weights between the nodes of the input layer and the first node of the hidden layer. Thus, calculation of the productory $\prod$ will occur between the n-results of the expression, as can be seen in Fig. 3.8C. In the example of Fig. 3.9, the output value of the first neuron erosion of the intermediate layer will be zero, as illustrated in Fig. 3.8D.

4.6 Image Retrieval in Medical Applications database

In this work, experiments were performed using the IRMA database [11,13,14]. The IRMA database was developed from a project conducted by the University of Aachen in Germany, which gathers images from other

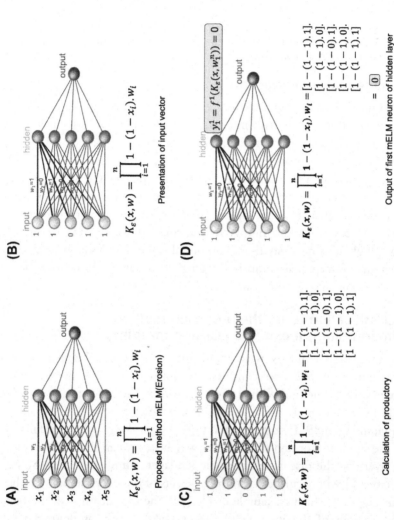

Figure 3.8 Example of classification process employing the proposed morphological extreme learning machine (mELM) (erosion) method.

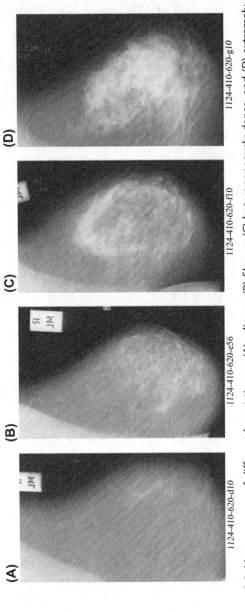

Figure 3.9 Mammograms of different breast tissues: (A) adipose, (B) fibrous, (C) heterogeneously dense, and (D) extremely dense.

databases available for consultation on the Internet. The database is composed of ROIs of mammograms classified by radiologists and resized to 128 × 128 pixels.

The database is composed of 2796 mammography images from four repositories:

- 150 images from the Mini-MIAS database [43];
- 2576 images from the Digital Database for Screening Mammography [20];
- 1 image from the Lawrence Livermore National Laboratory database; and
- 69 images from the Department of Radiology at Aachen University of Technology, Germany.

IRMA database images have four types of tissue density, classified into four types according to the BI-RADS classification [8]: adipose tissue (Type I), fibrous tissue (Type II), heterogeneously dense tissue (Type III), and extremely dense tissue (Type IV); as can be seen in Fig. 3.9.

The IRMA data set details the entire scanning procedure of breast image examination. In addition, it shows the direction of the examination: midlateral and craniocaudal. The IRMA data set specifies whether the image refers to the right or left breast. For this study, all images from the IRMA data set were used, considering all types of masses, totaling 2796 images. The proposed method identifies and classifies each image as benign, malignant, or normal (no lesion).

A lack of care can be observed when scanning mammography images taken by specialists. In many cases, the images have some elements that overlap the breast. Among them are adhesive tape, spatulas, and annotations (manuscript or digital), as well as grooves and fingerprint marks. Thus, the study of the breast region occupied by some of these types of external elements may become unfeasible, as can be seen in Fig. 3.10. To overcome this situation, IRMA uses only the ROI of each case, as shown in Fig. 3.11. The base ensures that there is only one lesion per ROI.

5. Results

In this section, we present results obtained with the proposed method, mELM, and with the following classifiers common in the state of the art: ELM linear kernel, ELM kernel Radial Basis Function (RBF), ELM with activation function RBF, ELM with sigmoid activation function, Bayesian networks, naive Bayes networks, MLP networks, RBF networks, Support

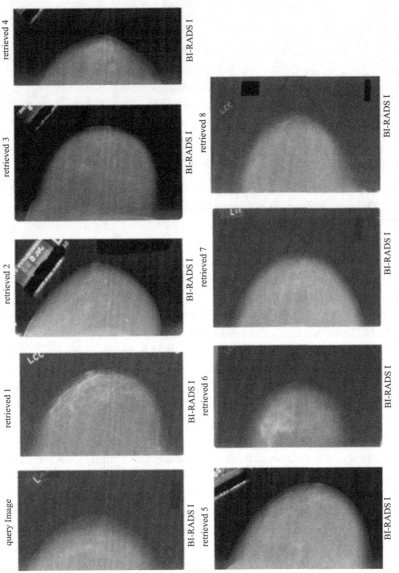

Figure 3.10 Example of lack of care when scanning mammography images by specialists.

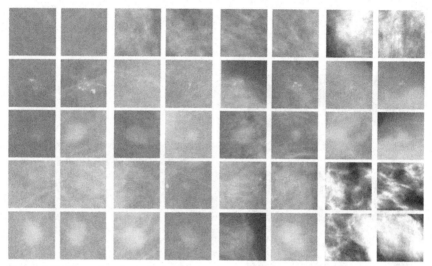

Figure 3.11 Example of regions of interest for mammography images from the Image Retrieval in Medical Applications database.

Vector Machine (SVM) linear kernel, SVM polynomial kernel degree 2, SVM kernel polynomial kernel degree 3, SVM polynomial kernel degree 4, SVM polynomial kernel degree 5, SVM kernel RBF, k-Nearest Neighbours (kNN) (k = 1), kNN (k = 3), kNN (k = 5), kNN (k = 7), kNN (k = 9), J48, random tree, and random forest.

A total of 2796 mammograms from the IRMA data set were used. The images contained in this data set consist of four types of tissue, according to the BI-RADS classification: adipose (Type I), predominately adipose (Type II), predominately dense (Type III), and dense (Type IV). Results were divided showing the classification precision and the κ index for each type of tissue and for the entire data set. All classifiers were evaluated using two different types of image descriptors, which served as input data for each technique. The two image descriptors used during the experiments were Haralick attributes (HA) and wavelet attributes combined with HA. The mELM, ELM, RBF, and MLP networks were configured with 100 neurons in the hidden layer. In the SVMs, the following kernels were used: linear, RBF, polynomial degree 2, polynomial degree 2, polynomial degree 4, and polynomial degree 5. The random forest classifier was configured with 20 trees. Regarding the kNN, experiments were performed varying the value of k as: $k = 1$, $k = 3$, $k = 5$, $k = 7$, and $k = 9$. Experiments with all classifiers identified each mammogram as benign, malignant, or normal.

Each analysis was accomplished using cross-validation with 10 folds. The process was repeated 30 times in relation to the synaptic connections between neurons, to obtain the results of mean and standard deviation.

The κ index was employed for each classifier for all performed experiments with each specific type of tissue and the entire database. The κ index has a range of $0-1$, 1 corresponds to an excellent classifier performance and 0 to very bad (Table 3.3).

5.1 Results and experimental analysis

In the following tables and box plots, there are only results obtained by the two best and two worst cases, in that order, for each classifier. To determine the best and worst cases, the first and second criteria are the arithmetic mean and standard deviation of the test accuracy, respectively. If there was more than one configuration with the same mean precision and standard deviation, the tiebreaker criterion was the training time.

Table 3.4 shows the results obtained for adipose tissue. The proposed model, mELM (erosion) had the best mean precision with an accuracy of 92.13%. The κ index for this method evaluated the model as excellent. The worst results were due to the classifiers: ELM RBF kernel and SVM polynomial kernel 5 degrees, when there were accuracies of 62.65% and 73.61%, respectively. Still, for the worst results, in agreement with the κ value, both techniques were evaluated as good. Fig. 3.12A presents the box plot for experiments performed with adipose tissue. In this graph, we can observe that the proposed models had a standard deviation very near 0. In the other two classical techniques, we can observe a higher value of standard deviation and the presence of an outlier, specifically for the ELM RBF kernel. Table 3.5 shows the nonparametric Wilcoxon test. For the results obtained with adipose tissue, it is possible to conclude that results obtained with this model are statistically distinct from those obtained by classical classifiers, because the hypothesis test is always 1 and the P value is always extremely low.

In experiments performed with predominately adipose tissue, Table 3.4 presents the proposed model mELM (dilation) that had the best accuracy, with a value of 91.41%. Our method was evaluated as having an excellent κ index. The worst results were due to the classical techniques: ELM RBF kernel and SVM polynomial kernel 5 degrees. The accuracy values were 39.26% and 70.74%, respectively. According to the κ index, the techniques were evaluated as regular and very good, respectively. Fig. 3.12B presents the box plot for experiments performed with predominantly adipose tissue.

Table 3.4 Results obtained by the two best and the two worst classifiers employing Haralick Attributes (HA).

Tissue	Feature extraction	Classifier	Test hit (%)	κ
I (adipose)	HA	mELM (erosion)	**92.13 ± 0.00**	**0.9113 ± 0.00**
	HA	mELM (dilation)	91.56 ± 0.00	0.9048 ± 0.00
	HA	SVM polynomial kernel 5 degrees	73.61 ± 4.58	0.6000 ± 0.07
II (predominately adipose)	HA	ELM RBF kernel	62.65 ± 3.39	0.5779 ± 0.04
	HA	mELM (dilation)	**91.41 ± 0.00**	**0.9034 ± 0.00**
	HA	mELM (erosion)	91.13 ± 0.00	0.8998 ± 0.00
	HA	SVM polynomial kernel 5 degrees	70.74 ± 4.44	0.5600 ± 0.07
III (predominately dense)	HA	ELM RBF kernel	39.26 ± 4.62	0.3140 ± 0.05
	HA	mELM (erosion)	**94.13 ± 0.00**	**0.9337 ± 0.00**
	HA	ELM sigmoid act. Function	93.35 ± 0.83	0.9243 ± 0.01
	HA	SVM polynomial kernel 5 degrees	73.94 ± 4.55	0.6100 ± 0.07
IV (dense)	HA	ELM RBF kernel	47.35 ± 6.34	0.4102 ± 0.06
	HA	mELM (erosion)	**91.27 ± 0.00**	**0.9015 ± 0.00**
	HA	mELM (dilation)	90.13 ± 0.00	0.8873 ± 0.00
	HA	Naive bayes network	62.02 ± 5.66	0.4300 ± 0.08
	HA	ELM RBF kernel	47.71 ± 3.43	0.4506 ± 0.04
All breast classifications	HA	SVM linear kernel	**65.27 ± 2.50**	**0.6200 ± 0.03**
	HA	mELM (erosion)	64.66 ± 0.00	0.6443 ± 0.00
	HA	ELM linear kernel	30.87 ± 0.53	0.3079 ± 0.01
	HA	ELM RBF kernel	10.51 ± 0.53	0.1024 ± 0.01

HA, Haralick attributes; *mELM*, morphological extreme learning machine. The values marked as bold are the best values, indicating the best configurations.

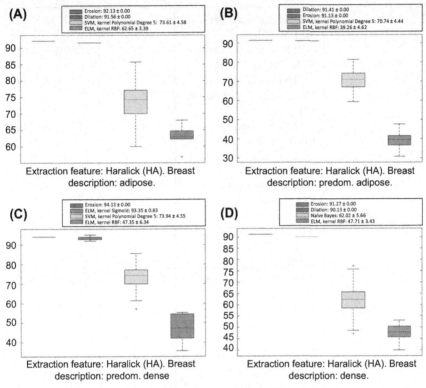

Figure 3.12 Box plots of accuracies obtained by two best and two worst classifiers. Feature extraction using Haralick attributes (HA). *ELM*, extreme learning machine.

This graph shows that our models had a standard deviation near 0. In the other two classical techniques, we can observe a larger value of standard deviation. Table 3.5 presents the nonparametric Wilcoxon test. By comparing the Wilcoxon test with the results obtained with predominantly adipose tissue, it can be concluded that the those obtained for the proposed model were statistically distinct compared with the classical classifiers, because the hypothesis test is always 1 and the P value is low.

Analyzing the experiments with predominately dense tissue, shown in Table 3.4, the model mELM (erosion) had better classification precision with a mean value of 94.13%. The proposed classifier was evaluated by the κ index as excellent. As for the worst results, the following classical techniques obtained the worst results: ELM RBF kernel and SVM polynomial kernel 5 degrees, with values of 47.35% and 73.94%, respectively. In agreement with the κ value, the techniques were evaluated as good and very good,

Table 3.5 Nonparametric Wilcoxon test comparing two best and two worst classifiers.

Tissue	Comparison	Hypothesis test	P value
I (adipose)	mELM (erosion) versus mELM (dilation)	1	2.78101e−132
	mELM (erosion) versus SVM (linear kernel)	1	1.20796e−38
	mELM (erosion) versus SVM (polynomial kernel 5 degrees)	1	8.83377e−114
	mELM (erosion) versus ELM (RBF kernel)	1	6.35092e−114
II (predominately adipose)	mELM (dilation) versus mELM (erosion)	1	2.78101e−132
	mELM (dilation) versus ELM (sigmoid act. function)	1	3.79431e−77
	mELM (dilation) versus SVM (polynomial kernel 5 degrees)	1	8.80274e−114
	mELM (dilation) versus ELM (RBF kernel)	1	6.35092e−114
III (predominately dense)	mELM (erosion) versus ELM (sigmoid act. function)	1	9.36891e−47
	mELM (erosion) versus SVM (linear kernel)	1	3.53302e−12
	mELM (erosion) versus SVM (polynomial kernel 5 degrees)	1	9.02723e−114
	mELM (erosion) versus ELM (RBF kernel)	1	6.35092e−114
IV (dense)	mELM (erosion) versus mELM (dilation)	1	2.78101e−132
	mELM (erosion) versus SVM (linear kernel)	1	0.023354
	mELM (erosion) versus naive Bayes	1	9.43394e−114
	mELM (erosion) versus ELM (RBF kernel)	1	6.35092e−114
All breast classifications	SVM (linear kernel) versus mELM (erosion)	1	0.00410445
	SVM (linear kernel) versus mELM (dilation)	1	2.05879e−23
	SVM (linear kernel) versus ELM (linear kernel)	1	7.81526e−100
	SVM (linear kernel) versus ELM (RBF kernel)	1	6.59731e−100

mELM, morphological extreme learning machine. Feature extraction used Haralick attributes.

respectively. Fig. 3.12C presents the box plot for experiments performed with predominately dense tissue. That graph shows that the model had a standard deviation near 0. In the other classical techniques, we can observe a higher value of standard deviation and the presence of an outlier, specifically for SVM with a sigmoid activation function. Table 3.5 presents the nonparametric Wilcoxon test. An analysis of the Wilcoxon test for the results obtained with the predominately dense tissue showed that the results achieved by the model were statistically distinct compared with the classical classifiers, because the hypothesis test is always 1 and the P value is low.

Observing the experiments with extremely dense tissue, shown in Table 3.4, the mELM (erosion) model had the best result with a mean accuracy of 91.27%. The proposed model was evaluated by the κ index as excellent. In addition, the mELM obtained very satisfactory accuracy. It is worth considering the difficulty of clinical analysis in extremely dense breast tissue. The least favored results were for the classical techniques of ELM RBF kernel and naive Bayes networks, with mean accuracies of 47.71% and 62.02%, respectively. The κ value evaluated these two techniques as good and very good, respectively. Fig. 3.12D shows the box plot for experiments performed with extremely dense tissue. It shows that the proposed models had a standard deviation near 0. The other two classic techniques had a standard deviation with a higher value and the presence of outliers, specifically for the naive Bayes networks. Table 3.5 shows the nonparametric Wilcoxon test. In that table, for results with extremely dense tissue, results obtained by the model were statistically distinct compared with the classical classifiers, because the hypothesis test is always 1 and the P value is low.

In the experiments performed with the entire data set (Table 3.4) (that is, encompassing all types of tissues) the SVM classifier with a linear kernel had the best result in terms of precision, with a mean accuracy 65.27%. The proposed method mELM (erosion) was in second place in terms of the classification rate, with a mean performance of 64.66%. The κ index classified both the SVM linear kernel and our mELM (erosion) method as very good. The worst results were achieved by the ELM RBF kernel and ELM linear kernel techniques. The accuracy was 10.51% and 30.87%, respectively. Still, for the worst results, the κ index evaluated the classifiers as bad and regular, respectively. Fig. 3.14A presents the box plot for experiments performed with all types of tissues. This graph shows that the proposed model had a standard deviation near 0. In the other classical techniques, a higher value of standard deviation and the presence of outliers, specifically for the winning technique (the SVM linear kernel) can be

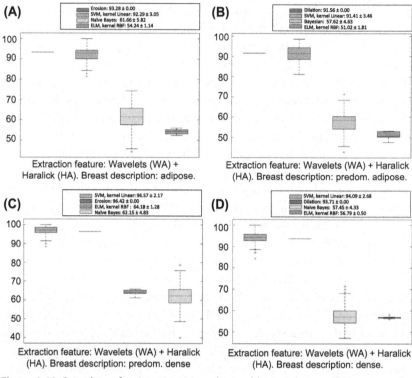

Figure 3.13 Box plots of ratings precision obtained by two best and two worst classifiers. Feature extraction employs wavelets (WA) and Haralick attributes (HA).

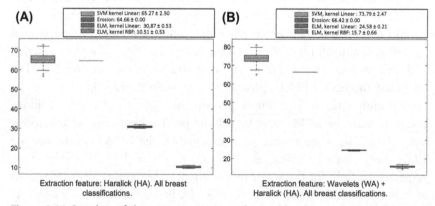

Figure 3.14 Boxplots of the ratings precisions obtained by the two best and the two worst classifiers. (A) Feature extraction employs only Haralick attributes (HA). (B) Feature extraction employs Wavelets decomposition cobined to Haralick attributes (HA). *ELM*, extreme learning machine.

noticed. Table 3.5 shows the nonparametric Wilcoxon test. For the results obtained with all types of tissue, it is possible to observe that the results achieved by the SVM linear kernel are statistically distinct from those obtained by the other classifiers, because the hypothesis test is always 1 and the P value is low in most cases.

Tables 3.5 and 3.7 show the nonparametric Wilcoxon tests between the proposed models and the main state-of-the-art classifiers. Samples are relative to the hit precisions during the test phase. For Tables 3.5 and 3.7, the P value is a scalar value [0, 1]. P is the probability of observing a test statistic as or more extreme than the observed value under the null hypothesis. If P is low, the observed result is statistically relevant.

In Table 3.6, for the results obtained with adipose tissue, our model, mELM (erosion), had the best classification performance with a percentage of correctness of 93.28%. The κ index for this method evaluated the proposed model as excellent. The worst results were due to the classifiers ELM RBF kernel and naive Bayes networks. The accuracy was 54.24% and 61.66%, respectively. Regarding the worst results, according to the κ index, both techniques were evaluated as good. Fig. 3.13A presents the box plot for experiments with adipose tissue. This graph shows that the proposed model had a standard deviation near 0. In the other classical techniques, we can observe a larger value of standard deviation and the presence of an outlier, specifically for the SVM linear kernel and for the naive Bayes networks. Table 3.7 shows the nonparametric Wilcoxon test. Results obtained with adipose tissue by the proposed model are statistically distinct from those by the classical classifiers, because the hypothesis test is always 1 and the P value is always low.

In experiments performed with predominately adipose tissue, Table 3.6 shows that the proposed model mELM (dilation) had the best accuracy, with a value of 91.56%. The proposed method was evaluated as have an excellent κ index. The worst results were due to the classic techniques: ELM RBF kernel and Bayesian networks. Accuracy values were 51.02% and 57.62%, respectively. According to the κ index, the techniques were evaluated as good and regular, respectively. Fig. 3.13B presents the box plot for experiments with fibrous (predominantly adipose) tissue. That graph shows that the proposed model had a standard deviation near 0. In the other classical techniques, there was a larger value of standard deviation and the presence of outliers, specifically in the Bayesian networks. Table 3.7 presents the nonparametric Wilcoxon test. Results obtained with fibrous tissue

Table 3.6 Results obtained by the two best and the two worst classifiers employing Wavelets combined with Haralick attributes (WA-HA).

Tissue	Feature extraction	Classifier	Test hit (%)	κ
I (adipose)	WA-HA	mELM (erosion)	**93.28 ± 0.00**	**0.9241 ± 0.00**
	WA-HA	SVM linear kernel	92.29 ± 3.05	0.8800 ± 0.05
	WA-HA	Naive Bayes	61.66 ± 5.82	0.4200 ± 0.09
	WA-HA	ELM RBF kernel	54.24 ± 1.14	0.4889 ± 0.01
II (predominately adipose)	WA-HA	mELM (dilation)	**91.56 ± 0.00**	**0.9050 ± 0.00**
	WA-HA	SVM linear kernel	91.41 ± 3.46	0.8700 ± 0.05
	WA-HA	Bayesian networks	57.62 ± 4.63	0.3600 ± 0.07
	WA-HA	ELM RBF kernel	51.02 ± 1.81	0.4561 ± 0.02
III (predominately dense)	WA-HA	SVM linear kernel	**96.57 ± 2.17**	**0.9500 ± 0.03**
	WA-HA	mELM (erosion)	96.42 ± 0.00	0.9598 ± 0.00
	WA-HA	ELM RBF kernel	64.18 ± 1.28	0.5886 ± 0.01
	WA-HA	Naive Bayes	62.15 ± 4.83	0.4300 ± 0.07
IV (dense)	WA-HA	SVM linear kernel	**94.09 ± 2.68**	**0.9100 ± 0.04**
	WA-HA	mELM (dilation)	93.71 ± 0.00	0.9285 ± 0.00
	WA-HA	Naive Bayes	57.45 ± 4.33	0.3600 ± 0.06
	WA-HA	ELM RBF kernel	56.79 ± 0.50	0.5375 ± 0.01
All breast classifications	WA-HA	SVM linear kernel	**73.79 ± 2.47**	**0.7100 ± 0.03**
	WA-HA	mELM (erosion)	66.42 ± 0.00	0.6618 ± 0.00
	WA-HA	ELM linear kernel	24.58 ± 0.21	0.2429 ± 0.00
	WA-HA	ELM RBF kernel	15.79 ± 0.66	0.1537 ± 0.01

mELM, morphological extreme learning machine.

by the proposed model are statistically distinct compared with the classical classifiers; the hypothesis test is always 1 and the P value is low.

In experiments with predominately dense tissue, shown in Table 3.6, the linear kernel SVM classifier had a better classification rate, with a value of 96.57%. The proposed mELM classifier (erosion) came in second place for accuracy, at 96.42%. The SVM linear kernel and mELM (erosion) were evaluated by the κ index as excellent. As for the worst results, the following classical techniques obtained the least favorable results: naive Bayes networks and the ELM RBF kernel, with values of 62.15% and 64.18%, respectively. According to the κ value, the techniques were evaluated as good. Fig. 3.13C presents the box plot for experiments performed with heterogeneously dense tissue. That graph shows that the mELM (erosion) had a standard deviation close to 0. In the other three classical techniques, we can observe a higher value of standard deviation and the presence of outliers, specifically for the SVM linear kernel, a technique with higher accuracy, and the naive Bayes network. Table 3.7 presents the nonparametric Wilcoxon test. Results obtained with predominately dense tissue achieved by the SVM linear kernel are statistically distinct compared with other classifiers, because the hypothesis test is always 2 and the P value is low for most cases.

Analyzing experiments conducted with extremely dense tissue, shown in Table 3.6, the linear kernel SVM had better results regarding the classification rate, with an accuracy of 94.09%. The proposed model, mELM (dilation), was in second place, with a percentage of correctness of 93.71%. For the mELM, the extremely dense tissue, which is considered difficult to analyze clinically, the proposed method achieved very satisfactory accuracy. The linear kernel SVM and the mELM (dilation) were evaluated by the κ index as excellent. The least favorable results were due to the following classical techniques: ELM kernel RBF and naive Bayes networks, with an accuracy of 56.79% and 57.45%, respectively. The κ value evaluated these two techniques as good and regular, respectively. Fig. 3.13D shows the box plot for experiments performed with extremely dense tissue. That box plot shows that the proposed model has a standard deviation near 0. The other three classical techniques had a standard deviation at a higher value and the presence of outliers, specifically for the SVM linear kernel (a technique with higher accuracy), naive Bayes networks, and ELM RBF kernel. Fig. 3.14B presents the box plot for experiments performed with all types of tissues.

Table 3.7 shows the nonparametric Wilcoxon test. Results with extremely dense tissue obtained by the SVM linear kernel are statistically

Table 3.7 Nonparametric Wilcoxon test comparing two best and worst classifiers using wavelets combined with Haralick attributes.

Tissue	Comparison	Hypothesis test	P value
I (adipose)	mELM (erosion) versus SVM (linear kernel)	1	3.44658e−12
	mELM (erosion) versus mELM (dilation)	1	2.78101e−132
	mELM (erosion) versus naive Bayes	1	9.70242e−114
	mELM (erosion) versus ELM (RBF kernel)	1	6.35092e−114
II (predominately adipose)	mELM (dilation) versus mELM (erosion)	1	2.78101e−132
	mELM (dilation) versus ELM (sigmoid action function)	1	7.12282e−114
	mELM (dilation) versus bayesian networks	1	8.9078e−114
	mELM (dilation) versus ELM (RBF kernel)	1	6.35092e−114
III (predominately dense)	SVM (linear kernel) versus ELM (erosion)	1	0.0490823
	SVM (linear kernel) versus mELM (dilation)	1	1.28758e−39
	SVM (linear kernel) versus ELM (RBF kernel)	1	2.79694e−100
	SVM (linear kernel) versus naive Bayes	1	3.66829e−100
IV (dense)	SVM (linear kernel) versus mELM (dilation)	1	5.97642e−07
	SVM (linear kernel) versus ELM (erosion)	1	3.9234e−32
	SVM (linear kernel) versus naive Bayes	1	4.73226e−100
	SVM (linear kernel) versus ELM (RBF kernel)	1	3.77904e−100
All breast classifications	SVM (linear kernel) versus mELM (erosion)	1	3.41118e−112
	SVM (linear kernel) versus mELM (dilation)	1	3.41118e−112
	SVM (linear kernel) versus ELM (linear kernel)	1	7.81884e−100
	SVM (linear kernel) versus ELM (RBF kernel)	1	6.60034e−100

mELM, morphological extreme learning machine.

distinct compared with the other classifiers, because the hypothesis test is always 1 and the P value is low.

Analyzing the experiments made with extremely dense tissue, shown in Table 3.6, the SVM linear kernel had better results regarding the classification rate, with an accuracy of 94.09%. The proposed model, mELM (dilation), was in second place, at 93.71% correct. For the mELM, for the extremely dense tissue, which is considered difficult to analyze clinically, the proposed method achieved very satisfactory accuracy. The SVM linear kernel and mELM (dilation) were evaluated by the κ index as excellent. The least favorable results were due to the classical techniques of ELM RBF kernel and naive Bayes networks, with accuracies of 56.79% and 57.45%, respectively. The κ value evaluated these two techniques as good and regular, respectively. Fig. 3.13D shows the box plot for experiments performed with extremely dense tissue. The proposed model had a standard deviation near 0. The other three classical techniques had a standard deviation with a higher value and the presence of outliers, specifically for the SVM linear kernel (a technique with higher accuracy), naive Bayes networks, and RBF ELM kernel. Table 3.7 shows the nonparametric Wilcoxon test. Results with extremely dense tissue obtained by the SVM linear kernel were statistically different compared with the other classifiers, because the hypothesis test is always 1 and the P value is low.

6. Conclusion

This work describes mELMs. The proposed method uses neural networks with hidden layers of random weights, with nodes based on nonlinear morphological operators of dilation and erosion. The main motivation was to construct new methods to support diagnosis by imaging to detect and classify breast lesions in mammogram images. The main objective of the proposed method was to combine (1) the ability of morphological neural networks to build complex decision surfaces with (2) the simplicity of training algorithms of hidden layer neural networks with random weights, such as ELMs.

In the experiments performed with IRMA mammography images, 2796 images were employed, organized into four types of tissues: adipose, fibrous, heterogeneously dense, and extremely dense. The analysis was performed for each type of tissue separately and for the entire data set. For the analysis, we compared results obtained using classical classifiers of state-of-the-art dilation, and erosion neurons, with two different types of feature extractions: (1) attributes of Haralick and (2) wavelets combined with Haralick. Results showed that using our morphological neurons improved the classification rate for most scenarios. In all configurations, the proposed method achieved a mean accuracy higher than 80%, and its classification performance was considered excellent in most cases, according to the κ index.

These results show that mELMs are competitive neural network architectures in relation to usual kernel approaches and activation functions. In synthesis, the dilation and erosion neurons proposed in this study can be employed to build other network architectures. Our morphological neurons can be applied to other classification problems as complex as detecting and classifying breast lesions.

6.1 Contributions

As main contributions of the proposed work, we can mention a study on classifying breast lesions in mammography images, focused on using ELM with morphological neurons in the hidden layer. Therefore, a morphological ELM was proposed, named mELM, containing dilation and erosion neurons in the hidden layer.

According to our experiments, we found that the proposed model, mELM, had significant improvements in relation to the recognition precision, compared with the main classifiers presented by the state of the art. Moreover, experiments were performed with four types of tissues (adipose, fibrous, heterogeneously dense, and extremely dense). When analyzing the results obtained with extremely dense tissue, the proposed method reached an accuracy of 93.71%. Extremely dense tissue is considered clinically difficult to analyze, and the proposed method was able to present satisfactory results for this type of tissue.

6.2 Future study

In addition to the contributions generated from this work, we can follow some lines of research from the proposed method. Future studies for the developed research involve constructing new methods to support the diagnosis of lesions in mammography images. There is also a to carry out new experiments with different mammogram databases to evaluate whether the results obtained with the IRMA data set can be generalized to other databases.

In addition, we intend to use the proposed morphological neurons (dilation and erosion) to create and evaluate the performance of other neural network architectures (for example, morphological MLPs). Finally, we intend to perform experiments with the proposed method in different fields of application, with the main objective of verifying whether the performance of the proposed method can generalize to solving other problems.

References

[1] American Cancer Society, Cancer Facts & Figures 2019, 2019.
[2] G.J.F. Banon, J. Barrera, Bases da Morfologia Matemática para a análise de imagens binárias, UFPE-DI, Brazil, 1994.
[3] BI-RADS, Breast Imaging Reporting and Data System (BI-RADSTM), fourth ed., American College of Radiology, 2003.
[4] A.M. Bosch, A.G. Kessels, G.L. Beets, J.D. Rupa, D. Koster, J.M. van Engelshoven, M.F. von Meyenfeldt, Preoperative estimation of the pathological breast tumour size by physical examination, mammography and ultrasound: a prospective study on 105 invasive tumours, European Journal of Radiology 48 (3) (2003) 285−292.
[5] E. Cambria, G.-B. Huang, L.L.C. Kasun, H. Zhou, Extreme learning machines [trends & controversies], IEEE Intelligent Systems 28 (6) (2013) 30−59.
[6] M.P. Coleman, M. Quaresma, F. Berrino, J.M. Lutz, R. De Angelis, R. Capocaccia, P. Baili, B. Rachet, G. Gatta, T. Hakulinen, A. Micheli, M. Sant, H.K. Weir, J.M. Elwood, H. Tsukuma, S. Koifman, G.A. E Silva, S. Francisci, M. Santaquilani, A. Verdecchia, H.H. Storm, J.L. Young, Cancer survival in five continents: a world-wide population-based study (CONCORD), The Lancet Oncology 9 (8) (2008) 730−756.
[7] H. Costa, J. Solla, J.G. Temporão, Ministério da Saúde, Instituto Nacional do Câncer. Controle do Câncer de Mama: Documento de Consenso, Rio de Janeiro, 2004.
[8] C.J. D'Orsi, Breast Imaging Reporting and Data System (BI-RADS), American College of Radiology, 1998.
[9] W. Da-Xi, F. Yuan, H. Sheng, An algorithm for medical imaging identification based on edge detection and seed filling, in: Computer Application and System Modeling (ICCASM), 2010 International Conference on. IEEE, 2010. V15-547-V15-548.
[10] E. De Abreu, S. Koifman, Fatores prognósticos no câncer da mama feminina, Revista Brasileira de Cancerologia 48 (1) (2002) 113−131.
[11] J.E.E. De Oliveira, A.M.C. Machado, G.C. Chavez, A.P.B. Lopes, T.M. Deserno, A.A. Araújo, MammoSys: a content-based image retrieval system using breast density patterns, Computer Methods and Programs in Biomedicine 99 (3) (2010) 289−297.
[12] C.E. DeSantis, C.C. Lin, A.B. Mariotto, R.L. Siegel, K.D. Stein, J.L. Kramer, R. Alteri, A.S. Robbins, A. Jemal, Cancer treatment and survivorship statistics, 2014, CA: A Cancer Journal for Clinicians 64 (4) (2014) 252−271 [S.l.].
[13] T. Deserno, M. Soiron, J. Oliveira, A. Araujo, Towards computer-aided diagnostics of screening mammography using content-based image retrieval, in: Graphics, Patterns and Images (Sibgrapi), 2011 24th SIBGRAPI Conference on IEEE, 2011, pp. 211−219.
[14] T.M. Deserno, M. Soiron, J. E. E. de Oliveira, A.A. Araújo, Computer-aided diagnostics of screening mammography using content-based image retrieval, in: SPIE Medical Imaging, International Society for Optics and Photonics, 2012, 831527-831527-9.
[15] C. Fiorentino, A. Berruti, A. Bottini, M. Bodini, M.P. Brizzi, A. Brunelli, U. Marini, G. Allevi, S. Aguggini, A. Tira, P. Alquati, L. Olivetti, L. Dogliotti, Accuracy of

mammography and echography versus clinical palpation in the assessment of response to primary chemotherapy in breast cancer patients with operable disease, Breast Cancer Research and Treatment 69 (2) (2001) 143−151.

[16] B.D. Fornage, O. Toubas, M. Morel, Clinical, mammographic, and sonographic determination of preoperative breast cancer size, Cancer 60 (4) (1987) 765−771.

[17] R.C. Gonzales, R.E. Woods, Digital Image Processing, Prentice Hall, New York, 2007.

[18] M. Hanni, I. Lekka-Banos, S. Nilsson, L. Häggroth, O. Smedby, Quantitation of atherosclerosis by magnetic resonance imaging and 3-D morphology operators, Magnetic Resonance Imaging 17 (4) (1999) 585−591.

[19] R.M. Haralick, K. Shanmugam, I. Dinstein, Textural features for image classification, IEEE Transactions on systems, man, and cybernetics 3 (6) (1973) 610−621.

[20] M. Heath, K.W. Bowyer, D. Kopans, The digital database for screening mammography, in: Proceedings of the 5th International Workshop on Digital Mammography, Medical Physics Publishing, 2000, pp. 212−218.

[21] J. Herrada, R.B. Iyer, E.N. Atkinson, N. Sneige, A.U. Buzdar, G.N. Hortobagyi, Relative value of physical examination, mammography, and breast sonography in evaluating the size of the primary tumor and regional lymph node metastases in women receiving neoadjuvant chemotherapy for locally advanced breast carcinoma, Clinical Cancer Research 3 (9) (1997) 1565−1569.

[22] G. Huang, Y. Chen, H.A. Babri, Classification ability of single hidden layer feedforward neural networks, IEEE Transactions on Neural Networks 11 (3) (2000) 799−801.

[23] G. Huang, Q. Zhu, C. Siew, Extreme learning machine: theory and applications, Neurocomputing 70 (1) (2006) 489−501.

[24] G. Huang, L. Chen, Enhanced random search based incremental extreme learning machine, Neurocomputing 71 (16) (2008) 3460−3468.

[25] G. Huang, H. Zhou, X. Ding, R. Zhang, Extreme learning machine for regression and multiclass classification, IEEE Transactions on Systems, Man, and Cybernetics, Part B (Cybernetics) 42 (2) (2012) 513−529.

[26] P. Jeatrakul, K.W. Wong, Comparing the performance of different neural networks for binary classification problems, in: Natural Language Processing, 2009. SNLP'09. Eighth International Symposium on. IEEE, 2009, pp. 111−115.

[27] S. Jenifer, S. Parasuraman, A. Kadirvel, An efficient biomedical imaging technique for automatic detection of abnormalities in digital mammograms, Journal of Medical Imaging and Health Informatics 4 (2) (2014) 291−296.

[28] J. Juhl, A.B. Crummy, Kuhlman, E. Janet, Interpretação radiológica, in: Paul & Juhl Interpretação Radiológica, Guanabara Koogan, 2000.

[29] G. Klir, B. Yuan, Fuzzy Sets and Fuzzy Logic, Prentice hall, New Jersey, 1995.

[30] R. Kruse, C. Borgelt, F. Klawonn, C. Moewes, M. Steinbrecher, P. Held, Multi-layer perceptrons, in: Computational Intelligence., Springer, 2013, pp. 47−81.

[31] J.R. Landis, G.G. Koch, The measurement of observer agreement for categorical data, Biometrics 33 (1) (1977) 159−174, https://doi.org/10.2307/2529310. PMid: 843571.

[32] L. Liberman, J.H. Menell, Breast imaging reporting and data system (BI-RADS), Radiologic Clinics of North America 40 (3) (2002) 409−430.

[33] I.K. Maitra, S. Nag, S.K. Bandyopadhyay, Identification of abnormal masses in digital mammography images, International Journal of Computer Graphics 2 (1) (2011) 17−30.

[34] S. Mallat, A Wavelet Tour of Signal Processing, Segunda Edição, Academic, Editora: New york, 1999.

[35] H. Meden, K.P. Neues, S. Röben-Kämpken, W.A. Kuhn, Clinical, mamographic, sonographic and histologic evaluation of breast cancer, International Journal of Gynecology and Obstetrics 48 (2) (1995) 193−199.

[36] Y. Miche, A. Sorjamaa, P. Bas, O. Simula, C. Jutten, A. Lendasse, OP-ELM: optimally pruned extreme learning machine, IEEE Transactions on Neural Networks 21 (1) (2010) 158–162.

[37] F. Monteiro, P. Siqueira, Correlação entre o exame clínico, a mamografia e a ultrasonografia com o exame anatomopatológico na determinação do tamanho tumoral no câncer de mama, Revista Brasileira de Ginecologia e Obstetrícia 30 (3) (2008) 107–112.

[38] M.Z. Nashed, in: Generalized Inverses and Applications: Proceedings of an Advanced Seminar Sponsored by the Mathematics Research Center, the University of Wisconsin—Madison, October 8–10, 1973, Elsevier, 2014.

[39] J.P.E.N. Pierie, C.I. Perre, L.M. Levert, P. Hooge, Clinical assessment, mammography and ultrasonography as methods of measuring the size of breast cancer: a comparison, The Breast 7 (5) (1998) 247–250.

[40] W.P. Santos, C.A.B. Melo, A.L.I. Oliveira, Mathematical morphology, in: Digital Document Analysis and Processing, Nova Science, New York, 2012, pp. 159–192.

[41] A. Shoma, A. Moutamed, A. Ameen, A. Abdelwahab, Ultrasound for accurate measurement of invasive breast cancer tumor size, Breast Journal 12 (3) (2006) 252–256.

[42] P. Soille, Morphological Image Analysis Principles and Applications, Springer-Verlag, 2004.

[43] J. Suckling, J. Parker, D. Dance, S. Astley, I. Hutt, C. Boggis, I. Ricketts, E. Stamatakis, N. Cerneaz, S.L. Kok, The mammographic image analysis society digital mammogram database, in: Proc. The 2nd International Workshop on Digital Mammography vol. 820, 1994, pp. 375–378. Amsterdam, Netherlands.

[44] M.B.R. Teixeira, Avaliação dos achados mamográficos classificados na categoria 4 do sistema BI_RADS® e sua correlação histopatológica, 2011.

[45] S.J. Thomas, I.R. Cowley, A comparison of four indices for combining distance and dose differences, International Journal of Radiation Oncology, Biology, Physics 82 (5) (2012) e717–e723.

[46] S. Ye, S. Zheng, W. Hao, Medical image edge detection method based on adaptive facet model, in: Computer Application and System Modeling (ICCASM), 2010 International Conference on. IEEE, 2010. V3-574-V3-578.

CHAPTER 4

4D medical image analysis: a systematic study on applications, challenges, and future research directions

E. Grace Mary Kanaga, J. Anitha, D. Sujitha Juliet

Department of Computer Science and Engineering, Karunya Institute of Technology and Sciences, Coimbatore, Tamilnadu, India

Contents

Advanced Machine Vision Paradigms for Medical Image Analysis
ISBN 978-0-12-819295-5
https://doi.org/10.1016/B978-0-12-819295-5.00004-4

1. Introduction

New diseases emerge every day and imaging science plays a vital role in the diagnosis of these diseases. Especially the latest four-dimensional (4D) medical imaging helps identify patient motion and abnormality in the body. Roentgen's invention of X-rays produced revolutionary progressions in the treatment of human disease. The state of the art in medicine is further improved by the invention of succeeding modalities like computer tomography (CT), ultrasound (US), single photon emission computed tomography, positron emission tomography (PET), and magnetic resonance imaging (MRI). However, constructing real-time images from these modalities with high resolution is not possible for helping in noninvasive surgeries. For instance, tumor sites located in the abdomen and thorax are affected by motion generated due to respiratory process, digestive tract motion, and vascular motion. Present imaging techniques are generally not quick enough to account for this motion in real time [1]. Three-dimensional (3D) scans show still pictures of the organs in three dimensions. 4D scans show that moving 3D images of the organ with time being the fourth dimension makes faster and accurate images than ever before. New technology is used in 4D imaging to capture the location and the motion of the body parts with respect to time. This is significant for precisely treating tumors situated on or near the body parts such as thorax and abdomen regions.

The summary of this chapter by section is given as follows:
• The first section gives a brief introduction of 4D medical imaging
• Section 2 discusses different 4D medical imaging modalities

- Sections 3, 4, and 5, present detailed exploration on the techniques and methods used, application domains, and challenges of 4D CT, 4D US, and 4D flow MRI
- The chapter concludes with open issues, challenges, and future trends in 4D medical image analysis

2. Different 4D medical imaging modalities

Several good surveys have been done by different authors to study 4D medical imaging, and each of them have presented their views from different perspectives, including advances in 4D medical imaging and radiation therapy [2], 4D registration and fusion techniques [1], software used in 4D imaging [3], different modalities of 4D imaging such as 4D CT [4], 4D MRI [5], 4D US [6], and its currents applications. Different 4D medical imaging modalities are listed in Fig. 4.1.

2.1 4D computer tomography

In CT, a special X-ray device is used to produce images from various angles of the body. The cross section of the organs and tissues are made available by processing these images. 4D CT is a special type of CT scan that produces multiple images over time. It permits playback of the scan as a video, so that physiological processes can be viewed and internal movement can be monitored. The time is the fourth dimension added to the traditional 3D CT [7]. The image in Fig. 4.2 gives the view of a 4D CT machine.

2.2 4D positron emission tomography scan

Faster and more accurate imaging is achieved in 4D PET-CT by combining PET with CT. It is designed to apprehend the internal

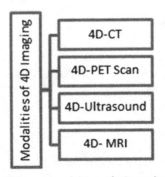

Figure 4.1 Different modalities of 4D medical imaging.

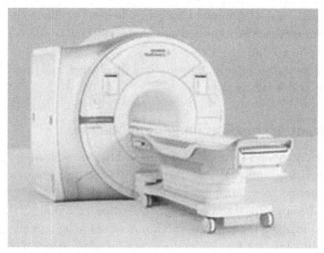

Figure 4.2 4D CT machine.

movement of organs and the metabolism of the tumor. Fig. 4.3 shows the image of a 4D PET scan machine. It creates the most complete and accurate information on the tumor and provides information on how the tumor moves with breathing and other body motions. It's good for imaging tumors in the chest, abdomen, and pelvis.

2.3 4D Ultrasound

US imaging uses sound waves to create an image. Two-dimensional (2D) US creates a cross-sectional view, however in a 3D ultrasound, number of

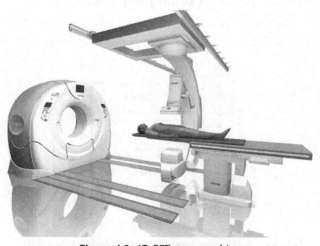

Figure 4.3 4D PET scan machine.

2D images is taken from different angles and merged together to form a 3D image. When it is viewed it looks more or less similar to a regular photograph. 4D is like 3D, however it enables us to see the movement also.

This noninvasive imaging technology is widely used in the area of obstetrics, gynecological, and interventional radiology (IR). In the gynecology sector, US imaging is used to capture the cornual ectopic pregnancy, endometrial cavity, congenital uterine anomalies, and adnexal lesions. Using a 4D US scan, it is possible to see the baby kicking or opening and closing his or her eyes [8]. Even though different US machines are available in the market, a sample 4D US scan machine is given in Fig. 4.4.

2.4 4D MRI

Radio waves and magnetic waves are used in MRI to capture the whole image of the body and subsequently it is free from unsafe radiation. The beams from the MRI machine move the nuclei of the human molecule into an alternate location and when these nuclei move back to their original location, they emit radio signals into the scanner to generate the image. These images are generated based on the intensity and location of the signal.

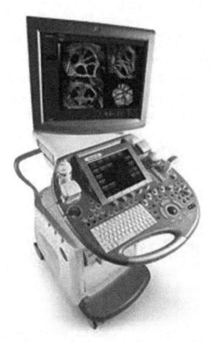

Figure 4.4 4D ultrasound machine.

Our body is composed of water, and water contains hydrogen particles. MRI scan uses these hydrogen particles to create images. The parts of the body that contain less hydrogen atoms (like bones) appear dark and the tissues with numerous hydrogen particles look brighter. Therefore it is more appropriate for analyzing spinal cord injuries and for discovering tumors in the brain. An increasingly exhaustive image of the heart and aorta can be created using the cutting-edge imaging technique, 4D flow MRI. In the fourth dimension, movement enables the physician to view the flow of the blood through the cardiovascular system more clearly. This helps the clinician to do better follow-up with cardiac patients [9].The 4D MRI machine used in Children's Hospital Colorado is shown in Fig. 4.5.

3. Exploration of 4D CT

Initially 4D CT has been primarily used for preparing radiation therapy planning. But recently many opportunities are opened in the diagnostic field for 4D CT [4]. The 4D CT from Canon medical systems is making high-hazard clinical cases simpler, more secure, and quicker. Infix 4D CT combines the most flexible angio suite with the advanced dynamic volume CT to obtain a full CT scan swiftly.

3.1 Application domains of 4D CT medical imaging

4D CT gives the medical team new capabilities for planning the intervention, treatment, and follow-up. Canon's signature wide detector CT technology with up to 16 cm coverage in a single rotation provides exceptional capability in a wide range of procedures including cardiac,

Figure 4.5 4D MRI machine. *(Courtesy: Children's Hospital Colorado.)*

neuro, interventional oncology, and trauma. It also brings a new dimension to procedures such as gastric-intestinal (GI) bleeding, bronchial artery embolization, and complex endoleak embolization or drainage. For example, locating a GI bleed can be very difficult in angio view or cone-beam CT due to motion artifacts caused by breathing, but a 4D CT provides high quality images [10]. Even though 4D CT is found useful in various health problems, a few of the application domains of 4D CT have been listed in Fig. 4.6.

3.1.1 Parathyroid

The most recent innovation in parathyroid imaging is parathyroid 4D CT. It produces high-resolution imaging when compared with any other type of parathyroid imaging. Parathyroid 4D CT is especially valuable when other imaging studies have neglected to demonstrate the affected parathyroid gland or when the life system of the neck has been misshaped by earlier medical procedure or concurrent thyroid illness [11]. The most significant job of parathyroid 4D CT is in the administration of reoperative cases. In such patients, the high resolution imaging given by parathyroid 4D CT causes us to reduce dissection during the medical procedure, all the while improving the health condition of the patients. Parathyroid 4D CT has made reoperative medical procedures both quicker and progressively fruitful, especially in challenging situations where numerous abnormal parathyroid glands are causing the patient's infection are proven by UCLA Endocrine Center, Los Angeles, CA.

3.1.2 Radiation oncology

• **Lung Cancer**

The main challenge in the treatment of non-small-cell lung cancer is the motion of tumor and normal organs since it has an effect on the delineation

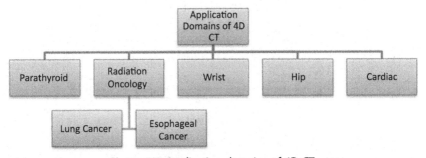

Figure 4.6 Application domains of 4D CT.

of the target and the normal tissues, the required margins, and dose distribution. The experimental study done by Slotman et al. [12] shows that 4D CT highly improves the target definition. Even though the exposure to radiation from 4D CT is six times when compared to a single conventional helical CT scan, the personalized and smaller volume generated from 4D CT highly justifies this additional exposure.

Wu, Lian, and Chen [13] have proposed a method to reconstruct a new 4D CT from a single breathing 3D CT on the treatment day (TD) with the direction from the high resolution 4D CT model built from the planning day, and used to estimate new motions on the TD. The steps of the method proposed by Wu et al. [13] are detailed in Fig. 4.7.

As per the abovementioned steps the authors have more precisely localize the moving tumor on the TD and it improves the lung cancer treatment.

Rasheed et al. have done a study with 17 patients to quantify the efficacy of abdominal compression plate on respiratory-induced motions using 4D CT to evaluate displacement and volume changes of the tumor, lungs, and heart [14]. The robustness of the mid-ventilation approach in the presence of irregular breathing patterns was evaluated by Aznar et al., which is an important factor for the calculation of patient-individualized margins based on 4D CT scan during lung cancer treatment [15].

- *Esophageal cancer*

Based on the literature [16] it is known that 4D CT is useful in detecting the variations in cardiac volume during radiotherapy for esophageal cancer.

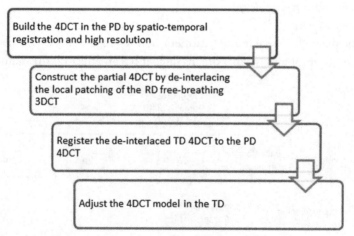

Figure 4.7 Steps to reconstruct 4D CT from 3D CT.

Repeated 4D CT has been performed by Wang et al. for 46 patients having esophageal cancer before radiotherapy and each 10 fractions during treatment. He has demonstrated that cardiac volume has been reduced altogether from an early treatment up to the middle stage. The heart volume changes viewed on 3D CT and 4D CT were consistent during radiotherapy.

3.1.3 Wrist
4D CT imaging helps for improved diagnosis and treatment of wrist ligament injuries. Many researchers have studied this area and proved that 4D CT improves the treatment of wrist injuries. Choi et al. [17] have done an analysis to determine the technical feasibility of 4D CT for analysis of the variation of radioscaphoid angle and lunocapitate angle during wrist radioulnar deviation, and they have proved that it is feasible.

The early diagnosis of tendon wounds in *Scapholunate interosseus* could assist the specialist with preventing injury that stimulates instability and ends in osteoarthritis. Leng et al. [18] have exhibited that the utilization of 4D CT in diagnosing *S. interosseus* tendon wounds with clinical doubt of *S. interosseus* tendon damage during spiral ulnar deviation, flexionextension, and dart hurler's movements. The achievability of utilizing 4D CT in the assessment of wrist biomechanics before and after surgery was demonstrated by Shores et al. [19].

3.1.4 Hip
4D CT has been put to use to view femoroacetabular impingement with a high exactness [20]. While customary CT evaluates the effect of pelvic tilt and position, which is a constraint of projectional strategies, 4D CT is expected to straightforwardly demonstrate the impingement of contradicting bony structures. In addition, the 3D CT dataset yields detailed pictures of the bony anatomy. Prior to the utilization of 4D CT, it was assumed that subluxation was tangled in pincer-type forbidden impingement. In any case, it was not convincingly demonstrated that 4D CT show that incomplete subluxation happens in all femoroace tabular impingement subtypes [4].

3.1.5 Cardiac
Coronary deterrent is the reason for ischemic coronary illness and prompts reduced heart supply and reduced contractility of the myocardium. Nowadays, high-resolution 4D CT has turned out to be accessible for

cardiovascular imaging and furnishes the clinician with superb anatomical pictures. In light of the investigation done by Lantz et al. [21], it has been demonstrated that 4D flow CT, in light of clinically accessible CT information, can deliver both subjectively and quantitatively comparative intracardiac blood flow designs in a cohort of patients with coronary illness when compared with the 4D flow MRI and can possibly be utilized in the appraisal of both procured and inborn coronary illness.

Another technique to identify 3D movement and strain from 4D cardiovascular CT pictures by compelling myocardial volume changes, force steadiness and movement smoothness presumptions have been proposed by Tavakoli and Sahba [22]. The strategy was approved by utilizing manual monitoring of the cardiovascular CT landmarks. The normal mistake for the manual following, by a specialist, was 2.9 ± 0.9 mm. Likewise the heart CT strain esteems were compared with the cardiovascular MRI and 2D B-mode echocardiography strain estimations of similar patients. It has been obvious that the movement and strain value processed from heart CT pictures concur with movement and strain esteems figured from echocardiography and labeled MRI pictures. Xiong et al. [23] have introduced another representation system for computer-aided diagnosis. The heart capacity or movement was followed by deforming the four-chamber heart model utilizing picture enlistment of 4DCT pictures.

3.2 Challenges in 4D CT

Although 4D CT has vast applications in different domains of imaging and diagnosis, it has a few limitations that need to be addressed. 4D CT generates a large volume of data that need reasonable effort and time to process [4]. 4D CT is used to calculate the internal target volume (ITV), which incorporates all possible locations of the tumor. In recent times, limitations of 4D CT in the context of treatment planning has been analyzed by comparing the ITV obtained in 4D CT to dynamic MRI images. It has been proven that variations in the ITV depend on the amplitude, tumor size, and breathing pattern. A stable ITV calculation method needs to be designed. The range of standard appearances is yet to be fully proven as 4D CT is a newly established technique. The researchers may work in these areas.

4. Exploration of 4D ultrasound imaging

4.1 4D ultrasound

In medicine, US, or ultrasonography, is a popular method that uses the high-frequency sound waves to observe images of structures in the internal human body [24]. During the examination, the physician or doctor moves a device called a probe or transducer over the area of the body to be studied. A small amount of gel is applied to the area to remove air pockets between the skin and the transducer. The probe emits the US waves that bounce from the internal tissues and produce the image of the structure. Different images have been produced due to the different densities of tissues, air, and fluid inside the body. The latest modern US diagnostics equipment has been progressively coming with the optimal patient examination techniques, effectively competing with methods such as CT and MRI.

4D US imaging allows physicians to gain information that can be used for detection and diagnosis with rich visual information and quantitative data. In obstetrics, the anomalies in fetal including brain, spine, heart, face, thorax, and limbs have been assessed for further diagnosis. Fusion imaging plays an important role that provides highly precise guidance in interventional radiology, where the GPS positioning is incorporated to capture the real-time response of needle position throughout interventional procedures and permits flexible adjustment of the needle. The advances in IR improve the quality and efficiency of the intervention procedures with cost savings. The benefits related to US imaging such as quality of care and cost has already been proven in several US applications.

4.1.1 Evolution from 2D to 4D

The traditional 2D US imaging processes the US waves in the single plane [25]. The waves that are reflected from the organ give a flat, black-and-white image. The movement of transducer allows viewing in numerous planes. So far 2D US imaging is used to give a complete assessment of fetal structure and morphology.

Further improvement in this technology helps to acquire volumetric data by capturing 2D images at different angles. The 3D US imaging deals with volume data acquisition, analysis, and display. The volumetric data can be viewed through computerized processing. It fills the gaps to generate a smooth 3D image using either rendering of images or multiplanar format. The virtual planes provide improved visualization of structures by adding 6% more chance of identifying defects that is not achievable by 2D imaging. It relies less on technician skill and experience for analysis of common fetal abnormalities. 3D imaging is helpful in identifying the structural congenital irregularities of the fetus during the 18−20 week scan.

4D imaging allows a live streaming video of the images that shows the movement of the fetal heart valves and blood flow in vessels whereas 3D imaging provides the visualization as static 3D images. It uses either a matrix array 3D transducer or a 2D transducer in which 20–30 volumes has been acquired rapidly. It has similar benefits as 3D, but additionally the movement of several moving organs also has been analyzed.

4.1.2 Steps in ultrasound image capturing

3D/4D US image capturing is defined in three steps [26]: acquisition, reconstruction, and display. US image acquisition is more flexible compared to CT or MRI. Image acquisition has been done in any of the three methods such as free-hand acquisitions, acquisitions with a motor-driven 3D transducer, and acquisitions with a 2D matrix array transducer. Free-hand acquisition results in a degradation in image quality and inaccurate quantification. Image acquisition using a 3D transducer has the main disadvantage of the bulkiness and weight of the 3D transducers compared with conventional 2D transducers. An acquisition with a 2D matrix array transducer is adopted in almost all 3D US image acquisition because it uses electronic scanning and solves the restrictions of 2D mechanical scanning. Reconstruction is the method where 2D images are translated into a series of 3D/4D representations. It can be done in either feature-based or voxel-based reconstruction. Feature-based reconstruction needs less information to process, which allows efficient 3D/4D rendering. But there may be a loss of image information due to the information reduction. In voxel-based reconstruction, the information in the 2D domain is interpolated into 3D/4D Cartesian volume. This method provides an improvement over feature-based but it produces large datasets that need high processing computers.

After reconstruction, the image has to be displayed with proper rendering. The rendering techniques are classified into surface rendering, multiplanar viewing, and volume rendering. The surface rendering uses a segmentation or classification where the segmentation is used to segregate voxels of similar features to represent a specific anatomic structure. The complexity of the segmentation algorithm varies from simple thresholding to complicated, depending on the properties of the image [27]. Multiplanar viewing offers a display of an arbitrary plane. The interface tools in the computer allow choosing a plane from the volume including the oblique. Volume-based rendering has been carried out using the ray-casting technique, maximum intensity projection, and minimum intensity projection. Recently two volume-based rendering techniques such as volume contrast imaging and inversion mode have been introduced to perform 4D rendering. The acquired image may have some defects that can be corrected by implementing various preprocessing techniques present in the 4D medical image processing such as slice timing correction, motion correction, spatial smoothing, and detrending.

Some of the 4D US machines available in the market [28] are VOLUSON S6 — BT14, GE Voluson E8 BT 13, GE Voluson S8, GE Voluson E8 BT10, GE Voluson E6 BT13.5, GE Voluson S6, Philips IE33 F Cart, PHILIPS IU22 G Cart, GE Voluson 730 PRO BT04, GE Voluson 730 Expert BT08, and GE Voluson P8. Fig. 4.8 shows a sample of the 4D US machine.

Some of the advantages of 3D/4D US imaging are
- Fetal heart screening and diagnosis with reduced time
- Volume data storage for screening, expert evaluation, and remote diagnosis
- Enriched parental affection with the baby
- Fetal anomalies, particularly of the face, heart, limbs, neural tube, and skeleton are identified precisely.

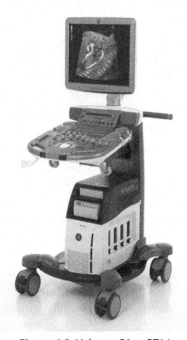

Figure 4.8 Voluson S6 — BT14.

4.2 4D ultrasound imaging in the assessment of fetal behavior

Due to the speckle noise nature of the US, surface rendering provides a low rendered image quality. This has been enhanced by performing pre-processing on the 2D US images. A 2D preprocessing for the 4D surface rendering has been proposed on the fetal US visualization that is implemented in the graphics processing unit (GPU) platform [29]. A despeckle filter with adaptive local statistical approach has been developed to remove the speckle noise and to enhance the edges. The experiment achieves acceptable rendering performance with better time performance on GPU. Maysanjaya et al. [30] perform a series of image processing techniques such as preprocessing, segmentation, shape-based feature extraction, and feature classification to classify the fetus gender on the US images using learning vector quantization and made a comparative analysis with other artificial neural network (ANN) methods.

Some common imaging problems and mistakes have been identified while performing the 4D imaging to assess fetal behavior, which is discussed below [31].

- **Images of fuzzy nature**

    This is the most common and least descriptive issue. Fig. 4.9A shows a sample fuzzy image. This occurs due to the wrong 4D setting in the machine. If the gain is too high, the fuzzy image is affected by image artifacts. If the gain is too low, the machine will not produce the details. The positioning of the transducer also plays an important role that reflects a bad imaging angle. The machine is not able to render the image clearly due to the overuse of the X, Y, and Z control presets that is shown in Fig. 4.9B.

- **Unrecognizable 4D with ideal 2D image**

    Generally, in the 2D image, the obstacles are not shown because it gives only a thin slice of images as shown in Fig. 4.10. But in the case of 4D, it renders the entire surface. If there is any obstruction between the face and the probe, it will create artifacts over the face image that makes it difficult to render the baby's face in 4D. But in 2D, sweeping the probe left-to-right will identify if there are any other obstacles in front of the face. Holding a probe also helps to get a clear image.

- **Obstacles in front of the face**

    Sometimes the feet, arms, and/or hands of the baby cover the face, which makes the image rendering difficult. The physician follows some standard techniques such as moving the probe in different angles, repositioning the mother, or giving the mother juice or something sweet to get the attention of the baby. Otherwise, adjust the size of the region of interest (ROI) box and reposition it to the spot that makes it easier to get the clear image.

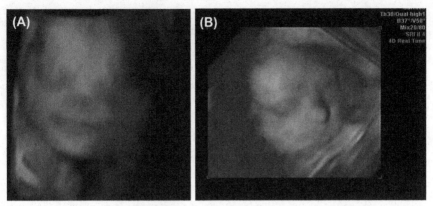

Figure 4.9 (A) Fuzzy image [8]. (B) Overuse of the axis controls degrades image quality [8].

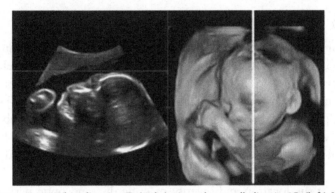

Figure 4.10 White line in 4D (right) gives the small slice in 2D (left) [8].

- *Difficulties in imaging the overweight patient*

As the US waves travel through the body, the sound is absorbed by the body. The image quality degrades due to attenuation if the patient is obese. This can be overcome by changing the penetration settings, by adjusting the gain, or by turning off the tissue harmonics. Also, place the probe as close as possible to the baby or reposition the mother on her side.

The steps that are performed to acquire a 4D US "babyface" imaging are shown in Fig. 4.11 and described as follows.

Step 1: Acquire an ideal 2D image by optimizing the machine settings and adjust the gain control. A good 2D image leads to a good 4D image.

Step 2: Set the ROI/render box/convex box over the image in the correct position with proper size and depth to get a good image. The image inside the box appears in 4D and outside the box does not.

Step 3: Check the presets for particular types of 4D modes in the machine to perform the surface rendering that obtains the best 4D babyface image.

Step 4: Adjust the gain to a lower value in 4D mode that will eradicate artifact in the image so the clear face can be obtained. If the image is too dark, adjust the gain by increasing it to make the face appear clear .

Step 5: Invert the image to get a correct orientation of the baby's face. This step mainly depends on the position of the baby and the orientation of the probe.

Step 6: Often return to 2D mode to reposition the probe to adjust the baby's movement or for better angles. It is easy to find the position of the baby in 2D rather than identifying in 4D. Also, it is less efficient to reposition in 4D due to the positioning of the ROI box and the rendering time.

Step 7: Even with good positioning, sometimes the image captured is poor. Further, the image is optimized by adjusting the proper settings that allow the machine to give the best 4D rendered images.

4.3 4D ultrasound imaging in neuroophthalmology

US imaging plays an important role in ophthalmology to evaluate eye circulation and eye structures for cataract patients. The recent development in 4D imaging helps in identifying additional information such as functional and structural changes in normal and pathological conditions. Titianova et al. [32] have presented a study on demonstrating the diagnostic abilities of 4D in eye pathology and neuroophthalmic syndromes. This study has been made on 15 healthy controls and 15 eye pathology patients with multimodal sonography. They have been reported that 4D imaging helps in identifying the location and severity of optic disc and optic nerve edema from other ophthalmic lesions. Ciurte et al. have developed a semi-supervised segmentation algorithm to segment the eye tumor from the ophthalmic imaging. Initially, the image is formulated with a graph of patches and the initial labels are provided by the user markers. The segmentation problem is formulated as a continuous min–cut problem and solved with a fast minimization scheme. They have evaluated their algorithm further to segment liver tumors, fetal head, and prostate.

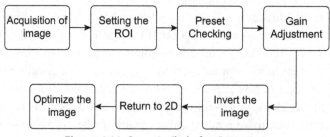

Figure 4.11 Steps in "babyface" imaging.

4.4 4D ultrasound imaging in neurology

Neurological disorders are syndromes of the brain, spine, and the nerves that join them. Neuroimaging helps to assess patients with neurological disorders [33]. Therapeutic US helps in the treatment of neurological diseases such as stroke, Parkinson disease, and chronic pain [34]. The recent development in US leads to a technology called functional US (fUS) [35,36], which offers high-sensitivity whole-brain imaging to assess the cerebral blood volume changes. The clinical applications of fUS are neuropediatry and neurosurgery. US has been used to detect the prenatal fetal brain anomalies between 16 and 32 weeks of pregnancy.

Children's cerebral palsy (CCP) is a neurological disorder that occurs in children, diagnosed at the age of 3. The development of 4D US helps to observe fetal movement in real time, which in turn helps to estimate quality and count of the spontaneous movement of fetal, stitches on the head, and the neurology thumb. Tomasovic et al. [37] have reviewed the epidemiology of CCP and its risks, diagnosis, significance, and treatments. The researchers have given insight on how 4D US plays a role to detect neurological damage early during fetal and postnatal development.

Kurjak et al. [38] have performed a study on the latest 4D sonographic on fetal behavior and present results of fetal neurobehavioral development assessment by Kurjak Antenatal Neurological Test in high-risk pregnancies. The authors have been performed an evaluation of fetal motoric patterns to estimate the qualitative features of movements and fetal face movements. They published a novel scoring system for fetal behavior based on 4D US.

Blahuta et al. [39] have presented a method to work with US images of the brain stem to find the defects in the substantia nigra (SN) that leads to Parkinson's disease (PD). A series of image processing techniques such as Otsu thresholding, morphological operators, and ANN have been carried out to help the doctor to diagnose PD by identifying the level of damage in the SN.

Image processing algorithm plays an important role in segmenting the carotid arteries from 3D/4D US images. A carotid US is used to observe the block in blood flow via carotid arteries that lead to the risk of stroke. The acquired US images suffer from various artifacts such as speckle noise, shadowing, false echoes, and refraction. Due to the presence of noise, the image needs to be filtered before processing. Mattsson and Eriksson [40] have devised a semiautomatic segmentation method to segment the carotid arteries from 3D and 4D US images. They have employed two adaptive filtering methods, Nagao-Ye filtering and Granlund-Knutsson filtering, to suppress the noise and to preserve the edge. The noises present in the image make the edge detection process more difficult. The authors utilize a Monga-Deriche-Canny edge detection process to separate the edge. Initially, a simple seeded region growing segmentation is applied to extract the rough region of carotid arteries. It is followed by an inflatable balloon model, which is a 3D segmentation technique adopted in many 3D/4D medical image segmentations.

4.5 Role of ultrasound in medical field

In the medical field, different fields use US to diagnose or screen the diseases in various parts of the body [41]. There are some procedural uses of US such as US-guided needle biopsy, needle aspiration, and US-assisted intravenous access. US can be used therapeutically, to break up kidney and gallbladder stones, treat cancer and musculoskeletal injuries, in drug delivery, hemostasis, or thrombolysis. A 4D registration technique named register-to-reference by tracking strategy is used to track the liver and provide supervision for transjugular intrahepatic portosystemic shunt (TIPS) interventions. The first step estimates the approximate transformation between the reference image and the incoming image during the tracking. During the second step, 4D image registration is applied between the reference frame and the approximately transformed input frame. Kim et al. [26] have discussed some of the abdominal applications of 3D/4D US.

Obstetrics: Access the fetus progression such as the number of fetuses, age, position, movement, breath and heart rates of the fetus, and the fluid amount in the uterus. The best time to take the 3D/4D US sonogram picture of the fetus in the womb is about 26 weeks. Doppler US has been used to examine the blood flow.

Gynecology: Vaginal US, pelvic US, or transvaginal US is used to diagnose the lower abdominal pain, ovarian cysts, uterine fibroids, uterine growths, and endometriosis.

Cardiology: To access the overall function of the heart, a heart US or echocardiography is used. It examines the blood flow through valves and chambers of the heart. It evaluates the heartbeat strength and the amount of blood pumped through it.

Blood vessels: Doppler US technology is used to identify blood clots in veins, narrowing of vessels (stenosis), or widening of vessels (dilatation).

Abdominal structures: The solid organs such as the liver, pancreas, bladder, gallbladder, and kidneys within the abdominal cavity have been evaluated through abdominal US.

Breast US: The interventional radiology helps to guide biopsy of breast masses in order to diagnosis breast cancer.

Neck US: The nodules, growths, and tumors in the thyroid and parathyroid glands have been diagnosed.

Knee US: It is used to evaluate the presence of a Baker's cyst in the back of the knee.

Skin US: US can be used to diagnose various types of skin diseases.

Eye US: The retina of the eye is examined to find whether the person has cataracts. It helps in cataract surgery and to diagnose retinal detachment.

4.6 Challenges in ultrasound imaging

US is an invaluable third eye that helps to monitor the fitness and development of the baby, but it cannot catch everything. In terms of processing the image, the challenges to be faced are denoising the image to remove the speckle noise, preserving and enhancing the organ edges, processing time constraints and implementation environment with high processing power, and significant cost value. Apart from this, there may be obstacles in US imaging due to the technical, software, and hardware issues. The lack of service information can negatively impact a biomed's ability to properly diagnose and fix a problem.

5. Exploration of 4D flow magnetic resonance imaging

5.1 4D flow MRI

Clinical evaluation of blood flow variations is indispensable in order to completely understand cardiovascular function and to diagnose the long-term risk related to the circulatory system. Congenital heart disease is considered one of the leading causes of morbidity and mortality worldwide [42] and the bicuspid aortic valve remains the most common congenital cardiac abnormality, with occurrence between 1% and 2% of the global population [43]. Anomalies from birth or subsequent intrusions or both may compel blood to flow in unpredicted directions and patterns. Doppler echocardiography method is capable of evaluating the blood flow using the color Doppler mode. This method provides dimensional 2D snapshot of unidirectional velocity and measures the flow velocity in the direction of the US beam. However, inconsistent readings owing to operator proficiency, patient body frame, and inadequate acoustic windows are the major limitations related to this method [44].

With the great development in the field of digital technology in the recent past, MRI has become an essential imaging modality in identifying and diagnosing cardiovascular diseases. MRI uses pulsed radio frequency and magnets to produce digital images for clinical diagnosis. This technique enables healthcare experts to know the structural and functional details related to heart, aorta, and surrounding blood vessels [45]. The traditional 2D phase-contrast MRI perhaps measures blood flow volumes, however the patients are expected to hold their breath during scanning. Since the imaging plane needs to be predetermined, the facts will comprise only irregular flow within those parameters. The conventional MRI has progressed from 2D phase contrast procedures to 3D diagnosis and now, the state-of-the-art 4D flow MRI find their position in clinical assessment. 4D flow MRI, on the other hand, permits patients to take breaths generously and blood flow is assessed retrospectively through any imaging planes [46].

The 4D flow MRI is a cutting-edge imaging technology that provides a complete picture of the heart and the blood flow through the circulatory system. This technology recommends rising potential for the noninvasive evaluation of blood flow in the heart and aorta. In the fourth dimension, movement allows the healthcare professional to visualize the blood flow accurately and identify the areas that demand closer follow-up.

4D velocity cardiovascular magnetic resonance (4D flow CMR) introduces phase contrast CMR with blood flow determining in all three spatial directions. 4D flow CMR assesses parameters like blood flow, its pressure, frictional flow of blood on the aortic wall, velocity, and turbulent kinetic energy throughout the heart and major blood vessels of the circulatory system. Since the results are provided in the form of visually colorful and dazzling images, MRI experts can easily comprehend the images and have confidence to make a decision about a curative approach [47]. This technology offers enormous insight into cardiovascular pathologies including aneurysm (a widened spot in the heart), hypertrophic cardiomyopathy (thick/weakened heart muscle), aortic bicuspid valve disease, cardiac tumor (growth on the surface of the heart), congenital heart disease, and heart failure.

5.2 4D flow MRI Processing and Analysis

As discussed previously, 4D MRI spins a new perspective on the medical imaging system, enabling the medical experts to observe the heart and blood flow to specific areas in an improved and zoomed-in version. Fig. 4.12 depicts the basic flow diagram MRI image processing and analysis process. This technology categorizes the occurrence of structure in MRI flow data and obtains the clinical indicator based on the identified structures. 4D flow datasets include anatomical data and velocity in three spatial directions referred to as Sx, Sy, and Sz. MRI investigation consists of series of perfusion and 4D flow acquisitions with multiple sets of MRI data. Series may be divided into magnitude and phase acquisition portions.

During image acquisition, 4D pulse sequences are utilized, which obtain a 3D volume set with phase contrast information. Therefore, it is termed as 4D phase contrast MRI. After data acquisition, the preprocessing of raw input images is performed for error correction. This stage includes the correction of phase error, antialiasing, and landmark identification. Later, visualization and quantification of flow such as arterial versus venous flow, mixture of visual characterization of blood flow information with anatomy have been performed on the resulting MRI data set. Fig. 4.12 depicts the complete process of 4D flow MRI in detail.

5.2.1 Data acquisition using flow-sensitive MRI

2D phase contrast (PC) MRI considers the acquaintance between MR signal phase attained during measurement and the blood flow velocity. Two different velocity-dependent signal phases are encoded using magnetic field gradients to measure blood flow velocity along a single direction. The two different phase images are subtracted from the acquisitions to eradicate the unnecessary background phase effects. The signal intensity from the resultant phase difference is exactly correlated to flow velocity, which further enables the expert to view and quantify the blood flow.

In a standard 2D PC MRI, the data acquisition is performed through a plane velocity encoding method by measuring the single-direction velocity orthogonal to the 2D imaging slice. For every cardiac time frame, one reference scan and a velocity scan are obtained through direct succession. The average of these two scans results in magnitude images and the subtraction of phase images results in quantitative blood flow velocities. This process is performed during 10−20 s breath-hold period. For patients with congestive heart failure and short breath, this breath-hold period may not be achievable. This is the major drawback in the implementation of 2D PC MRI. The image reconstruction stage provides a sequence of anatomical images that signify the temporal variations of morphology and blood flow over the circulatory system.

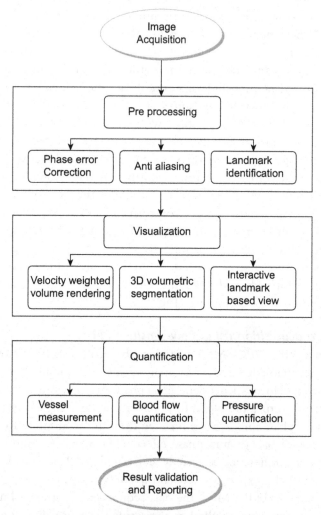

Figure 4.12 4D flow MRI processing and analysis.

One important parameter in PC MRI is the user-defined Venc velocity, which denotes the maximum possible flow velocity. When the primary velocity exceeds the Venc velocity, it will result in velocity aliasing, which is observed as a rapid variation from high to low velocity within the flow region. This aliasing artifact will compromise the precise flow visualization [48]. Also the velocity noise is directly associated with Venc velocity. As a result, high Venc may ease the issue of aliasing; on the other hand it will increase the velocity noise level. Therefore the selection of Venc should be carefully carried out to evade aliasing and to minimize the velocity noise. Typically the specifications for Venc in the thoracic aorta ranges from 150 to 200 cm/s, aorta with aortic stenosis or coarctation ranges from 250 to 400 cm/s, and intracardiac flow ranges from 100 to 150 cm/s.

In 4D flow MRI, velocity is determined along all three spatial directions all through the cardiac cycle, enabling a time-resolved 3D velocity field. The velocity measurements in three dimensions are attained by interleaved four-point velocity encoding that gains one reference image and three velocity-encoded images along three orthogonal (x, y, z) directions [49]. After completion of the 4D flow acquisition, four time-resolved (CINE) 3D datasets with magnitude data portraying the structure and three flow velocity directions Sx, Sy, and Sz are produced. Since enormous amount of data need to be collected, an effective data acquisition is very much essential to accomplish sensible scan times for 4D flow MRI in the clinical environment. Recent imaging approaches such as kt-BLAST, kt-SENSE, kt- GRAPPA, radial undersampling, and compressed sensing can assist in reducing the scan time [50]. Based on spatiotemporal resolution, pulse rate, and anatomic coverage, the scanning may be accomplished between 5 and 20 min for cardiovascular function.

Radial acquisition schemes combined with an undersampling [51] method has been proposed by Gu et al. to improve 4D flow MRI. This technique provides spatial resolution with significant volumetric coverage with better scan time. The inherent properties of the radial data acquisition approach minimize the incidence of motion artifacts and facilitate self-gating.

5.2.2 Data Preprocessing for Error Corrections

The image acquisition stage produces pulse series to run the MRI mechanism and obtains raw MRI. The 4D flow MRI captures the anatomy of the subject (magnitude) and velocity (phase). Since the data acquired is in the form of raw image, preprocessing is essential to reduce the phase offset errors owing to eddy currents, gradient field nonlinearity, and Maxwell terms, which may demean the quality of the images and provide inaccurate results [52].

The eddy current rectification approach is based on recognizing the structure with static tissue. These tissue structures evaluate the eddy current provoking linearly changing phase offset errors, which are then deducted from whole image. Phase offset errors for Maxwell terms and eddy currents can be rectified during reconstruction as investigated by Bernstein et al.

[53]. According to Bannas et al. [54], background phase correction is carried out using semiautomatic segmentation of the static tissue and verified by examining the derived angiogram for visual static tissue and through flow measurements of static tissue.

Apart from eddy current rectification and phase offset errors correction, image unwrapping, magnitude and phase aliasing correction, and artifact detection have also been performed during this phase.

5.3 4D blood flow visualization and Quantification

The visualization phase consists of a mixture of procedures such as fixing or locating the anatomical structures, producing −3D volumes/contours through image segmentation, differentiating arterial and venous blood flow representation, and identifying them with appropriate colors (blue and red). Recognition of suspected shunts signifying blood flow through appropriate colors is also done in this phase.

Most of the visualization techniques utilize 2D examination planes placed in the subject of interest. The 3D streamlines produced by these planes for cardiac time-frame signify the traces along the 3D blood flow velocity vector field. Another method frequently used for visualization in 4D MRI is color-coding by velocity magnitude. This method enables the visualization of regions with high systolic flow velocities. Time-resolved path lines/traces are the better choice for visual identification of the temporal evolution of 3D blood flow over one or more heartbeats. Color-coding of time-resolved path lines permits the visual identification of change in blood flow velocity over the cardiac cycle or to trace the flow pattern. A complete blood flow visualization in a 3D subject facilitates an improved perception of the underlying disease. The flow visualization greatly impacts the investigation with 4D flow MRI on disease diagnosis and patient administration.

During the quantification stage, quantization and comparison of various parameters are performed. This stage employs the concept of mass/flow conservation in order to quantize and compare the blood flow; that is, the blood flow into a segment of an artery or sinus or heart should usually match the blood flow exiting these organs. The mismatch between these blood flow values is the sign of a shunt or other critical anatomical trouble. 4D flow MRI allows quantification of standard blood flow parameters at any location contained by the 3D data volume. For this process, 2D analysis planes are placed in any artery or vein or organ of interest. The defined sketch of vessel segment provides peak velocity, total flow, retrograde flow, and pressure gradients. A number of researches have compared the 2D PC MRI with 4D flow MRI and proved the outstanding performance of 4D MRI based flow quantification [55]. Moreover, many researchers have investigated the scan rescan reproducibility and low inter- and intraobserver variability of 4D flow MRI for intracranial, thoracic, cervical, and abdominal applications.

5.4 Applications of 4D flow MRI

At present, MRIs play a vital role in assessing the heart conditions of patients such as aneurysms, atherosclerosis, tumors, cardiac failure, and heart valve diseases. However, with 4D flow MRI, more detailed research has been investigated in order to assess the mysterious parts of the cardiovascular system, such as movement of blood between heart chambers. Currently, 4D flow MRI is one of the major tools in the hands of the cardiologist to administer patients with bicuspid aortic valve issue and its related complications. This section deals with recently introduced vital applications of 4D flow MRI.

5.4.1 Evaluation of left ventricular diastolic function

The investigation of left ventricular (LV) diastolic function has been performed by Houriez et al. [56] using a transmitral inflow segmentation method. In this method, a rough transmitral flow velocity curve and two anatomical markers, specifically the mitral valve and the apex, were positioned manually. In order to initialize the segmentation process, the short axis slice is shown to draw the ROI around the transmitral flow. The time-resolved mean velocity curve is measured and the largest connected area on the peak velocity phase in terms of velocity sign (inflow) is detected and its barycenter is calculated. The biggest ROI is promulgated to the next slice along the LV long axis to perform the time propagation segmentation process until the apical region was reached.

5.4.2 Vessel segmentation in pancreas

In this research, Gu et al. [57] have demonstrated the application of deep-learning-based two-scale convolutional neural network (CNN) with distance and contour regularized level set evolution (DCRLSE), to segment the vessel in 4D-MRI pancreas datasets. In this study, CNN is employed to position and approximately segment the vessel. The DCRLSE structure is further utilized to improve the contours. The similarities among various patients are developed using the transfer learning method. After training the binary mask in one patient's network, the network weights are relocated to initiate the CNN training of the second patient. The CNN weights are adjusted on preferred breathing phases to get the least number of images required for new segmentation. This method has been successfully executed on 4D MRI to automatically delineate the blood vessels in the pancreas, which further limits surgery for pancreatic cancer patients.

5.4.3 Longitudinal monitoring of hepatic blood flow before and after TIPS

Portal hypertension is a familiar and possible fatal complication of end-stage liver cirrhosis. The patient may be treated through the placement of a TIPS. This shunt redirects the blood flow from the portal system straight into the systemic circulation, thereby reducing the pressure and the risk for variceal hemorrhage. The 4D MRI has been successfully used to monitor hepatic blood flow in patients with portal hypertension. However, Bannas et al. [54] has demonstrated that 4D flow MRI can offer comprehensive noninvasive longitudinal hemodynamic monitoring of hepatic blood flow before and after TIPS placement. Extensive anatomic coverage and comprehensive visualization of abdominal vasculature make 4D flow MRI a potential alternative to current techniques for monitoring the complex hemodynamics of the liver, including TIPS function and patency.

5.4.4 Assessment of uterine artery geometry and hemodynamics in human pregnancy

The possibility of attaining 4D flow MRI in pregnant subjects has been successfully investigated by Hwuang et al. [58]. In this study the uterine artery geometry and hemodynamics in human pregnancy has been assessed with 4D flow MRI. During the image acquisition stage, an ECG-gated multislice axial time-of-flight angiogram is obtained. The phase difference images from all the subjects are obtained and rectified through anti-aliasing correction. The noise in the images is eliminated through magnitude image thresholding. Pixel values below the threshold are discarded from magnitude and phase data. Velocity-based thresholding is also done to generate volumetric isosurfaces, from which four measurement planes are distributed along the uterine artery (UtA) and oriented vertical to the blood flow. The vessel is segmented and velocity profiles are extracted from each plane at each phase. Furthermore, research has proven that 4D flow MRI finds its applications in automatic segmentation of 4D MRI for cardiac functional measurements.

Along with congenital heart disease identification, 4D flow MRI discovers its purpose in diagnosing the stroke risk in patients affected with atrial fibrillation. Understanding the dynamics of blood flow enables healthcare professionals to recognize their place in the well-being of the patients and all domains of cardiovascular physiology. The robustness, high resolution, and exactness of 4D flow MRI provide greater growth in the medical world.

5.4.5 Future of 4D flow MRI

In the future, the effort to regulate 4D flow MRI acquisition parameters needs to be taken. The development of automated analysis tools and regularized evaluation metrics augment the ability for better studies and conversion to medical practice. Therefore, the possibility of 4D flow MRI to unravel composite questions associated with cardiovascular function will be exploited.

6. Machine learning techniques in 4D medical imaging

Machine learning (ML) techniques are widely used in medical imaging to improve accuracy of diagnosis. They are successfully applied in various domains like medical image diagnosis, risk assessment, and disease prognosis. ML in medical imaging is expected to have a great impact on medical image interpretation. Radiologists can use this as a decision support system to make their decisions in a more efficient and effective manner.

The rapid improvement of computation power and the availability of huge amounts of data made deep learning (DL) a prominent ML technique that can provide better learning than the conventional ML techniques. The following section discusses the various ML techniques used in medical imaging.

6.1 Machine learning approaches in 4D CT

One of the limitations of 4D CT imaging is the large volume of data, which is time consuming. This can be handled by the newly evolved ML methods. Not only various researchers have used different ML approaches to enhance the performance of 4D CT. Yuncheng et al. [59] have proposed a deep CNN approach for directly deriving 4D CT ventilation images without deformable image registration (DIR), thus enhancing the quality and accuracy of violation images. Li et al. [60] demonstrated that combining linear exhaustive optimal combination framework with DL algorithms has achieved an optimal matching index when compared with other traditional methods.

Li et al. 2015 [61] developed an effective motion extraction approach and an ML-based algorithm to estimate the average diaphragm motion trajectory. It can be used as an automatic robust tool to calculate diaphragm motion. The opportunities, requirements, and needs of ML in radiation oncology has been discussed by Feng et al. [62].

6.2 Machine learning approaches in 4D ultrasound

ML is the part of artificial intelligence that provides solutions to the various medical imaging applications such as computer-aided diagnosis, lesion segmentation, medical image analysis, image-guided therapy, annotation, and retrieval with 2D, 3D, and 4D data. Brattain et al. [63] presented a review on advances of ML in solving US image challenges. Most of the ML approaches adopted in US imaging are supervised learning where the model is trained with the available US images from the dataset to yield a desired output. ML algorithms are adopted for US images in the fields of detection or diagnosis, segmentation, registration, regression, and content retrieval. Several works of ML have been reported in the field of computer-aided diagnosis for US breast lesions classification. The texture features or morphological features extracted from these breast lesions are trained in ML classifiers such as multilayer networks, random forests, and support vector machines to analyze severity of the lesions in the US images. The assessment from computers and the knowledge of the radiologist together provide an improved specificity and sensitivity.

An automatic classification of ovarian tumors [64] from US images has been carried out by extracting the Fourier descriptors from the ROI and evaluated with various ML approaches. The design of the classifier can be further enhanced by integrating ensemble techniques.

The traditional CAD system has been migrated to the DL approaches where the features are extracted through the deep neural network instead of human-crafted features [65]. The DL approach provides more effective results than the hand-crafted feature learning approaches. It works in the field of breast cancer diagnosis, liver nodule diagnosis, thyroid nodule detection, fetal plane detection, and carotid classification. Recently, Akkus et al. [66] reviewed the DL approaches in optimizing the US image workflow and provided an insight to improve the diagnosis in US imaging.

6.3 Machine learning approaches in 4D flow MRI

In recent years, ML techniques have gained great interest in the field of 4D medical image analysis. Machines are programmed to perform analysis on the input data and to make intelligent decisions based on it. The integration of intelligence to the medical field receives great impact through visualization techniques, which reduce the necessity of medical professionals to handle mind-numbing tasks for disease diagnosis. Intelligent-based data visualization is efficient in inferring intricate decisions from the given input knowledge.

The 4D flow MRI dataset consists of a large number of time steps, usually in the thousands. Also a number of features are characterized by location, shape, and size. Therefore feature extraction is suggested to take place in a high-dimensional space. In the process of feature extraction in 4D flow MRI data, the feature of interest is extracted from the raw image and the feature representation is generated through the geometric representation of pulled-out features. In the study of flow visualization, Ma et al. proposed an intelligent system for 4D MRI feature extraction [67]. This visualization technique learns to extract the complex features and features of interest even in intricate 4D flow fields, based on the location of the features, their size, and shape [68]. In addition, the proposed intelligent visualization method performs feature extraction in high-dimensional space without specifically mentioning associations among the high dimensions, which further leads to effective and simple user interface.

An intelligent, high-dimensional feature extraction and classification system consists of a painting-based interface, which allows the user to mention the regions and features of interest through brushing. Fig. 4.13 shows the intelligent feature extraction process for 4D flow MRI. The neural network is trained to extract the features based on user commands and classify them accordingly. Finally the volume of extracted information is rendered and displayed by the user interface.

Many researchers have shown much interest in demonstrating the application of ML in 4D medical imaging. Margeta et al. [69] presented an

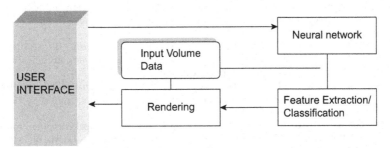

Figure 4.13 Intelligent feature extraction process for 4D flow MRI.

ML approach for automatic segmentation of LV from 4D cardiac MRI datasets. This method uses a layered approach in which the spatiotemporal features are segmented with decision forests.

Najarian et al. [70] have patented their research work on the development of ML-based automatic measurement of injury indices with brain CT image data. The ML method with the Gaussian mixture model is applied for feature extraction from multiple basis, and consists of blood amount, texture pattern, and other injury data. The extracted features offer the medical expert an estimation of intracranial pressure levels.

7. Conclusion and future trends

4D medical imaging analysis is a less explored field that needs more attention. This chapter discussed the fundamental techniques of 4D medical imaging. Different imaging modalities such as 4D CT, 4D US scan and 4D flow MRI, and their applications and corresponding challenges, have been dealt with in detail. From this survey it is clearly visible that 4D CT is very suitable for radiation oncology, which is affected by motion artifacts. Similarly, 4D US is very helpful in fetal study. 4D flow MRI is useful in accurately treating cardiac problems.

The main limitation is the need for huge storage and the time-consuming complex process. However, in the current technological era storage is not a big issue. Hence researchers need to concentrate on exploring and designing techniques that reduce time for imaging and processing. 4D medical imaging is in its infant stage and needs to be explored more. There is a noticeable scope for this technique. It needs to be developed and utilized in usual diagnostic imaging.

References

[1] P.X. Shajan, N.J. Muniraj, J.T. Abraham, 3D/4D image registration and fusion techniques: a survey, International Journal of Computer Science and Information Technologies 3 (4) (2012) 4829—4839.
[2] G. Li, D. Citrin, K. Camphausen, B. Mueller, C. Burman, B. Mychalczak, R.W. Miller, Y. Song, Advances in 4D medical imaging and 4D radiation therapy, Technology in Cancer Research and Treatment 7 (1) (2008) 67—81.
[3] R.A. Aryananda, et al., New three-dimensional/four-dimensional volume rendering imaging software for detecting the abnormally invasive placenta, Journal of Clinical Ultrasound 47 (1) (2019) 9—13.
[4] Y. Kwong, M. AO, G. Wheeler, J.M. Troupis, Four-dimensional computed tomography (4DCT): a review of the current status and applications, Journal of Medical Imaging and Radiation Oncology 59 (5) (2015) 545—554.

[5] J. Cai, Z. Chang, Z. Wang, W.P. Segars, F.F. Yin, Four-dimensional magnetic resonance imaging (4D-MRI) using image-based respiratory surrogate: a feasibility study, Medical Physics 38 (12) (2011) 6384—6394.

[6] M. Correia, J. Provost, M. Tanter, M. Pernot, 4D ultrafast ultrasound flow imaging: in vivo quantification of arterial volumetric flow rate in a single heartbeat, Physics in Medicine and Biology 7;61 (23) (2016) L48—L61.

[7] https://en.wikipedia.org/wiki/4DCT (Accessed on 29 may 19).

[8] https://utswmed.org/medblog/3d-4d-ultrasound (Accessed on 29 may 19).

[9] https://www.nm.org/conditions-and-care-areas/tests/four-dimensional-magnetic-resonance-imaging (Accessed on 29 may 19).

[10] https://eu.medical.canon/toshiba-introduces-infinix-4dct-a-revolutionary-add-on-to-the-angio-suite/ (Accessed on 29 may 19).

[11] https://www.uclahealth.org/endocrine-center/parathyroid-4d-ct-scan (Accessed on 29 may 19).

[12] B.J. Slotman, J. Frank, L. Waard, S. Senan, 4D imaging for target definition in stereotactic radiotherapy for lung cancer, Acta Oncologica 45 (7) (2006) 966—972.

[13] G. Wu, J. Lian, D. Shen, Improving image-guided radiation therapy of lung cancer by reconstructing 4D-CT from a single free-breathing 3D-CT on the treatment day, Medical Physics 39 (12) (2012) 7694—7709.

[14] M.C. Aznar, G.F. Persson, I.M. Kofoed, DE Nygaard, S.S. Korreman, Irregular breathing during 4DCT scanning of lung cancer patients: is the midventilation approach robust? Physica Medica 30 (1) (2014) 69—75.

[15] A. Rasheed, S.K. Jabbour, S. Rosenberg, A. Patel, S. Goyal, B.G. Haffty, A. Khan, Motion and volumetric change as demonstrated by 4DCT: the effects of abdominal compression on the GTV, lungs, and heart in lung cancer patients, Practical Radiation Oncology 6 (5) (2016) 352—359.

[16] X. Wang, J.Z. Wang, J.B. Li, Y.J. Zhang, F.X. Li, W. Wang, Y. Wang, Changes in cardiac volume determined with repeated enhanced 4DCT during chemo radiotherapy for esophageal cancer, Radiation Oncology 13 (1) (2018).

[17] Y.S. Choi, Y.H. Lee, S. Kim, H.W. Cho, H.T. Song, J.S. Suh, Four-dimensional real-time cine images of wrist joint kinematics using dual source CT with minimal time increment scanning, Yonsei Medical Journal 54 (18) (2013) 1026—1032.

[18] S. Leng, K. Zhao, M. Qu, K.N. An, R. Berger, C.H. McCollough, Dynamic CT technique for assessment of wrist joint instabilities, Medical Physics 38 (Suppl. 1) (2011) S50.

[19] J.T. Shores, S. Demehri, A. Chhabra, Kinematic "4 dimensional" CT imaging in the assessment of wrist biomechanics before and after surgical repair, Eplasty 13 (2013) e9.

[20] G.I. Wassilew, V. Janz, M.O. Heller, S. Tohtz, P. Rogalla, P. Hein, C. Perka, Real time visualization of femoroacetabular impingement and subluxation using 320-slice computed tomography, Journal of Orthopaedic Research 31 (2013) 275—281.

[21] J. Lantz, V. Gupta, L. Henriksson, M. Karlsson, A. Persson, C.J. Carlhäll, T. Ebbers, Intracardiac flow at 4D CT: comparison with 4D flow MRI, Radiology (2018) 1—8.

[22] V. Tavakoli, N. Sahba, Cardiac motion and strain detection using 4D CT images: comparison with tagged MRI, and echocardiography, The International Journal of Cardiovascular Imaging 30 (1) (2013) 175—184.

[23] G. Xiong, P. Sun, H. Zhou, S. Ha, B. o Hartaigh, Q.A. Truong, J.K. Min, Comprehensive modeling and visualization of cardiac anatomy and physiology from CT imaging and computer simulations, IEEE Transactions on Visualization and Computer Graphics 23 (2) (2017) 1014—1028.

[24] 3HCare Blog posts tagged with '4d ultrasound cost in india'. (Online) Available: www.3hcare.in/blog/tag/4d ultrasound cost in india. (Accessed 29 may 2019).

[25] S. Obruchkov, The technology and performance of 4D ultrasound, Critical Reviews in Biomedical Engineering 36 (2008) 257—304.

[26] S.H. Kim, B.I. Choi, Three-dimensional and four-dimensional ultrasound: techniques and abdominal applications, Journal of Medical Ultrasound 15 (4) (2007) 228–242 (cc).
[27] A. Fenster, D.B. Downey, 3-D ultrasound imaging: a review, IEEE Engineering in Medicine and Biology Magazine 15 (6) (1996) 41–51.
[28] Niranjan Ultrasound India 4D Ultrasound machines- Preowned Machines|Economical machines|Used 4D Machines, (Online) Available: http://www.ultrasoundindia.com/4d-machines/. (Accessed: 29 May 2019).
[29] A.F. Elnokrashy, Y. Kadah, 4D ultrasound adaptive image pre-processing, in: 35th National Radio Science Conference (NRSC), 2018, pp. 214–222.
[30] I.M.D. Maysanjaya, H.A. Nugroho, N.A. Setiawan, The classification of fetus gender on ultrasound images using learning vector quantization (LVQ), in: Makassar International Conference on Electrical Engineering and Informatics (MICEEI), 2014, pp. 150–155.
[31] Common 4D Imaging Problems and Mistakes - Providian Medical," (Online). Available: https://www.providianmedical.com/blog/common-4d-imaging-problems-mistakes/. (Accessed 29 May 2019).
[32] E. Titianova, S. Cherninkova, S. Karakaneva, B. Stamenov, Four-dimensional ultrasound imaging in neuro-ophthalmology, Perspectives in Medicine 1 (1) (2012) 86–88.
[33] W.J. Fry, Ultrasound in neurology, Neurology 6 (10) (1956) 693–704.
[34] G. Leinenga, C. Langton, R. Nisbet, J. Götz, Ultrasound treatment of neurological diseases: current and emerging applications, Nature Reviews Neurology 12 (3) (2016) 161.
[35] T. Deffieux, C. Demene, M. Pernot, M. Tanter, Functional ultrasound neuroimaging: a review of the preclinical and clinical state of the art, Current Opinion in Neurobiology 50 (2018) 128–135.
[36] C. Errico, B.-F. Osmanski, S. Pezet, O. Couture, Z. Lenkei, M. Tanter, Transcranial functional ultrasound imaging of the brain using microbubble-enhanced ultrasensitive Doppler, NeuroImage 124 (2016) 752–761.
[37] S. Tomasovic, M. Predojevic, 4D ultrasound-medical devices for recent advances on the etiology of cerebral Palsy, Acta Informatica Medica 19 (4) (2011) 228.
[38] A. Kurjak, M. Predojevic, M. Stanojevic, A. Talic, U. Honemeyer, A.S. Kadic, The use of 4D imaging in the behavioral assessment of high-risk fetuses, Imaging in Medicine 3 (5) (2011) 557.
[39] J. Blahuta, T. Soukup, P. Cermák, Image processing of medical diagnostic neuro-sonographical images in MATLAB, Recent researches in computer science, in: Proceedings of the 15th World Scientific and Engineering Academy and Society Circuits, Systems, Communications, and Computers Multiconference, 2011, pp. 15–17.
[40] P. Mattsson, A. Eriksson, Segmentation of carotid arteries from 3D and 4D ultrasound images, Institutionen för systemteknik (2002).
[41] Ultrasound Scan: Facts, Uses & Types (3D, 4D), (Online) Available: https://www.emedicinehealth.com/ultrasound/article_em.htm#what_are_the_diagnostic_or_screening_uses_for_ultrasound. (Accessed 29 May 2019).
[42] N.J. Pagidipati, T.A. Gaziano, Estimating deaths from cardiovascular disease: a review of global methodologies of mortality measurement, Circulation 127 (6) (2013) 749–756.
[43] L. Wang, L.M. Wang, W. Chen, X. Chen, Bicuspid aortic valve: a review of its genetics and clinical significance, Journal of Heart Valve Disease 25 (5) (2016) 568–573.
[44] A. Fyrenius, L. Wigstrom, A.F. Bolger, T. Ebbers, K.P. Ohman, Pitfalls in Doppler evaluation of diastolic function: insights from 3-dimensional magnetic resonance imaging, Journal of the American Society of Echocardiography 12 (1999) 817–826.
[45] Z. Stankovic, B.D. Allen, J. Garcia, K.B. Jarvis, M. Mark, 4D flow imaging with MRI, Cardiovascular Diagnosis and Therapy 4 (2) (2014) 173–192.

[46] C. Stuart, 4D Flow MRI: Another Dimension for Congenital Heart Disease, Cardiovascular Imaging, Strategies in Economics, Practice and Technology Magazine, 2017.

[47] A.J. Lewandowski, B. Raman, R. Banerjee, M. Milanesi, Novel insights into complex cardiovascular pathologies using 4d flow analysis by cardiovascular magnetic resonance imaging, Current Pharmaceutical Design 23 (22) (2017) 3262–3267.

[48] J. Bock, B.W. Kreher, J. Hennig, M. Mark, Optimized preprocessing of time-resolved 2D and 3D Phase Contrast MRI data, Proceedings of the International Society for Magnetic Resonance in Medicine 15 (2007) 3138.

[49] K.M. Johnson, M. Markl, Improved SNR in phase contrast velocimetry with five-point balanced flow encoding, Magnetic Resonance in Medicine 63 (2010) 349–355.

[50] A. Stadlbauer, W. van der Riet, G. Crelier, E. Salomonowitz, Accelerated time-resolved three- dimensional MR velocity mapping of blood flow patterns in the aorta using SENSE and k-t BLAST, European Journal of Radiology 75 (2010) e15–21.

[51] T. Gu, F.R. Korosec, W.F. Block, S.B. Fain, Q. Turk, D. Lum, Y. Zhou, T.M. Grist, V. Haughton, C.A. Mistretta, A Highspeed 3D phase-contrast method for flow quantification and high-resolution angiography, American Journal of Neuroradiology 26 (2005) 743–749.

[52] F. Beckers, A. Hsiao, J. Axerio, T. Taerum, D. Marc, Apparatus, Methods and Articles for 4D Flow Magnetic Resonance Imaging, 2019. US 2019/0069802.

[53] M. Bernstein, X. Zhou, J. Polzin, K.F. King, A. Ganin, N.J. Pelc, G.H. Glover, Concomitant gradient terms in phase contrast MR: analysis and correction, Magnetic Resonance in Medicine 39 (2) (1998) 300–308.

[54] P. Bannas, A. Alzate, K. Johnson, M. Woods, O. Ozkan, U. Motosugi, O. Wieben, S. Reeder, H. Kramer, Monitoring of hepatic blood flow before and after TIPS with 4D-flow MR imaging, Radiology 281 (2016) 574–582.

[55] W. AL, T.M. Grist, O. Wieben, Repeatability and internal consistency of abdominal 2D and 4D phase contrast MR flow measurements, Academic Radiology 20 (2013) 699–704.

[56] S. Houriez, et al., Evaluation of left ventricular diastolic function using 4D flow MR imaging, Computers in Cardiology 45 (2018) 1–4.

[57] S. Gou, Y. Lao, Z. Fan, K. Sheng, H.M. Sandler, R. Tuli, W. Yang, Automated vessel segmentation in pancreas 4D-MRI using a novel transferred convolutional neural network, Int Journal of Radiation Oncology 102 (3) (2018) e550–e551.

[58] E. Hwuang, M. Vidorreta, N. Schwartz, B. Moon, K. Kochar, M. Tisdall, J. Detre, W. Witschey, Assessment of uterine artery Geometry and hemodynamics in human pregnancy with 4D flow MRI and its correlation with Doppler ultrasound, Journal of Magnetic Resonance Imaging 49 (1) (2019) 59–68.

[59] Y. Zhong, Y. Vinogradskiy, L. Chen, N. Myziuk, R. Castillo, E. Castillo, T. Guerrero, S. Jiang, Jing Wang, "Deriving ventilation imaging from 4DCT by deep convolutional neural network", Medical Physics 46 (5) (2019) 2323–2329.

[60] X. Li, Z. Deng, Q. Deng, L. Zhang, T. Niu, Y. Kuang, A novel deep learning framework for internal gross target volume definition from 4D computed tomography of lung cancer patients, IEEE Access vol. 6 (2018) 37775–37783.

[61] G. Li1, J. Wei2, H. Huang1, C.P. Gaebler1, Y.1 Amy, J. O Deasy, Automatic assessment of average diaphragm motion trajectory from 4DCT images through machine learning, Biomedical Physics and Engineering Express 1 (2015) 045015.

[62] M. Feng, G. Valdes, N. Dixit, T.D. Solberg, Machine learning in radiation oncology: opportunities, requirements, and needs, Frontiers in Oncology 8 (2018) 110, https://doi.org/10.3389/fonc.2018.00110.

[63] L.J. Brattain, et al., Abdom Radiol (NY) 43 (4) (April 2018) 786–799.

[64] J. Martínez, et al., Evaluation of machine learning methods with Fourier Transform features for classifying ovarian tumors based on ultrasound images, PLOS One 14 (7) (July 2019).
[65] Q. Huang, F. Zhang, X. Li, Machine learning in ultrasound computer-aided diagnostic systems: a survey, BioMed Research International 1−10 (2018).
[66] Z. Akkus, et al., A survey of deep-learning applications in ultrasound: artificial intelligence-powered ultrasound for improving clinical workflow, Journal of the American College of Radiology 16 (9 Pt B) (2019) 1318−1328.
[67] M. Kwan-Liu, Machine learning to boost the next generation of visualization technology, IEEE Computer Graphics and Applications 27 (5) (2007) 6−9.
[68] F.-Y. Tzeng, K.-L. Ma, Intelligent feature extraction and tracking for large-scale 4D flow simulations, in: Proc. Int'l Conf. High Performance Computing Networking Storage and Analysis, 2005.
[69] J. Margeta, E. Geremia, A. Criminisi, N. Ayache, Layered spatio-temporal forests for left ventricle segmentation from 4D cardiac MRI data, in: O. Camara, E. Konukoglu, M. Pop, K. Rhode, M. Sermesant, A. Young (Eds.), Statistical Atlases and Computational Models of the Heart. Imaging and Modelling Challenges, STACOM 2011. Lecture Notes in Computer Science, vol. 7085, Springer, 2012.
[70] K. Najarian, G. Allen, W. Chen, K.R. Ward, Automated Measurement of Brain Injury Indices Using Brain CT Images, Injury Data, and Machine Learning, 2012. US 2012/018484.0 A1, Jul. 19, 2012.

CHAPTER 5

Comparative analysis of hybrid fusion algorithms using neurocysticercosis, neoplastic, Alzheimer's, and astrocytoma disease affected multimodality medical images

B. Rajalingam[1], R. Priya[2], R. Bhavani[2]
[1]Department of CSE, Priyadarshini College of Engineering & Technology, Nellore, Andhra Pradesh, India; [2]Department of CSE, Annamalai University, Chidambaram, Tamilnadu, India

Contents

Advanced Machine Vision Paradigms for Medical Image Analysis
ISBN 978-0-12-819295-5
https://doi.org/10.1016/B978-0-12-819295-5.00005-6

1. Introduction

Image fusion is basically an emerging technique of blending the important and complementary information of multiple images without any loss of information. Various input images either in same domain or various domains are merged together to develop an image containing the larger, relevant, reliable, and consistent information in comparison to all input images in a single fused image. The resulting fused picture will be more detailed, accurate, concise, and complete than the original images from the source. The basic idea behind image fusion is to integrate low detail multisensor images captured from a common scene to obtain a fused image with a high spatial resolution multispectral image. It is an efficient approach of extracting the more informative values from a set of images. It effectively increases the spatial and spectral resolution optimality. Image fusion is also an effective way to reduce the increasing volume of information by representing the useful and descriptive information from multimodal source images in a single image only. With rapid improvement in various domains of imaging technologies and modern instrumentation, multisensory system has become a reality in various applications such as machine vision, military applications, high-speed object tracking, automatic vehicular systems, remote sensing, medical imaging, and more. With such advancement in real-time applications, image fusion has proved itself an efficient and powerful tool to increase the human and machine perception and to decrease the storage space requirement minimizing the cost.

Medical image fusion is a rapidly developing and emerging application of image fusion to handle various medical issues retrieved from multimodal medical images. Medical image fusion (MIF) is the process of combining multiple images from single or multiple image tools with meaningful information into a single image that retains useful information and better describes the scene. MIF helps increase the reliability of images and decrease the redundancy and storage cost. This improves the value and provides a clear visual effect for the diagnosis, evaluation, treatment of medical problems, and historical recording of clinical images. This technique has gained vital importance in tumor diagnosis in brain, mouth, breast, and so on. For the fusion process in MIF, multiple image acquisition can be done using a common source or using different imaging modalities. MIF using two or more imaging tools is known as multimodal MIF. MIF is basically a concept of improving the image content and quality by merging images captured from different imaging tools as magnetic resonance imaging (MRI), computed tomography (CT), positron emission tomography (PET), single photon emission computed tomography (SPECT), X-ray, and so on. All the aforementioned tools provide the images with different spectral features. In case of clinical diagnosis, use of a single image is not a sufficient requirement for the physician. Thus for the sake of accuracy in diagnosis, more than one image with different and complementary features are fused together. This eliminates the limitation of diagnosis using single sensor image.

1.1 Levels of medical image fusion

MIF should be done at three levels depending on the merging state or abstraction level.

1.1.1 Pixel-level fusion

Also known as signal level fusion, the lowest level of fusion, pixel-level fusion, deals with the information in the source image associated with each pixel and generates a fused image with the corresponding pixel values depending on certain rules and methods. It can be done on the field of space as well as frequency. It is performed for the reduction of contrast.

1.1.2 Feature-level fusion

This deals with descriptive property data that have already been derived from the source images such as pixel size, edge, and texture. Such extracted features and object labels are fused with additional composite features to obtain the fused medical image. It is also known as fusion of object level and applies to detection or classification of objects.

1.1.3 Decision-level fusion

The fusion of probabilistic judgment data is the highest level of fusion or symbol level object fusion. It deals with the decision of local decision-makers operating on the results of the processing of feature-level image data derived from individual sensors.

1.2 Multimodal medical images

With the advancement in technology and medical imaging tools, medical imaging has become an emerging domain in medical diagnosis and analysis. Varieties of imaging methods are available in the medical field, each possessing a different characteristic property. Various medical imaging methods include MRI, CT, PET, SPECT, and so on. The complementary properties of two or more modality medical images are combined, developing a single image consisting of fine details of each image. This is known as multimodal MIF.

1.2.1 Computed tomography

For bone imaging, CT images are very clear and have relatively low soft-tissue contrast. X-rays are used for this imaging tool. Its main advantage is high resolution and short scan times. Nature of X-ray probe, number of X-rays generated, and restriction on slices scanned limits the performance of CT scan.

1.2.2 Magnetic resonance imaging

MRI is a noninvasive type of imaging technique and is efficiently used in brain diagnosis. These images can provide better information of the pathological soft tissue and the relevant vessel. This is used to efficiently extract the abnormal region present in brain representing the presence of reflective brain tumor. It is also used for imaging of soft tissues of eyes and heart with high accuracy as it does not emerge any radiation and does not harm the body. One more advantage is that it is safe for pregnant women and the fetus. Its limitation lies in its sensitivity for movement, which makes it inefficient for detecting tumor in moving organs.

1.2.3 Positron emission tomography

PET is an efficient tool for nuclear imaging. It can provide better information on blood flow with low spatial resolution. Its function is based on the operation of positrons. Due to molecular imaging, it possesses high sensitivity. It is used for brain diagnosis and treatment.

1.2.4 Single photon emission computed tomography

SPECT is a powerful tool for nuclear imaging. It shows the blood flow to various organs in the human body. It is efficiently used for brain diagnosis, lung cancer detection, neck and head cancer detection, multimodality fusion, and so on. It possesses poor image quality as is affected by image noise, and it requires postprocessing to enhance the image quality.

1.3 Medical image fusion techniques

Multimodal medical imaging techniques are used in various clinical diagnoses. The commonly used multimodalities in medical imaging are given below:

- MRI-SPECT
- MRI-PET
- MRI-CT

1.3.1 MRI-SPECT fusion

This type of imaging modality has great scope in field pathological identification. MRI images provide the anatomical structure and edge details while SPECT images contain functional and metabolic information. The fused MRI-SPECT provides the localization of the pathology as well as structural and metabolic behavior in a single frame.

1.3.2 MRI-PET fusion

This type of imaging modality is effectively used in the field of clinical diagnosis. MRI images provide the anatomical structure and hard tissue information while the PET image provides the metabolic behavior and blood flow. The fused MR-PET can localize the pathology and provide an enhanced vision of functional behavior.

1.3.3 MRI-CT fusion

This imaging modality is widely used in clinical diagnosis in which MRI images provide soft tissues information. The CT image provides the information of hard tissues and bone structure. The fused MR-CT provides the soft tissues and bone structure in a single image frame.

1.4 Dataset descriptions

In this chapter the sample study sets used in the experimentation are obtained from online databases (http://www.med.harvard.edu,

https://radiopaedia.org). The following disease-affected input multi-modality medical images were taken for the experimental work.
• Neurocysticercosis
• Astrocytoma
• Alzheimer's disease
• Anaplastic astrocytoma
• Degenerative disease (mild Alzheimer's disease)
• Metastatic brochogenic carcinoma

1.4.1 Neurocysticercosis

Neurocysticercosis (NCC) can be fatal; it affects the brain and is the disease's most severe form. NCC is considered a neglected parasitic infection, one of a group of diseases that leads to severe disease among infected individuals and is often overlooked by health care providers. A person gets NCC in the feces of a person who has an intestinal pork tapeworm by swallowing microscopic eggs that passed through. A person eats undercooked, infected pork, for example, and gets an intestinal tapeworm infection. In her feces she passes tapeworm eggs. She may contaminate food or surfaces with feces containing these eggs if she does not wash her hands properly after using the bathroom. If they eat contaminated food, these eggs may be swallowed by another person. The eggs hatch and become larvae that find their way into the brain once inside the body. These larvae are responsible for NCC [1].

1.4.2 Neoplastic disease

Neoplastic disease is a disease wherein cells divide rapidly, causing them to form abnormal tissues called neoplasm. These abnormal growths, also known as tumors, can form in any part of the body. Neoplastic disease causes two types of tumor growth. Symptoms of neoplastic disease greatly depend on where the neoplasm is located. Anemia, shortness of breath, abdominal pain, persistent fatigue, loss of appetite, chills, diarrhea, and fever are some common symptoms of neoplastic diseases. The following risk factors that may lead to the development of malignant neoplastic disease are excessive alcohol consumption, obesity or being overweight, smoking, genetics, disorders of the immune system, chemical toxins, excessive exposure to radiation. chemotherapy, surgery, and radiation therapy are the types of treatment available in the medical field [2]. Fig. 5.1A shows neoplastic disease-affected MRI T2 image and Fig. 5.1B shows neoplastic disease-affected PET FDG image [3].

(A)   **(B)**

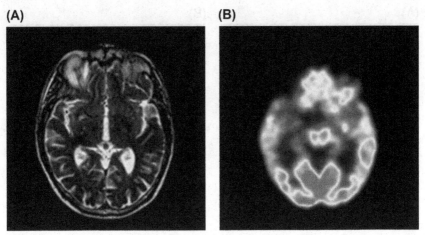

Figure 5.1 (A) Neoplastic disease affected MRI T2 image; (B) Neoplastic disease affected PET FDG image.

1.4.3 Astrocytoma

Astrocytoma is a type of brain cancer. Astrocytes arise in the cerebrum in a particular type of glial cells, star-shaped brain cells. Normally, this type of tumor does not grow outside the brain and spinal cord and usually does not affect other organs. In the brain, astrocytomas can cause seizures, headaches, and nausea. In the area affected by the growing tumor, astrocytomas that occur in the spinal cord can cause weakness and disability. It may be a slow-growing tumor, or it may be a rapidly growing aggressive cancer. Persistent headaches, double or blurred vision, vomiting, loss of appetite, changes in mood and personality, changes in ability to think and learn, new seizures, and speech difficulty of gradual onset [4]. Fig. 5.2A shows the astrocytoma disease-affected MRI T2 image and Fig. 5.2B shows the astrocytoma disease-affected SPECT TC image [5].

1.4.4 Alzheimer's disease

This is a progressive form of dementia, which destroys memory and other important functions of the mind. At first, someone with Alzheimer's disease may notice a small amount of confusion and memory difficulty. People with the disease may eventually even forget important people in their lives and experience dramatic changes in their personality. Alzheimer's disease accounts for 60% to 80% of cases of dementia, according to the Alzheimer's Association. At 65 years of age, most people with the disease were diagnosed [6]. Fig. 5.3A shows Alzheimer's disease-affected MRI T2 image and Fig. 5.3B shows Alzheimer's disease-affected SPECT TC image.

(A)   (B)

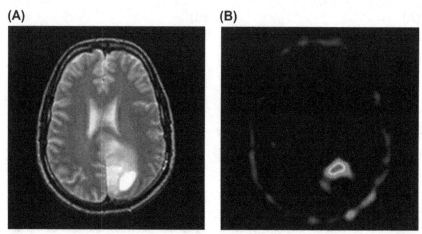

Figure 5.2 (A) Astrocytoma disease affected MRI T2 image; (B) Astrocytoma disease affected SPECT TC image.

(A)   (B)

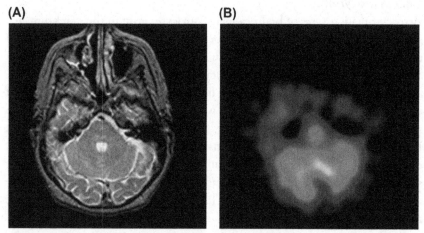

Figure 5.3 (A) Alzheimer's disease affected MRI T2 image; (B) Alzheimer's disease affected SPECT TC image.

1.5 Categories of multimodality images

In this work, various medical images have collected from Harvard medical school and Radiopedia a whole-brain database that consists of CT, MRI T1, MRI T2, SPECT T1, SPECT TC, SPECT CBF, PET, and PET FDG. Fig. 5.4 illustrates the categories of multimodal medical images.

- **MRI T1** — T1-weighted
- **MRI T2** — T2-weighted

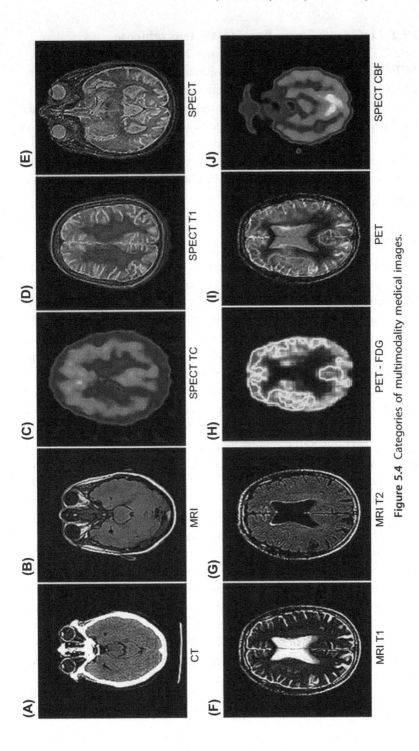

Figure 5.4 Categories of multimodality medical images.

- **PET FDG** — PET with **fluorine-18 deoxyglucose**
- **SPECT T1** — SPECT with **thallium-201**
- **SPECT TC** — SPECT with perfusion agent **Tc99m-HM-PAO**
- **SPECT CBF** — SPECT with cerebral blood flow; perfusion

This chapter is structured as follows: the literature survey on multimodal MIF is listed in Section 2. The proposed fusion methods were discussed in Section 3. The performance evaluation criteria for this experiment are explained in Section 4. Section 5 discusses the results of experiments and comparative analysis of performance. Finally, the conclusion is given in Section 6.

2. Literature survey

James et al. [7] provides an updated list of methods and summarizes the broad scientific challenges facing MIF. Gupta [8] suggested nonsubsampled shearlet transform (NSST) domain CT and MRI MIF using the adaptive neural spiking model. Daniel [9] suggested a homomorphic wavelet fusion called optimum homomorphic wavelet fusion using gray wolf optimization (GWO) hybrid genetic algorithm. Daniel et al. [10] proposed an optimum spectrum mask fusion with traditional GWO algorithm for clinical object fusion. Bhadauria et al. [11] suggested a noise reduction system for both CT and MRI medical images that fuses images via curvelet transform processing. Hermessi et al. [12] suggested a fusion process in the shearlet domain for CT and MRI clinical images based on convolutional neural network. Shahdoosti et al. [13] suggested multimodal medical image Fusion (MMIF) tetrolet transformation. Heba et al. [14] investigate some of the MIF techniques and explore the major advantages and disadvantages of these techniques in developing hybrid techniques that improve the quality of the fused image. Xi et al. [15] proposed an MMIF algorithm for medical care assessment together with sparse representation and pulse coupled neural network (PCNN). Xia et al. [16] suggested a new Multimodal Medical Image (MMI) fusion scheme using both multiscale transformation features and deep convolutional neural network (DCNN). Chavan et al. [17] proposed the non subsampled rotated wavelet (NSxRW) transform image fusion used to analyze and review NCC after treatment. Sharma et al. [18] suggested NSST-based image fusion algorithm with simplified PCNN model. Sreeja et al. [19] proposed a fusion algorithm to fuse the clinical image and improve the fused image quality. Xua [20] proposed the clinical object fusion discrete fractional wavelet transform (DFRWT) model. Liu et al. [21] suggested tensor structure and NSST to remove geometric characteristics and apply a single optimization method to fuse objects. Liu et al. [22] proposed a fusion algorithm based on NSST leveraging decomposition based on the moving picture.

3. Proposed work

This chapter is experimenting with some traditional and hybrid fusion algorithms for different types of medical input images. Existing methods require the ability to collect photographs of superior quality. The proposed algorithm is used to combine the two spectral domain algorithms to enhance the visual quality of the output. The two-level conversions on origin images were implemented before fusion processing. Such findings provide the best quality, superior handling of rounded shapes, and enhanced input image characterization.

3.1 Generalized MIF scheme

The generalized diagram of MIF consists of different input image modalities of the same patient having complementary information. The generalized MMIF system has four major components: source modality images, registration of source images, fusion using fusion rules, and evaluation of fused images for visual quality. It uses two different modality images, CT/2MRI, MRI/PET, and MRI/SPECT as source images. These images are coregistered using geometric transformations using manual and interactive registration methods. The registration process plays an important and crucial role in fusion. The success of fusion process also depends on precise and accurate registration. After registration, the fusion process is achieved in spectral domain using appropriate fusion rules. Decomposition is a process of splitting the input image into different frequency bands, generally transform-based techniques that are used for image decomposition. The decomposed bands of complementary features can be fused together using fusion rules such as averaging. MMIF efficacy is evaluated using indicators of quantitative and qualitative efficiency. Without adding false information, the fused picture will carry all the relevant data from source modalities. The resulting image should be superior visually and free of artifacts and distortions. The algorithm's efficiency is estimated using fusion parameters, and with the help of radiologists, the quality of the fused images is reviewed with respect to the source images. The MMIF process includes detailed

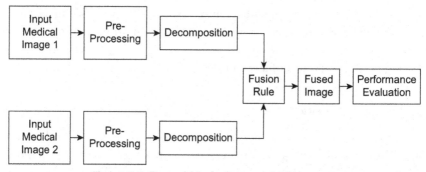

Figure 5.5 General block diagram of MIF system.

features and allows the radiologist or neurologist to prepare a disease for treatment. Fig. 5.5 describes the MIF framework general block diagram.

3.1.1 Input image modalities

In this chapter, CT, MRI, PET, and SPECT medical images are used as pilot study datasets. These images belong to the same patient and the same slice positions.

3.1.2 Medical image registration

The second stage of the fusion process registration of source modality images aligns them such that anatomical structures coincide with each other. It is a very important step in image fusion because the effectiveness of the fusion process depends entirely on the correct registration of the image. It involves voxel alignment of one modality image with another. This image registration process helps to achieve perfect fusion of anatomical structures from both input modalities.

3.1.3 Fusion process

In the spectral domain, the features are chosen. Using one of the selected transformations, source modality images are decomposed into the spectral domain. Anatomical structures in both modalities may be differently localized or oriented. The physics behind the acquisition of both input modalities are different, which results in variations of spatial resolution and size. But these images carry rich and complementary information, which needs to be combined. These fused images present better visual quality compared to input modalities, and hence the radiologist can interpret them with ease. The fused images also provide better visualization of abnormalities compared to source images. Proposed algorithm features are combined using appropriate fusion rules designed considering the human visual system.

3.1.4 Evaluation [17]

The proposed fusion techniques are tested on various sample study sets. The details of study sets, the processing system, and evaluation of algorithms are in this research work. Depending on the visual quality of the fused images, the efficiency and effectiveness of the proposed algorithms are evaluated. The fused images are evaluated with the help of expert radiologists using subjective (qualitative) evaluation and the estimation of fusion metrics as objective (quantitative) evaluation. Also described in this work are the criteria for subjective evaluation and different fusion parameters used to estimate objective evaluation.

3.1.4.1 Performance evaluation metrics

Multimodality MIF algorithms are evaluated using a quantitative evaluation method, which is a challenging task due to unavailability of ground truth. The values of the parameters vary as the study set changes. Large numbers of metrics provide different assessments of algorithms. However, the selection of fusion metrics is the choice of fusion application. The visual quality is tested using such fusion metrics. Some of the fusion metrics/ parameters used in this research work is presented next. These parameters are very useful in validation of quality of fused images objectively.

A. Fusion Factor (FusFac) [17]

Fusion factor can be used to calculate the resemblance of fused image to source images. It provides approximation of the content provided by source images to the fused image. It is determined using Eq. (5.1) on the basis of mutual data estimation. Here, $MI_{A,B}$ means the reciprocal knowledge that is determined using Eq. (5.2) between image A and image B. Here, p(.) is the feature of distribution of likelihood. FusFac's higher value implies the fused image's better quality.

$$\text{FusFac} = MI_{input1,Fus} + MI_{input2,Fus} \tag{5.1}$$

$$MI_{A,B} = \sum_{i,j} p_{A,B}(i,j)\log\frac{p_{A,B}(i,j)}{p_A(i)_B(j)} \tag{5.2}$$

B. Fusion Symmetry (FusSym) [17]

This indicates the similarity of the fused object to the source objects. Reciprocal data between source images and fused image is estimated. Use Eq. (5.3) to calculate this. If the value of *FusSym* is lower, the fused image is visually stronger.

$$FusSym = abs\left(\frac{MI_{Input1,Fus}}{MI_{Input1,Fus} + MI_{Input2,Fus}} - 0.5\right) \tag{5.3}$$

C. Image Quality Index (IQI) [17]

It is a measure of the differences between images of the origin and object fused. It is calculated by Eq. (5.4). Thus, the average and standard deviation is the norm and the standard deviation. To reflect better quality of fused image, the value of IQI should be close to 1.

$$IQI(A, B) = \frac{2\sigma_{A,B} \cdot 2\mu_A\mu_B}{(\sigma_A^2 + \sigma_B^2)(\mu_A^2 + \mu_B^2)} \tag{5.4}$$

D. Edge Quality Measure (EQM) $(EQ_{a,b}^f)$ [17]

The edges are critical for the analysis of medical images. To generate the fused image, the proposed system uses edge-related functionality. The fusion metric is an approximation of the fused image's conservation of edges. The EQM is calculated using Eq. (5.5). Here, *EI* (edge index) and S_{xy} (window) are estimated using Eqs. (5.6) and (5.7), respectively. Two reference images a and b reconstruct the fused object f. The value of 0 represents the loss of edge information, while 1 indicates that the fused image preserves edge information.

$$EQ_{a,b}^f = \frac{EI}{S_{xy}} \tag{5.5}$$

$$EI = \sum_{x=0}^{N-1}\sum_{y=0}^{M-1} EQ_{a,f}(x, y)w_a + EQ_{b,f}(x, y)w_b \tag{5.6}$$

$$S_{xy} = \sum_{i=0}^{N-1}\sum_{j=0}^{M-1} w_a(i, j) + w_b(i, j) \tag{5.7}$$

E. mean Structural Similarity Index Measure (mSSIM) [17]

The mSSIM parameter shows structural similarities between the image fused and the image source. Using Eqs. (5.8) and (5.9), mSSIM is calculated. The mean intensity here is μm, and the standard deviation is σm. The iterative parameters are constants, C1 = 6:50 and C2 = 58:52. In the fused images, the similarities will be maintained if mSSIM approaches value 1.

$$mSSIM(i,j) = \frac{1}{M} \sum_{k=1}^{M} SSIM(i_k, j_k) \qquad (5.8)$$

$$SSIM(i,j) = \frac{\left(2\mu_i\mu_j + C_1\right)\left(2\sigma_i\sigma_j + C_2\right)}{\left(\mu_i^2 + \mu_j^2 + C_1\right)\left(\sigma_i^2 + \sigma_j^2\right) + C_2)} \qquad (5.9)$$

F. Cross Entropy (CEn) [17]

It is a measure of the difference between the images of the origin and the fused object. The relative value of the fused image for source images is calculated using the parameter called CEn estimated using Eq. (5.10). A and B are two origin images here, p (.) is a distribution function of probability, and N is the highest gray value in an image. The fused image is of enhanced quality, if CEn has lower value.

$$CEn(A, B) = \sum_{i=0}^{N-1} P_A(i) \log_2 \frac{P_A(i)}{P_B(i)} \qquad (5.10)$$

G. Correlation Coefficient (*Rcorr*) [17]

It is the closeness of the fused object to the modalities of the origin. Using the formula it is estimated (11). Here, fs is the image source and ffus is the image fused. If Rcorr is close to value 1, the fused image and source images will be similar.

$$Rcorr(i,j) = \frac{2 \sum_{i=0}^{M-1} \sum_{j=0}^{N-1} f_s(i,j) \cdot f_{fus}(i,j)}{\sum_{i=0}^{M-1} \sum_{j=0}^{N-1} |f_s(i,j)|^2 + \sum_{i=0}^{M-1} \sum_{j=0}^{N-1} |f_{fus}(i,j)|^2} \qquad (5.11)$$

3.2 Proposed hybrid fusion algorithms

Five different hybrid fusion methods are discussed in this chapter. The proposed hybrid algorithms are explained in the following sections.

3.2.1 Hybrid Fusion Algorithm Based on Dual Tree Complex Wavelet Transform (DTCWT)—sNSST

1. Get the images from the two sources.
2. Resize input frames to 256 × 256.
3. Multimodal medical images are transformed into complex coefficient sets by a dual tree complex wavelet. Thresholds are determined for each degree of decomposition for both sets of coefficients.
4. Absolute difference is calculated from the corresponding threshold of all wavelet coefficients.
5. Source pictures are subdivided based on the fusion law of NSST.
6. Using NSST, low pass and high pass coefficients are determined.
7. Absolute differences in the related parameters of both the clinical input images are compared and the coefficient with a greater value of absolute difference from the threshold is chosen to form the fused image coefficient set.
8. Finally, reverse DTCWT and reverse NSST are applied to the set of the fused coefficient to obtain the image of the output. Fig. 5.6 shows the overall structure for the hybrid fusion algorithm (DTCWT—NSST).

3.2.2 Hybrid Fusion algorithm Based on Nonssubsampled Contourlet Transform (NSCT)—sNSST

1. Get the images from the two sources.
2. Resize image data to 256 × 256.
3. Calculate the NSCT spectral domain's high pass and low pass subband coefficients.
4. Combine the low pass and high frequency coefficients of the subband.
5. Refer the NSST fusion law to the coefficients of subbands.
6. For the final output, the input image is decomposed by contourlet transform. Apply the reverse NSCT and reverse NSST. Fig. 5.7 illustrates the block diagram of the NSCT—NSST-based hybrid fusion technique.

3.2.3 Hybrid Fusion algorithm Based on dfDFRWT—DTCWT

1. Get the images from the two inputs.
2. Resize input frames to 256 × 256.

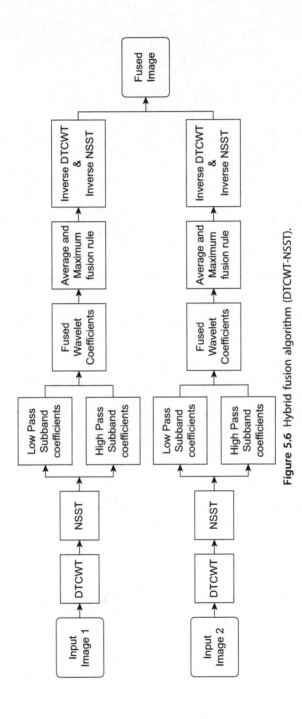

Figure 5.6 Hybrid fusion algorithm (DTCWT-NSST).

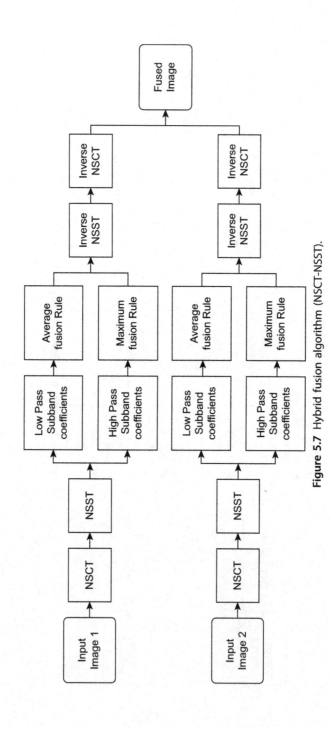

Figure 5.7 Hybrid fusion algorithm (NSCT-NSST).

3. Obtain by DFRWT high-pass directional subband coefficients and low-pass subband input image coefficients at each scale and direction.
4. Multimodal clinical images are converted into complex coefficient sets by a dual tree complex wavelet. Thresholds are determined for each rate of decomposition for both coefficient sets.
5. The absolute difference is determined from the corresponding limit of all wavelet coefficients. Absolute differences of the corresponding coefficients are compared between the input medical image and the coefficient with a greater value of absolute difference from the threshold is selected to form a coefficient set of the outcome.
6. Finally, reverse DFRWT and reverse DTCWT are added to the defined fused coefficient to obtain the final result. Fig. 5.8 shows the overall structure of the DFRWT−DTCWT-based hybrid algorithm.

3.2.4 Hybrid Fusion algorithm Based on sNSCT−dfDFRWT

1. Get the images from the two inputs.
2. The width of the input images is 256 × 256.
3. The NSCT subband coefficients are determined and the coefficients are fused.
4. Apply the DFRWT spectral domain algorithm-based fusion law.
5. Every image input is decomposed by transforming the contourlet.
6. Finally, to get the output image, apply the inverse NSCT and inverse DFRWT. Fig. 5.9 describes the proposed structure for the NSCT−DFRWT-based hybrid method.

3.2.5 Hybrid Fusion algorithm Based on sNSCT−DTCWT

1. Get the images from the source.
2. Resize input frames to 256 × 256.
3. Obtain NSCT's high-pass directional subband parameters and low-pass subband input image matrices at each scale and direction.
4. The decomposition was performed by the non subsampled pyramid filter bank (NSPFB) and non subsampled directional filter bank (NSDFB) on the basis of complete multiscale and multidirection.
5. Use DTCWT to decompose multimodal medical images into complex coefficient sets.
6. Thresholds are calculated for each level of decomposition for both sets of coefficients.

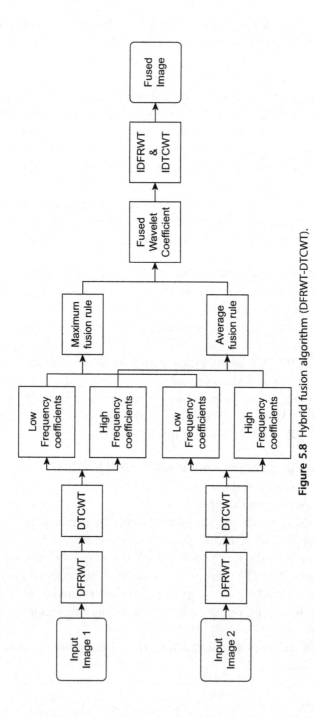

Figure 5.8 Hybrid fusion algorithm (DFRWT-DTCWT).

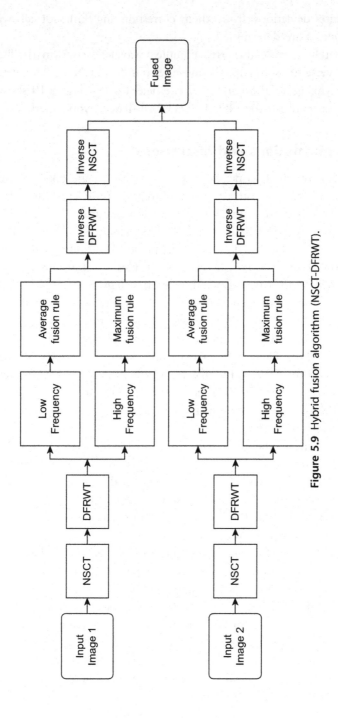

Figure 5.9 Hybrid fusion algorithm (NSCT-DFRWT).

7. Absolute deviations from their corresponding limit of all wavelet coefficients are determined.

8. Ultimately, inverse dual tree complex wavelet transform (IDTCWT) and inverse nonsubsampled contourlet transform (INSCT) add the final output image to the combined coefficient array. Fig. 5.10 shows the block diagram for the NSCT—DTCWT-based hybrid method.

4. Implementations and discussions

For the experimental work, various medical images are taken. To obtain the output image, the conventional and hybrid fusion algorithms are used. The clinical image multimodal database is obtained from The Whole Brain Atlas-Harvard Medical School and Radiopedia.org. Each input image is resized to 256 × 256 for the execution phase. The findings of traditional and hybrid algorithms are discussed in Tables 5.1 through 5.5 for the experimental performance evaluation metrics. Figs. 5.11, 5.13, 5.15, 5.17, and 5.19 illustrate the experimental results; a and b describe the source images, and c, d, e, f, g, and h describe the output images.

Fig. 5.12 show the comparative analysis for the NSST—DTCWT-based hybrid algorithm. The results of experiments are compared with discrete wavelet transform (DWT), PCNN, DFRWT, NSST, and NSCT methods. The proposed NSST-DTCWT have higher value for FusFac, IQI, EQM, and mSSIM and lower value for FusSym and Rcorr when compared with other existing conventional approaches.

Fig. 5.14 shows the comparative analysis for the NSST—NSCT-based hybrid algorithm. The results of experiments are compared with DWT, curvelet transform (CVT), DFRWT, NSST, and DTCWT methods. The proposed NSST—NSCT have higher value for FusFac, IQI, EQM, and mSSIM and lower value for FusSym and Rcorr when compared with other existing conventional approaches.

Fig. 5.16 shows the comparative analysis for the DTCWT—DFRWT-based hybrid algorithm. The results of experiments are compared with DWT, CVT, DFRWT, NSST, and DTCWT methods. The proposed DTCWT—DFRWT have higher value for FusFac, IQI, EQM, and mSSIM and lower value for FusSym and Rcorr when compared with other existing conventional approaches.

Fig. 5.9 shows the comparative analysis for the NSCT—DFRWT-based hybrid algorithm. The results of experiments are compared with DWT,

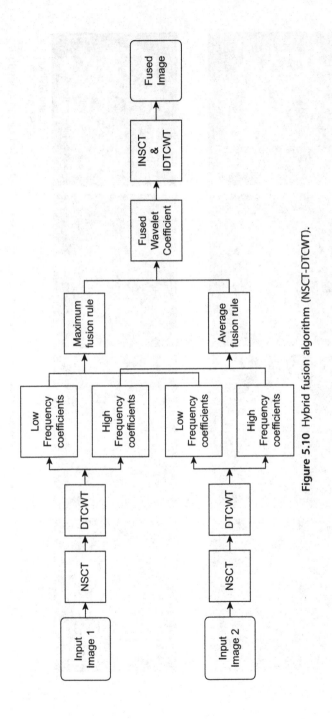

Figure 5.10 Hybrid fusion algorithm (NSCT-DTCWT).

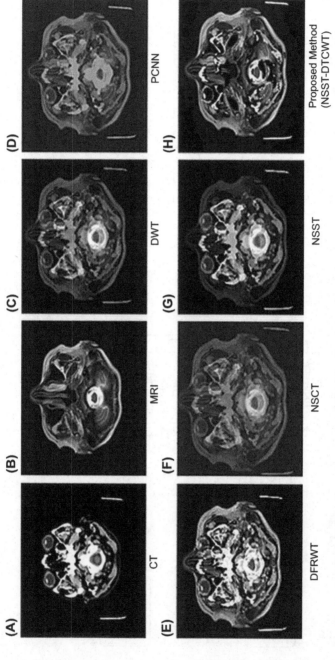

Figure 5.11 Experimental results of neurocysticercosis disease affected images for NSST-DTCWT-based hybrid algorithm.

Table 5.1 Performance metrics values obtained from neurocysticercosis disease affected images for NSST-DTCWT-based hybrid algorithm.

Method	FusFac	FusSym	IQI	$EQ^f_{a,b}$	mSSIM	CEn	Rcorr
DWT	4.1813	0.2981	0.6534	0.6492	0.6872	1.2011	0.7212
PCNN	4.3023	0.2515	0.6832	0.6981	0.7381	1.1812	0.7491
DFRWT	4.0262	0.2982	0.7112	0.7591	0.7781	1.1072	0.8042
NSCT	4.4741	0.2324	0.6882	0.8221	0.7871	0.9981	0.8116
NSST	4.6982	0.1987	0.6983	0.8581	0.8096	0.9467	0.8371
Proposed (NSST-DTCWT)	5.4291	0.1089	0.7201	0.9293	0.9197	0.7054	0.9018

Table 5.2 Performance metrics values obtained from neoplastic disease affected images for NSCT-NSST-based hybrid algorithm.

Method	FusFac	FusSym	IQI	$EQ^f_{a,b}$	mSSIM	CEn	Rcorr
DWT	3.1513	0.4052	0.6981	0.8192	0.7172	1.3127	0.7512
CVT	3.3223	0.3815	0.7012	0.8273	0.7516	1.2511	0.7719
DFRWT	3.4762	0.3682	0.7291	0.8517	0.7768	1.1023	0.8012
NSST	3.7141	0.3216	0.7431	0.8712	0.7912	0.9981	0.8271
DTCWT	3.8282	0.2821	0.7812	0.8814	0.7991	0.9812	0.8318
Proposed (NSST-NSCT)	4.0191	0.1542	0.9012	0.9312	0.8512	0.6981	0.8912

Table 5.3 Performance metrics values obtained from DTCWT-DFRWT-based hybrid algorithm.

Method	FusFac	FusSym	IQI	$EQ^f_{a,b}$	mSSIM	CEn	Rcorr
DWT	3.2981	0.4671	0.6762	0.6217	0.6872	1.3721	0.7012
PCNN	3.4781	0.4128	0.6989	0.6892	0.7072	1.2833	0.7426
DFRWT	3.7981	0.3721	0.7017	0.7263	0.7476	1.1073	0.7923
NSCT	3.8192	0.2982	0.7391	0.7638	0.7827	1.0231	0.8183
NSST	3.9912	0.2012	0.7562	0.7982	0.8017	0.9982	0.8387
Proposed (DTCWT-DFRWT)	4.5182	0.1324	0.8417	0.8989	0.8992	0.7298	0.9012

CVT, DFRWT, NSST, and DTCWT methods. The proposed NSCT–DFRWT have higher value for FusFac, IQI, EQM, and mSSIM and lower value for FusSym and Rcorr when compared with other existing conventional approaches (Fig. 5.18).

Table 5.4 Performance metrics values obtained from NSCT-DFRWT-based hybrid algorithm.

Method	FusFac	FusSym	IQI	$EQ^f_{a,b}$	mSSIM	CEn	Rcorr
DWT	1.2562	0.7083	0.7832	0.6921	0.6782	1.9827	0.6782
CVT	1.3612	0.6086	0.8342	0.7093	0.6982	1.8721	0.7162
DFRWT	1.5771	0.6023	0.8472	0.7324	0.7052	0.9982	0.7821
NSST	1.7892	0.5098	0.8764	0.7542	0.7261	0.8972	0.7998
DTCWT	1.8018	0.5009	0.8989	0.7892	0.7452	0.8231	0.8016
Proposed (NSCT-DFRWT)	2.0521	0.3202	1.6521	0.9172	0.9882	0.4982	0.9873

Table 5.5 Performance metrics values obtained from NSCT-DTCWT-based hybrid algorithm.

Method	FusFac	FusSym	IQI	$EQ^f_{a,b}$	mSSIM	CEn	Rcorr
DWT	3.1661	0.5882	0.7891	0.7181	0.7276	2.0510	0.5021
CVT	3.3411	0.6165	0.8219	0.7318	0.7416	1.9520	0.6210
DFRWT	3.4862	0.6371	0.8526	0.7621	0.7856	1.6820	0.6820
NSST	3.6741	0.6882	0.8893	0.7982	0.7922	1.5031	0.7306
DTCWT	3.5882	0.6683	0.8763	0.7768	0.8035	1.3045	0.7501
Proposed (NSCT-DTCWT)	4.2991	0.8621	0.9012	0.8127	0.8856	0.8620	0.9103

Fig. 5.20 shows the comparative analysis for NSCT–DTCWT-based hybrid algorithm. The results of experiments are compared with DWT, CVT, DFRWT, NSST, and DTCWT methods. The proposed NSCT–DTCWT have higher value for FusFac, IQI, EQM, and mSSIM and lower value for FusSym and Rcorr when compared with other existing conventional approaches.

Tables 5.1–5.5 illustrate the comparative analysis for various performance measurement values of fus fact, fus symry, img qty idx, mSSIM, CEn, EQM, and corre coeff for the traditional and proposed hybrid fusion techniques. For an efficient image fusion technique, the limits for the performance metrics values of fusion factor should get maximum value, the image quality index, mSSIM, edge quality measure and correlation coefficient should be getting maximum value. The value should be nearest to 1 and get lower value for fusion symmetry and cross entropy is declared as the fused output image is better quality. The proposed hybrid fusion algorithm

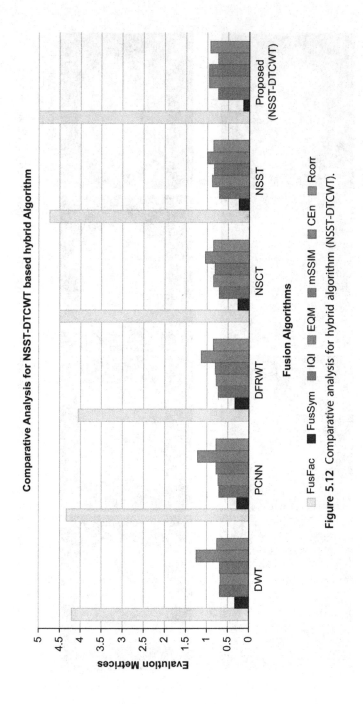

Figure 5.12 Comparative analysis for hybrid algorithm (NSST-DTCWT).

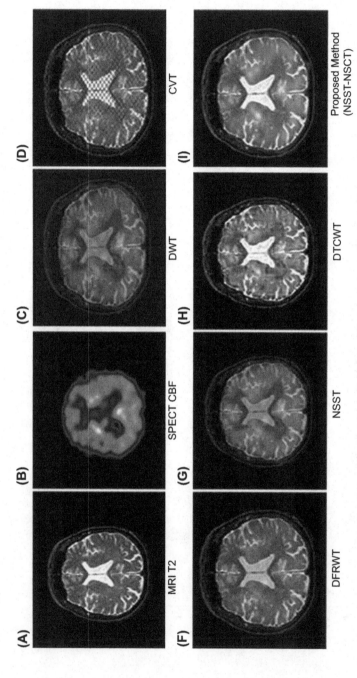

Figure 5.13 Experimental results of neoplastic disease affected images for NSCT-NSST-based hybrid algorithm.

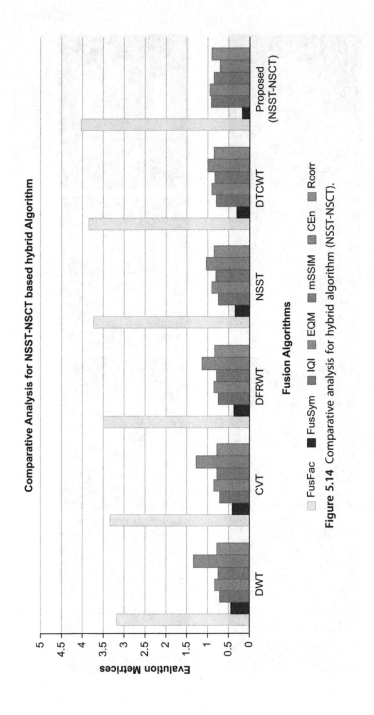

Figure 5.14 Comparative analysis for hybrid algorithm (NSST-NSCT).

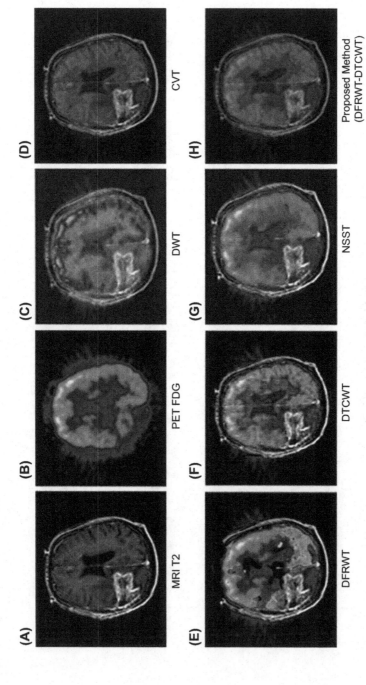

Figure 5.15 Experimental results of astrocytoma disease affected images for DFRWT-DTCWT-based hybrid algorithm.

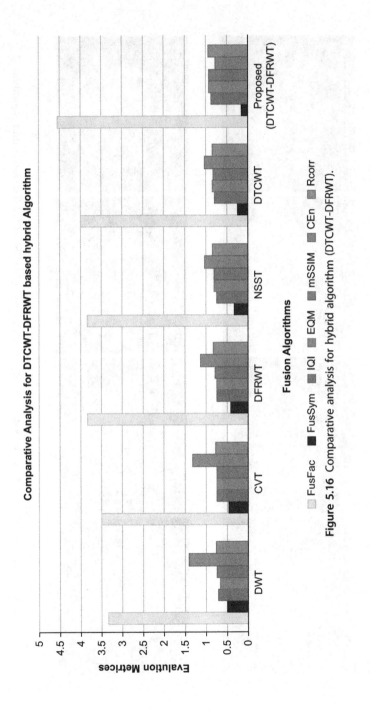

Figure 5.16 Comparative analysis for hybrid algorithm (DTCWT-DFRWT).

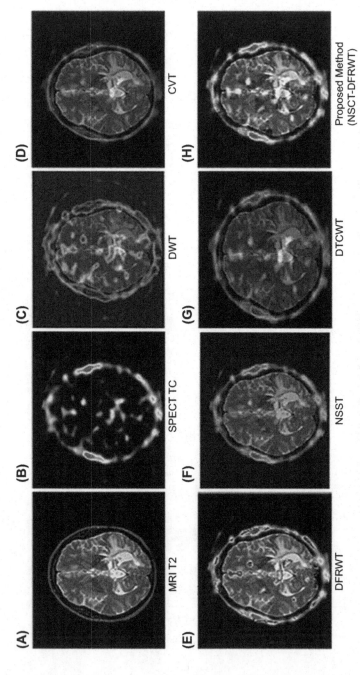

Figure 5.17 Experimental results of neoplastic disease affected images for NSCT-DFRWT-based hybrid algorithm.

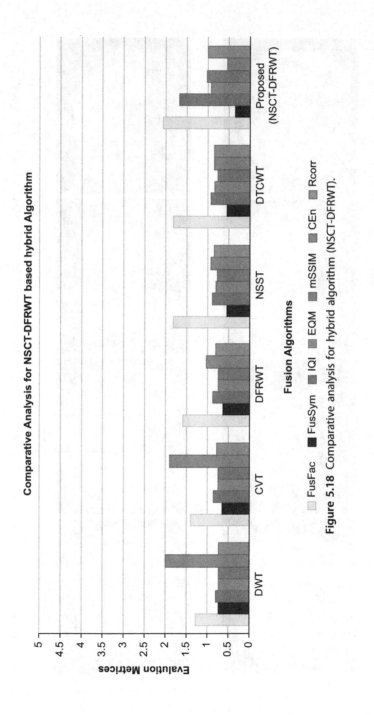

Figure 5.18 Comparative analysis for hybrid algorithm (NSCT-DFRWT).

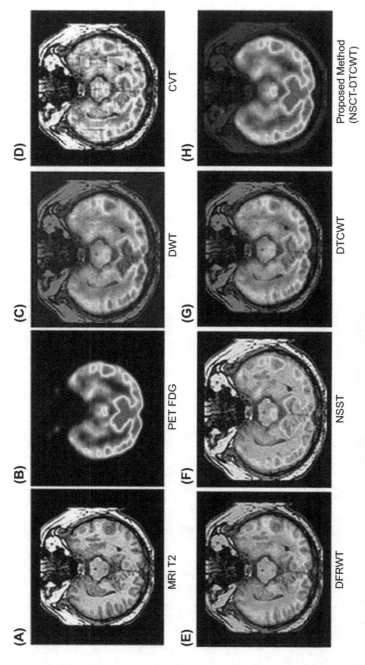

Figure 5.19 Experimental results of Alzheimer's disease affected images for NSCT-DTCWT-based hybrid algorithm.

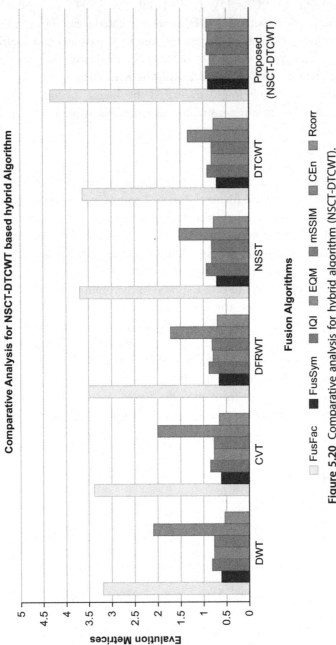

Figure 5.20 Comparative analysis for hybrid algorithm (NSCT-DTCWT).

is compared with other traditional fusion algorithms like principal component analysis (PCA), DWT, CVT, DFRWT, DTCWT, NSCT, and PCNN. All of these methodologies are incorporated using fusion rules as an average for low-pass subband parameters and high-pass subband coefficients selection of maximum value. On the basis of qualitative and quantitative parameter analysis, the proposed algorithm is evaluated. As a qualitative analysis, the expert radiologists evaluated the image quality of the fused images because the fusion constraints are estimated as predictive analysis.

5. Summary

This chapter presented a summary of the various conventional and hybrid fusion algorithms' clinical image fusion and comparative analysis. MIF is an active procedure that is useful for diagnosis, medical assessment of disease stages, and treatment evaluation in NCC, neoplastic disease, and Alzheimer's and astrocytoma diseases. The fusion algorithm is an aid to radiologists in accurate representation, better perception, and accurate description of lesions and disease acquired in the brain of NCC, neoplastic, and Alzheimer's and astrocytoma disease patients. This chapter discussed the comparative analysis for hybrid fusion algorithm of multimodality medical images to analyze and review the NCC, neoplastic, and astrocytoma and Alzheimer's diseases. A multimodality photo simulation experiment tested the proposed hybrid fusion algorithm. Multimodal MIF combines all relevant and unique data from multiple input images into a single composite image that facilitates more accurate diagnosis and better outcomes. The proposed hybrid fusion algorithm gives better results.

References

[1] A.A. James, B.V. Dasarathy, Medical image fusion: a survey of the state of the art, Information Fusion 19 (2014) 4—19. Elsevier.
[2] E. Daniel, Optimum wavelet based homomorphic medical image fusion using hybrid genetic — grey wolf optimization algorithm, IEEE Sensors (2018) 1558—1748.
[3] E. Daniel, J. Anithaa, K.K. Kamaleshwaran, I. Rani, Optimum Spectrum Mask Based Medical Image Fusion Using Gray Wolf Optimization, Biomedical Signal Processing and Control 34 (2017) 36—43. Elsevier.
[4] H.S. Bhadauria, M.L. Dewal, Medical image denoising using adaptive fusion of curvelet transform and total variation, Computers and Electrical Engineering 39 (2013) 1451—1460.
[5] H. Hermessi, O. Mourali, E. Zagrouba, Convolutional neural network-based multimodal image fusion via similarity learning in the shearlet domain, Neural Computing and Applications (2018). Springer.

[6] H.R. Shahdoosti, A. Mehrabi, Multimodal image fusion using sparse representation classification in tetrolet domain, Digital Signal Processing (2018). Elsevier.
[7] M. Heba, M. El-Sayed, Rabaie, W.A. Elrahman, E. Fathi, Medical Image Fusion Techniques Based on Combined Discrete Transform Domains, Arab Academy for Science, Technology & Maritime Transport, IEEE, 2017, pp. 471−480.
[8] J. Xi, Y. Chen, A. Chen, Y. Chen, Medical image fusion based on sparse representation and PCNN in NSCT domain, Computational and Mathematical Methods in Medicine (2018). Hindawi.
[9] K.-Jian Xia, H.-Sheng Yin, J.-Qiang Wang, A novel improved deep convolutional neural network model for medical image fusion, Cluster Computing (2018). Springer.
[10] S. Chavan, A. Mahajan, S.N. Talbar, S. Desai, M. Thakur, A. D'cruz, Nonsubsampled rotated complex wavelet transform (NSRCxWT) for medical image fusion related to clinical aspects in neurocysticercosis, Computers in Biology and Medicine (81) (2017) 64−78. Elsevier.
[11] S.D. Ramlal, J. Sachdeva, C.K. Ahuja, N. Khandelwal, Multimodal medical image fusion using non-subsampled shearlet transform and pulse coupled neural network incorporated with morphological gradient, Signal, Image and Video Processing (2018). Springer.
[12] S.H. Sreeja, An improved feature based image fusion technique for enhancement of liver lesions, Biocybernetics and Biomedical Engineering (2018). Elsevier.
[13] X. Liu, W. Mei, H. Du, Structure tensor and nonsubsampled sheasrlet transform based algorithm for CT and MRI image fusion, Neurocomputing 235 (2017) 131−139. Elsevier.
[14] X. Liu, W. Mei, H. Du, Multi-modality medical image fusion based on image decomposition framework and nonsubsampled shearlet transform, Biomedical Signal Processing and Control 40 (2018) 343−350. Elsevier.
[15] https://radiopaedia.org/articles/neurocysticercosis, 2017 (accessed).
[16] www.healthline.com/health/neoplastic-disease, 2018 (accessed).
[17] www.aans.org/Patients/Neurosurgical-Conditions-and Treatments/Astrocytoma-Tumors, 2018 (accessed).
[18] www.mayoclinic.org/diseases-conditions/alzheimers-disease, 2018 (accessed).
[19] www.cdc.gov, 2018 (accessed).
[20] www.ncin.org, 2018 (accessed).
[21] https://braintumoralliance.org, 2018 (accessed).
[22] https://hellodoktor.com, 2018 (accessed).

CHAPTER 6

Binary descriptor design for the automatic detection of coronary arteries using metaheuristics

Ivan Cruz-Aceves[1], Fernando Cervantes-Sanchez[2],
Arturo Hernandez-Aguirre[2], Martha A. Hernández-González[3],
Sergio Solorio-Meza[3]

[1]CONACYT − Centro de Investigación en Matemáticas (CIMAT), Guanajuato, Gto, Mexico; [2]Centro de Investigación en Matemáticas (CIMAT), Guanajuato, Gto, Mexico; [3]Unidad de Investigación, UMAE 1 Bajio, IMSS, León, Gto, Mexico

Contents

1. Introduction

Automatic segmentation of coronary arteries represents the main challenge for systems that perform computer–aided diagnosis in medical imaging. Although x-ray procedures for coronary angiography are the most widely used strategy in clinical practice, they present different problems for working with computational methods, such as nonuniform illumination

Advanced Machine Vision Paradigms for Medical Image Analysis
ISBN 978-0-12-819295-5
https://doi.org/10.1016/B978-0-12-819295-5.00006-8

and low contrast between tubular structures and the image background. In general, specialized vessel detection methods work under the assumption that vessel-like structures can be approximated as tubular objects with different vessel widths and directions.

In the literature, various automatic methods have been introduced for vessel detection, most of them following a Gaussian assumptions in the spatial image domain. Methods based on the second-order derivatives of a Gaussian function (Hessian matrix) use the properties of the dominant eigenvalues to compute a vesselness measure [1,2]. These methods are competitive for detecting vessels at different diameters and angular resolutions using a vesselness measure to classify vessel and nonvessel pixels. However, a main drawback of those methods is the number of parameters to be tuned to obtain competitive performance; another drawback is the second-order derivative, because it is highly sensitive to noise.

Another type of vessel enhancement method is based on matching templates. Gaussian matched filters (GMF) were introduced by Chaudhuri et al. [3] for segmenting vessel-like structures in retinal fundus images using the green channel. The GMF method works under the assumption that vessel-like structures can be detected by using a predefined Gaussian kernel as the matching template. To enhance vessel-like structures at different angular resolutions, a filter bank of directional filters is convolved with the input image, and to produce the enhanced image, the maximum response at each pixel is recorded. To form the Gaussian template, the GMF method uses the parameters of the number of oriented filters, the width and the height of the matching template, and the spread of the Gaussian profile. In general, those four parameters have been empirically determined for different works. Chanwimaluang et al. [4] used the original parameters of the GMF method to segment retinal vessels. Cinsdikici and Aydin [5] increased the number of directional filters to detect retinal vessels. Kang et al. [6] proposed different strategies to classify the Gaussian filter response, in which the GMF was modified in terms of the number of oriented filters and considering the spread value of the Gaussian profile. This work was proposed for segmenting coronary arteries. Moreover, to avoid empirically determined parameters, Al-Rawi et al. [7] introduced an improved version of the GMF, establishing a range of values for each Gaussian parameter and using an exhaustive full-search strategy to determine the best set of parameters according to a training set. This method was later improved by Al-Rawi and Karajeh [8] using a genetic algorithm (GA) to perform parameter tuning of the Gaussian method.

Some state-of-the-art vessel detection methods are based on mathematical morphology techniques. Eiho and Qian [9] proposed using the top-hat operator to segment coronary arteries, which was later improved by Qian et al. [10] by introducing the multiscale top-hat operator. This method is useful to detect vessels at different diameters. Lara et al. [11] introduced a semiautomatic segmentation method using a differential-geometry strategy working with region-growing to segment the coronary artery tree. The main benefit of the mathematical morphology methods is the competitive results under the accuracy metric and computational time, along with a low number of parameters to be tuned.

In the literature, the most widely used technique from mathematical morphology is the top-hat operator for working with nonuniform illuminated images to detect vessel-like structures. The single-scale top-hat operator works with a binary template, also called a structuring element, formed by two parameters: size and shape. Determination of the size and shape of the parameters is commonly addressed by an empirical process or by using a priori knowledge about the object of interest.

Because the design of the binary descriptor for working with the top-hat operator is a nonpolynomial problem $(O(2^n)$, where n represents the total number of pixels of the structuring element, also the called binary template), it has not been explored properly. In the current chapter, a comparative study is proposed of three different metaheuristics to address the problem of designing binary descriptors for automatic coronary artery segmentation. GAs, the Univariate Marginal Distribution Algorithm (UMDA), and iterated local search (ILS) are compared in terms of vessel detection and computational time. The method for vessel segmentation consists of two steps. In the first stage, the binary descriptor is automatically designed using metaheuristics instead of empirically determined parameter values. In this step, the vessel enhancement results obtained from the metaheuristics are compared with those acquired by deterministic methods using the area under the receiver operating characteristic (ROC) curve as an evaluation metric (Fig. 6.5). Finally, in the second step, the filter response obtained by the binary descriptors is classified as vessel and nonvessel pixels using a comparative analysis of five state-of-the-art automatic thresholding methods in terms of the accuracy metric.

The organization of the chapter is as follows. Section 2 introduces the fundamentals of the top-hat transform for image enhancement and three different metaheuristics to solve combinatorial optimization problems. The proposed method based on the design of binary descriptors for vessel enhancement is presented in Section 3. The computational results of the proposed method and its comparison with deterministic structuring elements are presented in Section 4, and conclusions are given in Section 5.

2. Background

Because of the suitable results in vessel detection obtained using mathematical morphology operators, the top-hat transform for image enhancement and three different metaheuristics for the design of binary descriptors are interesting in the current work. In this section, the metaheuristics and top-hat transform are described in detail.

2.1 Morphological top-hat transform

The top-hat transform is a mathematical morphology operator that is useful for working with nonuniform illumination in different types of images [12]. Because the top-hat transform is composed of the elemental operators of dilation and erosion, in gray-scale images these two operators can be viewed as the maximum and minimum filters, respectively. The top-hat transform performed on an input image f can be defined as:

$$\text{TopHat} = f - \max(\min(f)). \qquad (6.1)$$

To perform the top-hat operator, two parameters have to be tuned: the shape and size of the structuring element (binary descriptor). In general, these two parameters are empirically determined by the expert, because determination of the optimal binary descriptor represents a problem of $O(2^n)$, in which n is the total number of pixels of the structuring element.

To illustrate the enhancement results of applying different structuring elements on x-ray angiograms, Fig. 6.1 introduces four binary descriptors based on diamond and disk shapes with different sizes. Both two descriptors are the most commonly used ones in the literature for working with vessel-like structures.

2.2 Iterated local search

The metaheuristic of ILS is based on a local search strategy using a single solution along the iterative process [13]. ILS is a low−computational time method used to improve the quality of local optima, which is useful in high-dimensional problems. Generally, the process performed by the ILS method starts with a random initial solution (binary encoding) within the predefined search space, and the stopping criterion can be a number of

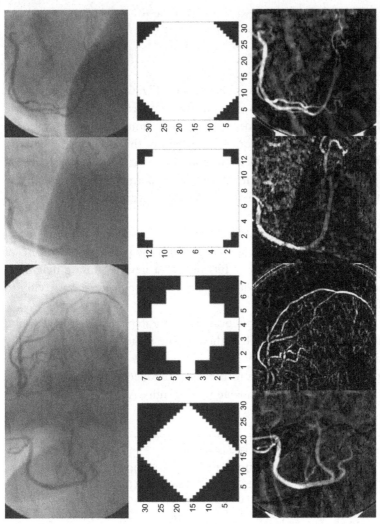

Figure 6.1 First row: Subset of x-ray coronary angiograms. Second row: Structuring elements of diamonds, sizes 15 and 3, and disk-shaped elements with size 7 and 17 pixels, respectively. Third row: Top-hat response obtained by applying the structuring element of the second row on the angiogram of the first row.

iterations. The fundamental idea of the ILS is governed by the steps of local search, perturbation, and the stopping criterion.

To illustrate the local search and perturbation steps, the test optimization function known as the Ackley function in two dimensions is used:

$$f(x) = -20exp\left(-0.2\sqrt{\frac{1}{2}\sum_{i=1}^{2}x_i^2}\right) - exp\left(\frac{1}{2}\sum_{i=1}^{2}cos(2\pi x_i)\right) + exp(1) + 20$$

$$(6.2)$$

The step of the local search is illustrated in Fig. 6.2. The individuals are encoded with binary values to perform the local search in each bit of the string. These binary values are decoded to continuous value to be evaluated in the objective function to acquire the fitness of the individual. The local search strategy consists of the permutation of one bit at a time over the best individual of the previous iteration. This permutation is iteratively performed over the best individual for each iteration until a stopping criterion is met.

The perturbation step is illustrated in Fig. 6.3 using the contour line of the Ackley function. The main idea to perform the perturbation consists of applying a strong permutation of bits to find a new promising neighborhood. In this step, the perturbation is applied through iterations trying to escape from a local minimum.

The steps of permutation and local search are iteratively performed until a stopping criterion is met, such as the number of iterations or the stability of the single solution.

According to this description, the ILS pseudocode is shown in Algorithm 1; the source code is available in Appendix A.

Individuals	Fitness	First local search		Second local search	
11101011	9.121	00010110	4.505	00010100	3.082
10101011	7.975	10010110	5.579	10010100	4.310
⋮		01010110	3.632	01010100	**1.764**
		00110110	3.632	00110100	1.764
11001011	7.335	00000110	4.643	00000100	2.637
00010110	**4.505**	00011110	8.284	00011100	6.283
11001101	8.003	00010010	4.505	00010000	4.310
⋮		00010100	**3.082**	00010110	4.505
11001100	6.593	00010111	4.504	00010101	3.833

Figure 6.2 Local search process using a binary representation of the Ackley function.

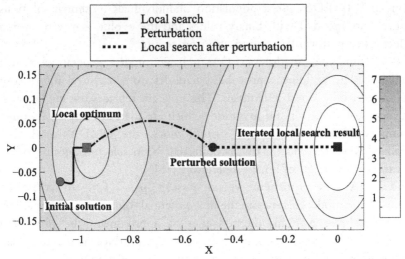

Figure 6.3 Perturbation process to avoid local minima problem using the contour line of the Ackley function.

Algorithm 1 Iterated local search

Require: D = dimension of the problem, N_{iter} = number of iterations
1: Initialize $t = 0$, $X^t \sim U(0,1)$
2: **while** stopCrit $\neq$ **true do**
3: $\quad X_*^t = Perturb(X^t)$ %Random selection
4: $\quad X_*^t = Localsearch(X_*^t)$
5: $\quad X^t = Accept(X^t, X_*^t)$
6: $\quad t = t + 1$
7: **end while**
8: **return** $X^t, f(X^t)$

In general, the metaheuristics based on a single solution obtains promising results in lower computation than the metaheuristics based on a population of solutions such as the UMDA and GAs, which are described subsequently.

2.3 Univariate marginal distribution algorithm

In evolutionary computation, the Estimation of Distribution Algorithms (EDAs) are a family of stochastic optimization strategies that use statistical procedures to solve numerical problems in the discrete and continuous domain [14]. EDAs use a population of individuals (potential solutions) commonly encoded with binary values and the evolutionary operator of selection to perform the optimization procedure.

The fundamental idea of EDAs is based on the generation of new individuals by building a probabilistic model from statistical information about a set of selected individuals. This concept replaces the evolutionary operators of crossover and mutation, which are used in most evolutionary computation methods. In the current work, the UMDA based on a probability vector and binary encoding has been selected because of the nature of the design of binary descriptors [15].

UMDA uses probability vector $\mathbf{p} = (p_1, p_2, ..., p_n)^T$ to create the probabilistic model to generate the new potential solutions using a marginal probability rate p_i. This method tries to approximate the probability distribution of the best solutions in $\mathbb{P}_t$ as the product of the univariate frequencies assuming that the binary features are independent.

The evolutionary process performed by UMDA consists of the steps of selection, estimation of probability distribution, and generation of new promising solutions. The selection stage is applied to generate a subset composed of the best potential solutions according to the fitness value. This process is generally computed using proportional selection:

$$\mathbb{P}^s(x) = \frac{\mathbb{P}(x)f(x)}{\sum_{\widetilde{x}\in\Omega} \mathbb{P}(\widetilde{x})f(\widetilde{x})}. \tag{6.3}$$

The second step corresponding to the estimation of the univariate marginal probabilities $\mathbb{P}$ to build the probability model for independent features can be performed:

$$\mathbb{P}(x) = \prod_{i=1}^{n} \mathbb{P}(X_i = x_i), \tag{6.4}$$

where $x = (x_1, x_2, ..., x_n)^T$ is the binary values of the i th bit encoding in the potential solutions, and X_i is the i th random value of the vector X. In the last step, from the probability vector a new population is generated and evaluated using the fitness function.

These three stages are iteratively performed until a stopping criterion is met. Considering this description, the UMDA algorithm can be implemented using the following pseudocode.

Algorithm 2 Univariate marginal distribution algorithm

Require : D = number of dimensions
n_{pop} = number of individuals
N_{gen} = number of generations
n_{sel} = selected subset
1: Initialize $t = 0$, $X^t \sim U(0, 1)$
2: Evaluate $F^t = f(X^t)$
3: $[x_{best}, X^t]$ =Sort X^t depending of the fitness values
4: **while** stopping criterion $\neq$ **true do**
5: **for** $i = _{n_{sel}} 1 .. D$ **do**
6: $p_i = \sum_j x_{i,j}$
7: **end for**
8: Set $P = [p_1, p_2, ..., p_D]$
9: Sample $X^{t+1} \sim P$
10: Elitism $X^{t+1} = \left[X^{t+1}_{1:(n_{pop}-1)}, x_{best} \right]$
11: $t = t + 1$
12: Evaluate $F^t = f(X^t)$
13: $[x_{best}, X^t]$ =Sort X^t depending of the fitness values
14: **end while**
15: **return** x_{best}

2.4 Genetic algorithms

The GA is a well-known optimization method that emulates genetic evolution [16]. The GA is composed of a set of potential solutions called individuals, in which each individual is encoded using binary values and evaluated using an objective function through a number of generations. The best individual found with this iterative process is called the elite individual; it represents the best solution for the optimization problem. The strategy of the GA is based on the three evolutionary operators of selection, crossover, and mutation. The selection operator ensures strong solutions will survive the evolutionary process to produce stronger offspring. The most commonly used selection strategy is the roulette wheel. This strategy is based on the sum of the fitness values of the current population, and the selection probability for each individual is the rate that its fitness value contributes to the global sum.

The crossover operator combines the genes of selected individuals trying to generate stronger offspring. In general, two new individuals are formed from two randomly parents belonging to the selected subset, keeping the number of individuals in the population constant for the next generation in the evolutionary process. The new individuals are evaluated using the fitness function and with the restriction that if a children is better in terms of fitness than the parent, it is considered a new potential solution. Finally, the mutation operator is carried out for each individual to avoid stagnation in local minima problems.

Considering the previous description, the GA can be implemented by using the following procedure:

1. Initialize number of iterations G and population size N.
2. Set crossover value CR and mutation percentage MR.
3. Initialize N individuals into the search space (randomly).
4. Evaluate individuals using the fitness function.
5. For each iteration $g = \{1, \ldots, G\}$:
   (a) Perform selection operator
   (b) Perform crossover operator
   (c) Perform mutation operator
   (d) Evaluate new individuals according to objective function
   (e) Replace individuals with the worst fitness.
6. Stop if converge criterion is met (e.g., stability or number of generations).

3. Proposed method

3.1 Design of binary descriptors using Metaheuristics

In the literature, methods based on the top-hat operator have obtained suitable performance for the detection of vessel-like structures; however, in many instances the discrete parameters of the size and morphological shape of the structuring element have been empirically determined or by using trial and error. Consequently, the search space of $O(2^n)$ computational complexity, which is n, the total number of pixels of the structuring element, cannot be explored properly.

To explore the high-dimensional space of the binary descriptor and determine its optimal behavior, in the current work, the metaheuristics of ILS, UMDA, and GAs have been adopted. Fig. 6.4 presents six binary descriptors for vessel detection obtained using the three previously mentioned metaheuristics. These asymmetric binary descriptors are used as

Figure 6.4 Six morphological binary descriptors of size $= 25 \times 25$ pixels obtained using metaheuristics for the vessel detection problem.

binary structuring elements to perform the top-hat transform on x-ray angiograms.

The proposed method to design binary descriptors for vessel detection consists of three stages. The first step is the definition of a predefined size of the binary descriptor. This is a fundamental step, because in many cases, the size of the element depends on the vessel-like structures and is related to the detection performance. In the second step, the metaheuristics are used according to their particular strategies to generate candidate binary descriptors with different pixel distribution by exploring the high dimensional search space. The number of potential solutions is related to the parameters of the metaheuristics, such as the number of generations and number of individuals in the population. In the last step, to determine the optimal binary descriptor for working with the top-hat operator in terms of vessel detection, area (A_z) under the ROC curve is used to evaluate the top-hat filter response. The binary descriptor with the highest A_z value will be selected as the optimal to detect vessel-like structures according to a training set. *In the proposed method, the main advantage is that the search space is explored properly, whereas the binary descriptor can be automatically determined avoiding empirical values or* a priori *knowledge of the problem.*

Moreover, the top-hat filter response obtains a gray-scale image with uniform illumination and enhanced vessel-like structures. To classify vessel and nonvessel pixels from the filter response, a thresholding strategy is required. In this work, five automatic thresholding methods are compared using the accuracy metric. Finally, in the postprocessing step, length filtering is applied to eliminate all isolated regions around the coronary tree, which is the main structure to be segmented in x-ray angiograms for angioplasty or to detect potential cases of coronary stenosis.

3.2 Evaluation measures

To assess the top-hat filter response in vessel detection, also called vessel enhancement, area (A_z) under the (ROC) curve is computed. The ROC curve represents a plot between the true-positive fraction (TPF) also known as Sensitivity and the false-positive fraction (FPF), also computed as the inverse of the specificity value. Because the filter response is a gray-scale image, the values of TPF and FPF are obtained using an exhaustive sliding threshold, and the area under the curve is computed by the Riemman sum method. This metric is in the range $[0, 1]$, where 1 is the maximum performance and 0 is the worst detection rate.

Moreover, to evaluate the vessel segmentation (binary image) step, the accuracy measure has been selected. In the literature, the accuracy measure is the most representative metric to assess image binary classification (vessel and nonvessel pixels), which can be defined as:

$$Accuracy = \frac{TP + TN}{TP + FP + TN + FN}, \tag{6.5}$$

where TP and TN are the fractions of vessel and nonvessel pixels correctly classified, and FP and FN, the fractions of incorrectly segmented pixels.

4. Computational experiments

All computational experiments in the current chapter were carried out on a computer with an Intel Core i3, 4 GB of RAM, and a 2.13-GHz processor. The database of x-ray images consists of 100 gray-scale coronary angiograms of size 300×300 pixels from different patients. To form the ground-truth images, the database was outlined by an expert cardiologist and the ethics approval letter was provided by the Instituto Mexicano del Seguro Social, Unidad Medica De Alta Especialidad Leon T1. To assess the performance of the computational experiments, the database was divided into the training and testing sets of 50 angiograms each. Because the metaheuristics are stochastic optimization techniques, all computational experiments were performed using 30 runs for statistical analysis.

Table 6.1 Statistical comparison with 30 trials of three metaheuristics using the training set.

Method	Maximum	Minimum	Mean	Standard deviation	Median
Iterated local search	**0.9682**	0.9575	0.9627	0.0112	0.9636
Genetic algorithm	0.9663	0.9582	0.9604	0.0246	0.9621
Univariate Marginal Distribution Algorithm	0.9612	0.9564	0.9592	0.0110	0.9598

4.1 Results of vessel enhancement

For an analysis of the performance of the metaheuristics on the binary descriptor design for morphological operators, a statistical comparison of ILS, UMDA, and GA is presented in Table 6.1. To perform the analysis, the parameters of the ILS were tuned according to I. Cruz-Aceves et al [17] with a dimension of 25^2 and a stopping criterion of stability; the UMDA was established as 30 individuals using 30 iterations with a selection rate of 0.7 according to I. Cruz-Aceves et al. [15]. On the other hand, considering that GA is a population method similar to UMDA, and the best trade-off between detection performance and computational time, the GA parameters were established to be a selection rate of 0.7 and mutation rate of 0.05 using 30 individuals and 30 generations. This statistical analysis reveals that the ILS is more robust than population-based methods, because this test's solutions obtained low variations in range and standard deviation. Furthermore, in terms of the computational time in the training step, the

Table 6.2 Comparison between top hat–based on metaheuristics and five vessel detection methods in terms of A_z value with training set of angiograms.

Detection method	Area under receiver operating characteristic curve (A_z)
Kang et al. [6]	0.9004
Chaudhuri et al. [3]	0.9108
Cinsdikici et al. [5]	0.9156
Wang et al. [2]	0.9422
Univariate Marginal Distribution Algorithm (top-hat)	0.9612
Eiho and Qian [9]	0.9635
Genetic algorithm (top-hat)	0.9663
Iterated local search (top-hat)	**0.9682**

Table 6.3 Comparison between vessel detection methods using A_z value as evaluation metric with testing set of angiograms.

Detection method	Area under receiver operating characteristic curve (A_z)
Kang et al. [6]	0.8960
Cinsdikici et al. [5]	0.9058
Chaudhuri et al. [3]	0.9066
Wang et al. [2]	0.9401
Univariate Marginal Distribution Algorithm (top-hat)	0.9558
Eiho and Qian [9]	0.9577
Genetic algorithm (top-hat)	0.9602
Iterated local search (top-hat)	**0.9614**

UMDA obtained 240 s per image, the GA obtained 312 s, and the ILS obtained 142 s. In the testing step, applying the morphological top-hat operator on the binary descriptor designed by metaheuristics, no significant differences were obtained at 0.44 s, on average

On the other hand, to compare the performance of the binary descriptors based on metaheuristics, Table 6.2 shows state-of-the-art methods using the training set. The comparison was carried out with methods based on the Hessian matrix, Gaussian templates, and the deterministic top-hat operator, in which the GMF-based methods obtained the lowest performance, and the top hat—based methods achieved the highest A_z values including the deterministic and stochastic design.

Because the previous comparative analyses were performed on the training set for tuning purposes in the binary descriptors based on metaheuristics, in Table 6.3, an analysis is carried out on the testing set. In this analysis, the methods have behavior similar to that of the results of the training set. The top hat—based methods present the highest detection performance compared with the other seven vessel enhancement methods, especially the method based on the metaheuristic ILS. Consequently, the binary descriptor design based on the ILS was selected for further analysis.

To illustrate the qualitative results obtained from the comparative analysis, Fig. 6.6 shows a subset of x-ray angiograms along with the ground-truth, and the filter responses of the five deterministic methods and the ILS (top-hat).

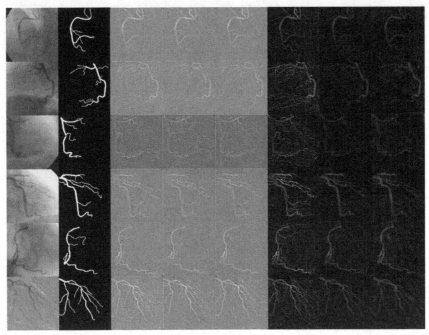

Figure 6.5 Vessel enhancement results. First and second rows: angiograms and ground-truth image, respectively. The remaining six rows present the results of the methods [2,3,5,6,9] and the method based on the iterated local search, respectively.

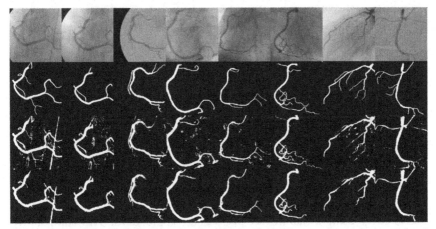

Figure 6.6 Vessel segmentation results obtained by the proposed iterated local search—top-hat method. The first and second rows show a subset of x-ray angiograms and the ground-truth image, respectively. The third row presents the results using the intraclass thresholding method on the images of the first row. The last row shows the final segmentation result applying length filtering as a postprocessing step on the images in the first row.

Table 6.4 Comparison of five thresholding methods to segment the top-hat filter response based on the iterative local search.

Thresholding method	Accuracy
Ridler and Calvard [18]	0.9219
Rutherford—Appleton Threshold Selection (RATS) [19]	0.9485
Statistical moments [20]	0.9532
Histogram concavity [21]	0.9584
Interclass variance [22]	**0.9621**

4.2 Results of vessel segmentation

Because the top-hat filter response based on the ILS is a gray-scale image, it must be classified as vessel and nonvessel pixels. In Table 6.4, automatic thresholding methods are compared in terms of segmentation accuracy using the test set of angiograms. The computational results reveal that Otsu's method based on intraclass variance obtains the highest classification rate.

To illustrate the obtained segmentation results, Fig. 6.6 presents a subset of angiograms. In this last step, length filtering is useful to eliminate isolated regions of pixel classified as vessels by the thresholding method. This is suitable to obtain the coronary tree while increasing segmentation accuracy.

The proposed method based on the ILS for an automatic binary descriptor design avoids an empirical process to determine the best morphological parameters by exploring high-dimensional space using metaheuristics. The experimental results show that the proposed method is robust and competitive with respect to comparative vessel detection methods; therefore, it may be suitable for systems that perform computer-aided diagnosis in clinical practice.

5. Concluding remarks

In this chapter, an automatic binary descriptor design for the top-hat operator has been addressed by comparing three metaheuristics to segment coronary arteries in gray-scale x-ray angiograms. The metaheuristics of ILS, UMDA, and GAs have been compared in terms of the area (A_z) under the ROC curve using a training set of 50 x-ray angiograms. This comparative analysis was tested for 30 runs, in which the highest performance was obtained by the ILS with $A_z = 0.9682$. In addition, the best binary descriptor obtained with metaheuristics was compared with five well-known vessel enhancement methods using an independent test set of 50 images, in which the best area under the ROC curve was obtained by ILS with $A_z = 0.9614$. Moreover, to segment the top-hat filter response obtained based on the ILS, five state-of-the-art automatic thresholding methods were compared using the accuracy measure, in which the intraclass variance method achieved the highest value (0.9621). According to the experimental results, the automatic design of binary descriptors for working with morphological operators may be suitable for systems that perform vessel segmentation as part of medical analysis. Because the use of metaheuristics is efficient for exploring the high-dimensional $(O(2^n))$ search space of binary descriptors, for future work, more sophisticated metaheuristics or evolutionary computation techniques might be explored or proposed.

Appendix A

Local search code in MATLAB programming language used to design binary descriptors for use with the morphological top-hat operator for vessel detection in x-ray angiograms.

```
1 function []=LocalSearchRand ( )
2 LS( 2 5, 0 , 1 , 2 5 0 0 ) ; %random search with a priori
information
3 clear all ; close all ; clc ;
4
5 function [ f ,X]=LS(n , apriori , runs , iterations )
6 %Local Search Parameters
7 % n : number of rows
8 % Iterations : Stopping criterion
9 % apriori : 1 a priori information , 0 randomly information
10 % runs : number of independent runs .
11 for run=1 : runs
12 genes=power (n , 2 ) ;
13 first _ poblacion=10 ;
14 elitista _ res=0 ;
15 elitista _ gen=[] ;
16
17 if ( apriori == 0)
18 P=randi ( [ 0 , 1 ] , first _ poblacion , genes ) ;
19 for i=1 : first _ poblacion
20 ind=P( i , 1 : genes ) ;
21 ind _ CC = ObjConexo ( ind ) ;
22 X=fitness ( ind_CC) ;
23 if (X>elitista _ res )
```

```
24 elitista _ res=X;
25 elitista _ gen=ind _ CC ;
26 end
27 end
28 end
29 for iter=1 : iterations
30 gen _ aux=elitista _ gen ;
31 if ( rand ()<0 . 5 )
32 SE _ final 2=vec2mat ( gen aux , sqrt (
length ( gen aux ) ) ) ;
33 siz=size ( SE _ final 2 ) ;
34 while true.
35 valx=round ( ( siz ( 1 ) −1) * rand ()
+1);
36valy=round ( ( siz ( 2 ) −1) * rand ()
+1);
37 SE_aux=SE_f inal 2 ;
38 SE_aux ( valx , valy )=1 ;
39 end
40 end
41 else
42 SE_final2=vec2mat ( gen_aux , sqrt (
length ( gen_aux ) ) ) ;
43 siz=size ( SE_final2 ) ;
44 while true
45 valx=round ( ( siz ( 1 ) −1)* rand ()
+1) ;
46 valy=round ( ( siz ( 2 ) −1)* rand ()
+1) ;
47 SE_aux=SE_final2 ;
48 SE_aux ( valx , valy ) = 0 ;
49 end
50 end
51 end
52 res_aux=fitness ( gen_aux ) ;
53 if ( res_aux>elitista_res )
54 elitista_res=res_aux
55 elitista_gen=gen_aux ;
56 end
57 end
58 Show_results ( elitista_gen , apriori , run ) ;
59 end
```

Acknowledgments

This research was completely supported by the Consejo Nacional de Ciencia y Tecnología (CONACYT) under Reference Cátedras-CONACYT No. 3150−3097.

References

[1] A. Frangi, W. Niessen, K. Vincken, M. Viergever, Multiscale Vessel Enhancement Filtering, Medical Image Computing and Computer-Assisted Intervention (MIC-CAI'98), vol. 1496, Springer LNCS, 1998, pp. 130−137.

[2] S. Wang, B. Li, S. Zhou, A segmentation method of coronary angiograms based on multi-scale filtering and region-growing, in: International Conference on Biomedical Engineering and Biotechnology, 2012, pp. 678−681.

[3] S. Chaudhuri, S. Chatterjee, N. Katz, M. Nelson, M. Goldbaum, Detection of blood vessels in retinal images using two-dimensional matched filters, IEEE Transactions on Medical Imaging 8 (1989) 263−269.

[4] T. Chanwimaluang, G. Fan, S. Fransen, Hybrid retinal image registration, IEEE Transactions on Information Technology in Biomedicine 10 (2006) 129−142.

[5] M. Cinsdikici, D. Aydin, Detection of blood vessels in ophthalmoscope images using MF/ant (matched filter/ant colony) algorithm, Computer Methods and Programs in Biomedicine 96 (2009) 85−95.

[6] W. Kang, W. Kang, Y. Li, Q. Wang, The segmentation method of degree-based fusion algorithm for coronary angiograms, in: 2nd International Conference on Measurement, Information and Control, 2013, pp. 696−699.

[7] M. Al-Rawi, H. Karajeh, Genetic algorithm matched filter optimization for automated detection of blood vessels from digital retinal images, Computer Methods and Programs in Biomedicine 87 (2007) 248−253.

[8] M. Al-Rawi, M. Qutaishat, M. Arrar, An improved matched filter for blood vessel detection of digital retinal images, Computers in Biology and Medicine 37 (2007) 262−267.

[9] S. Eiho, Y. Qian, Detection of coronary artery tree using morphological operator, Computers in Cardiology 24 (1997) 525−528.

[10] Y. Qian, S. Eiho, N. Sugimoto, M. Fujita, Automatic extraction of coronary artery tree on coronary angiograms by morphological operators, Computers in Cardiology 25 (1998) 765−768.

[11] D. Lara, A. Faria, A. Araujo, D. Menotti, A semi-automatic method for segmentation of the coronary artery tree from angiography, XXII Brazilian Symposium on Computer Graphics and Image Processing (SIBGRAPI) (2009) 194−201.

[12] H. Hassanpour, N. Samadiani, S. Salehi, Using morphological transforms to enhance the contrast of medical images, The Egyptian Journal of Radiology and Nuclear Medicine 46 (2015) 481−489.

[13] E.G. Talbi, Metaheuristics. From Design to Implementation, John Wiley & Sons, 2009.

[14] M. Hauschild, M. Pelikan, An introduction and survey of estimation of distribution algorithms, Swarm and Evolutionary Computation 1 (2011) 111−128.

[15] I. Cruz-Aceves, S. Ivvan-Valdez, A novel evolutionary morphological descriptor for the segmentation of coronary arteries, in: 2018 IEEE Latin American Conference on Computational Intelligence (LA-CCI), 2018, pp. 1−5.

[16] M. Mitchell, An Introduction to Genetic Algorithms, The MIT Press, Cambridge, 1997.

[17] I. Cruz-Aceves, F. Cervantes-Sanchez, M. Hernandez-Gonzalez, A new binary descriptor for the automatic detection of coronary arteries in X-ray angiograms, in: Proceedings of the SPIE, 14th International Symposium on Medical Information Processing and Analysis 10975, 2018, pp. 1—7.

[18] T. Ridler, S. Calvard, Picture thresholding using an iterative selection method, IEEE Transactions on Systems, Man, and Cybernetics 8 (1978) 630—632.

[19] J. Kittler, J. Illingworth, J. Foglein, Threshold selection based on a simple image statistic, Computer Vision, Graphics, and Image Processing 30 (1985) 125—147.

[20] W. Tsai, Moment-preserving thresholding: a new approach, Computer Vision, Graphics, and Image Processing 29 (1985) 377—393.

[21] A. Rosenfeld, P. De la Torre, Histogram concavity analysis as an aid in threshold selection, IEEE Transactions on Systems, Man, and Cybernetics 13 (1983) 231—235.

[22] N. Otsu, A threshold selection method from gray-level histograms, IEEE Transactions on Systems, Man, and Cybernetics 9 (1979) 62—66.

CHAPTER 7

A cognitive perception on content-based image retrieval using an advanced soft computing paradigm

K. Martin Sagayam[1], P. Malin Bruntha[1], M. Sridevi[2], M. Renith Sam[1], Utku Kose[3], Omer Deperlioglu[4]

[1]Department of ECE, Karunya Institute of Technology and Sciences, Coimbatore, Tamil Nadu, India; [2]Department of Computer Science and Engineering, National Institute of Technology, Trichy, Tamil Nadu, India; [3]Department of Computer Engineering, Suleyman Demirel University, Isparta, Merkez, Turkey; [4]Department of Computer Programming, Afyon Kocatepe University, Afyonkarahisar, Merkez, Turkey

Contents

Advanced Machine Vision Paradigms for Medical Image Analysis
ISBN 978-0-12-819295-5
https://doi.org/10.1016/B978-0-12-819295-5.00007-X

1. Introduction

In research fields for the past decades, image retrieval has been used extremely. In the early 1980s, medical images were explored for diagnosing disease from input data. With the rise of digital image acquisition and storage systems in clinical routine, there is a demand for new access methods. Still, most picture archiving and communication systems use only textual information to access a patient's image data, which has mainly been entered manually, whereas content-based image retrieval (CBIR) automatically extract content descriptions of each image as well as stores and compares upon a query. Mainly the users do not want to retrieve images that still refer to the basis of similarity in appearance. They need to locate images of a particular type of object or events.

The CBIR features such as three-dimensional (3D) calibration, color, shape, and texture are used in the manipulation of the details of an image and store the required details in the database as per user request. The storing level will be lesser in the data rate as the abstraction keeps only the required features. Figs. 7.1 describes the key terms used by a CBIR system to identify the query that is being searched for a particular image. As the user specifies the search by defining it through more words, the system locates the specified image to provide the desired result. The objective of our work mainly focuses on the image retrieval from big medical databases providing the precise result, which therefore helps doctors plan for that particular patient treatment.

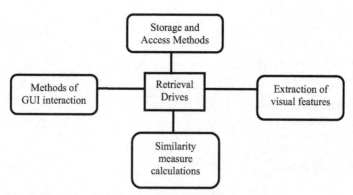

Figure 7.1 Basic components of content-based image retrieval system.

2. Related works

Over last few decades, there is extensive growth in the use of digital imaging techniques that led to an ever-growing collection of images. Retrieving images from large databases is a challenging problem. Much research has been carried out to address the challenges of image retrieval such as properties of the contents, correlation, computational complex, accurate retrieval, noise, and so on. Earlier, query-b0y-image content is developed. The textual annotations are based on language and the variations in annotation will pose a challenge to image retrieval. CBIR model [6] is used to retrieve an image from a larger database. Traditional methods of image indexing for larger databases are proved to be insufficient and extremely time consuming. CBIR usually indexes images by low-level visual features such as color, shape, and texture. The feature plays a vital role in image retrieval. Hence, the authors in Ref. [9] did make a brief comparative study on the image retrieval techniques, by using various feature extraction methods such as color histogram, Gabor transform, color histogram and Gabor transform, contourlet transform, and color histogram and contourlet transform. In Ref. [8], features of magnetic resonance imaging (MRI) are extracted using discrete cosine transform (DCT). The author proved that the DCT-based feature extraction provides good result. In Ref. [10], the authors used various methodologies for CBIR using relevance feedback. The author concludes that the relevance feedback technique in the CBIR system gives better retrieval performance. Wavelet transform is used in Ref. [1] for CBIR. The results show that the proposed method is efficient and fast.

A computer-aided diagnosis (CAD) system is the predominant method for the decision-making process for radiologists [2]. It is to reduce the false positives and discomfort effort for the diagnosis of a lesion. Content-based medical-image retrieval (CBMIR) is the decision-making task for clinicians by retrieving the most relevant cases and images from the digital medical-image database. CBMIR for personal study and cross-referencing similar images in a large medical-image database have been explored. Later, machine learning—based framework [4,7] has been developed for image retrieval and also for medical-image retrieval based on human perceptual similarity and semantic of query. The data are classified using naïve Bayes, random forest, support vector machine (SVM), k-nearest-neighbors (kNN), and so forth. In Ref. [11], the kNN classifier is used for CBIR of a CAD scheme. They utilize the features such as shape factors, radial length statistics, histogram, and local pixel value fluctuations from both the mass region and the whole breast area. They achieved good result.

The authors in Ref. [12] have found out that circumscribed margins are produced as a result by using the signified Zernike method for image retrieval. Also, the clarity of the inner and outer regions of the mass was brought by the edge-detection method. In scale–invariant feature transform (SIFT) [13], visual words are applied in CBIR approach to detect mass or nonmass rather than diagnosis from mammograms. The proposed method is efficient and scalable.

The main approach behind the retrieval systems use feature extraction from image and a classifier to differentiate normal and abnormal conditions [14]. In this way, all the features that define the object including shape factors, Zernike moments, as well as histogram and Haralick features are extracted and optimal feature subsets are selected for classification.

The feature extraction methodologies take two different parts from most systems. They are shape features and texture features that quantify characteristics and properties of the area around the boundary of a mass and its core. CBIR has a big influence on this case, which offers decision-making to radiologists to select the most appropriate image for their purpose from the reference database.

Agarwal et al. [24] introduced a feature descriptor 3D local ternary cooccurrence pattern (3D-LTCoP) for retrieving biomedical images. A Gaussian filter bank was used to evaluate statistical geometry of all images. 3D-LTCoP and 3D local ternary pattern (LTP) are combined. This method has been evaluated using OASIS MRI database and the average precision of 3D-LTCoP + 3D-LTP is 64.96% and 3D-LTCoP is 62.73%.

Recently, deep neural networks [3,5] have been adopted in medical images and yield state–of–the-art performance. Using deep neural networks allows automatic feature extraction and general, expressive representation learning for different computer vision tasks, including medical imaging. Adnan et al. [25] utilized deep convolutional neural network in CBIR systems to reduce semantic gap. It is reported that 24 different classes of medical images are involved in the experimental work with average precision of retrieval 0.69.

Wu has described a two-stage learning method to train multimodal mappings that projects the multimode data to low-dimensional embeddings that preserve both feature and semantic information, whereas Yang has explained more clearly about the aurora images taken with all-sky-imagers (ASI) [26,27]. After drawing out the results from ASI and aurora, a salient region determination scheme is proposed and embedded into the mask region based convolutional neural network (R–CNN) framework. Gu [28] has proposed a novel end-to-end, deep framework for image retrieval, clustering-driven unsupervised hashing, to recursively learn discriminative clusters by soft clustering model and produce binary code with high similarity response. The approach taken by Mahmood Sotoodeh [29] was to extract discriminative features for color image retrieval [29]. The local texture descriptors, based on radial mean local binary pattern (RMLBP), are called color RMCLBP and prototype data model. RMLBP has a strong and rigid noise descriptor that extracts texture features of grayscale images for classification. A linguistic description-based approach for a patient's image data retrieval using their outward descriptions and given input using parts of speech and attributes ontology was proposed by Khan [30]. The rankings are sorted according to the need of the patient.

This work focuses on CBIR using advance soft computing paradigm to yield a breakthrough performance for image retrieval tasks.

3. Methodology

The need of efficient image retrieval techniques is required for managing large image databases. The CBIR system for image retrieval from the database depending on their similarity level of the input images is comprised of the following given methods. First, it begins with the user giving the desired search queries for a particular image. After the query is set, it is sent onto the database to provide the better results. Second, it enters the main MRI database to retrieve the particular one. The median filter is used for the noise reduction of the image in the preprocessing stage. Now, it enters the important feature extraction process of gray-level cooccurrence matrix (GLCM), which calculates how often the pairs of pixels with specific values and spatial relationship occur in the image. Next, the detection performance is improved by the local binary pattern (LBP) whereas the Merthiolate-Iodine-Formaldehyde (MIF) techniques describes the objects after segmentation. This falls under the extraction category whereas the next process is a little more similar, but only that it selects the best results for the requirement. Then a subset is formed by the SVM classifier to provide the explanatory variables for the pattern recognition. Once the classified query feature vector matches with the

Euclidean search, the resultant images are set in order for display. Finally, the retrieval result is shown to the user.

3.1 MRI brain image database

The brain data images from the well-know organization open access series of image studies (OASIS) website [15]. There are three types of datasets that were involved and we have selected only one for our work. The central. xnat.org hosted the OASIS datasets by providing for the community open access to the very remarkable database of neuroimaging by processing the image data across a different spectrum made accessible to any platforms involving cognitive research and cognitive decline.

Described in Table 7.1 are the three types of OASIS datasets found. Stage-1 OASIS, cross-sectional, and stage-2 OASIS, longitudinal have been used for conjecture-based data surveys and developments in segmentation algorithms. Stage-3 OASIS is the recent release, aimed to make MRI datasets easily made available to the research field. By assembling and giving these multi-modal datasets, it has been therefore hoped to facilitate any of the future discoveries in basic and clinical neuroscience. Stage-3 OASIS is a clinical, cognitive, and biomarker dataset for any of the normal aging and Alzheimer's Disease.

3.2 Pre-processing

The pre-processing stage is the essential step towards retaining the important information. The filtering and preparation of image will take a considerable amount of processing time. Image pre-processing includes cleaning, normalization, transformation, feature extraction and selection, etc. In order to the improve the quality of the image, the raw image is preprocessed so as to improve the efficiency and ease of the mining process. Preprocessing has a major impact on the quality of feature extraction and a profound output of image analysis. A dataset has a common feature descriptor method that corresponds to mathematical normalization in preprocessing.

3.2.1 Median filtering

The median filter is the filtering technique used for noise removal from images and signals. Median filter is very crucial in the image processing field as it is well known for the preservation of edges during noise removal. The prior duty of the filter is to scan every input data interceding the overall entries with the median function known as "window" method. The window tends to be a little bit complex over the

Table 7.1 OASIS brain datasets

OASIS	Subjects	MRI sessions	PET sessions
1 Cross-sectional MRI data in young, middle-aged, nondemented, and demented older adults	416	434	—
2 Longitudinal MRI data in nondemented and demented older adults	150	373	—
3 Longitudinal neuroimaging, clinical, and cognitive dataset for normal aging and Alzheimer's disease	1098	2168	1608

higher-dimensional signals. The number of medians is set according to the number of windows, falling under odd and even categories.

3.3 Feature extraction

A feature is the occurrence of a property with characteristics that is being surveyed. They are usually seen in numeric and pictorial representations. The concept is mainly focused on variables found in statistics, such as histograms, phonemes, and so on. The key point in the reduction process is feature extraction. It starts by constructing combinations of data and then measures them into the required values for providing the right set of information for the user. The analysis for the given input data is very important as it has to separate the valid and void files, providing a reduced feature vector. Determining the particular subset with these vectors is known as feature selection. The features that have been selected contain the required information from the large data set to help users complete their task by giving an accurate result.

3.3.1 Gray-level cooccurrence matrix

GLCM is a statistical scheme of investigating textures of the medical image that considers the spatial relationship of the pixels. This is also known as gray-level spatial-dependence matrix. The specified matrix is formed when GLCM characterizes the image texture by measuring the pixel pairs with given values in a specified spatial relationship in the image.

Texture is related with the spatial distribution of gray tones. Practically speaking, texture is an inborn characteristic of virtually any surface. It encompasses significant statistics about the structural arrangement of surfaces and their connection to the adjacent neighbors. It is not tough for humans to discriminate and define textures in a pragmatic way. However, for digital computers, it is not so easy to define and analyze them.

The textural properties of images are indicating essential information for classification purposes. Hence, for texture, it is imperative to develop features. Since texture information is very significant, extraction of textural features is a crucial step in image processing applications like classification, content-based image retrieval.

Textural features can be extracted by different approaches such as statistical method, structural method, model-based method, and transform-based method. Spatial distribution plays a vital role for measuring the intensity values by calculating local features at each point in the image, and taking statistical data from the local features, statistical-based feature extraction methods are employed.

This statistical-based feature extraction technique can be categorized into three different types. The orders are from least to higher order statistics. The properties of individual pixel values with respect to neighbor pixels are estimated in first-order statistics method. The properties of two or more pixel values with respect to neighbor pixels are determined in second-order and higher-order statistics methods.

One of the widespread second-order statistical features for analyzing textures are obtained from the cooccurrence matrix. So GLCM is a popular statistical tool for extracting second-order texture information from images. It is a matrix where the number of rows and number of columns are decided by the number of distinct intensity levels in the image. If there are five different intensity levels, then the size of the GLCM matrix is 5×5. This method calculates how often a pair of pixels with definite intensity values and in a specified spatial relationship with another intensity level within the region of interest and thereby a matrix will be created. Generally, this matrix is calculated based on two parameters. They are relative distance between the pair of pixels (d) measured in pixel number and their relative orientation (θ). The relative orientation (θ) can be represented in four directions such as 0 degree, 45 degree, 90 degree, and 135 degree.

Robert Haralick, in his paper [21], listed 14 textural features. They are angular second moment, contrast, correlation, variance, inverse difference moment, sum average, sum variance, sum entropy, entropy, difference variance, difference entropy, information measures of correlation (I), information measures of correlation (II), and maximal correlation coefficient [21].

3.3.2 Local binary patterns

Ever since its founding in 1996, LBP is known to be a classifying function that decodes the binary patterns into a visual image to get a clear idea for the user. It is the most profound feature that is used when going for texture classification.

LBP was designed for monochrome still images in the beginning. Recently, it has been extended for multichannel color images and also for videos. It was introduced by Ojala [22]. This operator is an image operator that transforms a given image into an array of integer labels. This describes even small-scale appearances (textures) of the given image. Further analysis can be done by the statistics obtained during initial operation.

In LBP, it is assumed that two complementary aspects with local texture are required, a pattern and its strength. It works in a 3 × 3 pixel. In this 3 × 3 block, the pixels are thresholded by its central pixel value. They are multiplied by powers of two (decimal) and added to get the label for the center.

3.3.2.1 Calculation of local binary pattern

Table 7.1 a gives a local 3 × 3 matrix. In the given matrix, 7 is the value for center pixel. Each 3×3 window in the image is processed to extract using the local binary patterns (LBP). This work represents thresholding the center pixel of that window with its surrounding pixels using the window mean, window median or the actual center pixel, as thresholds. It is given by below equation, where I_thresh is the threshold value and I_n are the intensities of the surrounding window pixels with (n=0,1,...,7).

10	12	9
6	7	18
5	11	16

1	1	1
0		1
0	1	1

Example (3x3 neighborhood)

Binary Values

1	2	4
128		8
64	32	16

1	2	4
0		8
0	32	16

Weights

Representation

In this example, the center pixel value is 7. The neighborhood pixels are compared with the center pixel and if the value is greater than or equal to 1, then binary value 1 is given. If it is less, binary value 0 is allocated. The 3 × 3 weight matrix is constructed based on the powers of two and this is multiplied with binary values. The resultant matrix, called Representation, is obtained. The 3 × 3 neighborhood values are summed and an LBP of 63 is obtained.

The performance of LBP tends to improve when it is combined with the histogram of oriented gradients descriptor for certain datasets. An LBP is said to be uniform if the binary pattern contains 0−1 or 1−0 transitions. The histogram separates the bins according to the uniformity of the patterns. Depending upon the uniform patterns, the feature vector length tends to reduce from 256 to 59.

3.3.3 Moment invariant feature

For our part of the work in the image analysis, we use the MRI scans that have moments, and those image moments contain the pixel intensities and functions and are chosen to have proper interpretation. When we are to derive invariants concerning particular transformation classes, this process is known as moment invariant.

Table 7.2 describes two of the most important equations used for the moment variations. These moments are estimated to be invariant only when they represent a shape in a discrete image, which are blended with normalized spatial moments. Invariant moments are the very well-known feature for pattern recognition functions.

Table 7.2 Important moment equations.

Moment	Equation
Invariant	$\gamma = \frac{p+q+2}{2}$ which is then substituted into the main equation as $\eta_{p,q} = \frac{\mu_{p,q}}{(\mu_{0,0})^{\gamma}}$ where p and q are the normalized moment orders in the horizontal and vertical directions, and $\mu_{p,q}$ is the spatial central moment of order (p,q).
Central	$\mu_{p,q} = \sum\limits_{i=0}^{nrow-1} \sum\limits_{j=0}^{ncol-1} \left((j - c_j)^p \cdot (i - c_i)^q \cdot M_{i,j} \right)$ where n row and n col are the number of rows and columns of the input image M, and (c_j, c_i) is the center of mass of the image.

3.4 Feature selection

Feature selection is the area where the required features are selected either manually or automatically to draw out the output required for the user. Feature selection, also known as variable (subset) selection, is the selection process for model constructions for a more simplified version for the user. The selection algorithm is the combined structure of search methods for new subsets along with estimates of different feature subsets. For the choice of evaluation on the algorithm, we have used the filtering method. These filtering methods have higher rate of usage to the go-between measure rather error rate to settle the feature subset. This is the fastest way for the feature set to compute. The main data is set to contain some features that are either redundant or irrelevant, and based on the assertion that it can be removed without any loss of information. The filtering methods only select the variables that are redundant, which then do not consider any variable relationship.

3.4.1 Differential evolution

Differential evolution is the most optimal method used by iteration when going for primal solutions with respect to the quality measures. Optimal solution is not guaranteed, but the produced result will be without any assumptions. It is mainly used in the multidimensional real-valued functions, which do not use the gradient to draw out the primal solution. The main function is that the candidate solution keeps on creating a new stack until it matches the best score for the problem at hand.

3.5 Feature vector

A feature vector contains information describing an image with important characteristics such as a particular object or class in a feature space. A feature vector is a collection of features extracted from the image in the form of a one-dimensional matrix. It can be used to describe an entire image (global feature) or a feature present in a location in the image space (local feature). For example, in fingerprint recognition, a feature vector is a collection of minutiae extracted from the fingerprint. Often this is used for tasks like comparison, classification, and such instead of the original image. Many of the present algorithms have many requirements of these numerical depictions since they accommodate processing along with statistical analysis. The image representation is done with the feature values that operate parallel to the pixels present in the image along with texts, representing the frequencies. These vectors are also directly analogous to the vectors that are used for explanatory variables in the statistical strategies. From our work, we were able to find a transfer function that has logic on the input vector from the sample space to transform it into a feature vector.

3.6 Feature subset matrix

For this part of the step, we will look into feature subset selections for a matrix. The subset evaluation is done with the most features, which is much more satisfactory. In this work, we have mainly focused on the filtering method. The filters tend to blend in with the program to reason the logic of the candidate solution. The scoring metric is graded for the assessment of the subset of features. For this scoring metric, two of the most popular filters are used to classify the queries, correlation and mutual information. They are intended to bring out the best possible outcomes. However, producing the metrics for the simple function that satisfies the metric properties is done using the variation of information.

We have surveyed a few feature selection-oriented applications that are currently found in the modern literature as mentioned in Table 7.3.

3.7 SVM classifier

For classifying and regression analysis, SVM is a suitable machine learning approach. This can be trained by learning algorithms and is dependent on supervised learning models. Parallel partitions are generated by an SVM. This is accomplished by generating two parallel lines for each category of

Table 7.3 Applications of some of the feature selection methods.

Approach	Algorithm	Classifier
Filter	Feature selection using feature similarity	Independent (Phuong 2005 [16])
Filter + wrapper	Hill climbing	Naive Bayesian (Long 2007 [17])
Filter	Symmetrical Tau (ST)	Structural associative classification (Shaharanee and Hadzic 2014)
Filter	Welch's t-test	Kernel support vector machine (Zhang 2015 [18])
Filter	Infinite feature selection	Independent (Roffo 2015 [19])
Filter	Eigenvector centrality FS	Independent (Roffo and Melzi 2016 [20])

data. This uses all attributes in a high-dimensional space. SVM separates the space in a single pass to generate flat and linear partitions. The steps involved in SVM are as follows.

The first step involves dividing the two categories by a clear gap, which has to be as wide as possible. This is achieved by partitioning by hyperplane. The given data are separated into classes by these hyperplanes, which, in a high-dimensional space, have the largest margin. The longest distance between closest data points of these classes are represented by the margin between these two classes. The generalization error can be minimized by keeping the margin as large as possible. This is done after training maps the new data to the same space to predict which category they belong to.

By training data, the new data can be categorized into different partitions. An advantage of SVM is that it provides the largest flexibility of all the available classifiers. SVM classifiers are similar to probabilistic approaches but at the same time, they do not consider dependencies among attributes [23].

3.7.1 Algorithm

SVM algorithm can be understood by considering two cases as follows.

Separable case − To separate the data into two classes, it is possible to have infinite boundaries.

Nonseparable case − Two classes of data are not separated in reality but they overlap each other.

3.7.1.1 Separable case

As mentioned, infinite boundaries are possible in this case. The optimal hyperplane is defined as the boundary that gives the largest distance to the nearest observation. This can ensure the fit and robustness of the model. The following equation is used for finding the optimal hyperplane.

$$m \cdot x + b = 0$$

where $m \cdot x$ is the scalar product of m and x. This equation should satisfy the given two conditions.

Example

It should separate the two classes X and Y very well so that the function defined by

- $f(x) = m \cdot x + b$ is positive if and only if $x \in X$
- $f(x) \leq 0$ if and only if $x \in Y$

An advantage of this approach is that it can exist as far as possible from the observations being made and this testifies to the robustness of the model. The distance x to the hyperplane is given by $|m \cdot x + b| / \|m\|$ from an observation. The width is given by $2/\|m\|$ between two observations. This is known as margin and has to be the largest. There are support points known as closest points and hyperplane is dependent on this set of points. When the number of these points decreases, the generalization capacity of SVM tends to increase.

3.7.1.2 Nonseparable case

When the two classes overlap and are not perfectly separated a new term measuring the classification error must add to each of the given two conditions.

- For every j, $y_j \, (m \cdot x_j + b) \geq 1$ (correct separation)
- $1/2 \, \|m\|2$ is minimal (greatest margin)

On the wrong side of the boundary, for each observation xj, one has to define these conditions. This can be achieved by measuring the distance of separation from the margin boundary on the side of its class.

The next step is the normalization of the distance by dividing it by $1/\|m\|$ (half margin). A term called slack variable j is introduced. An error term (ξ) is introduced in the model, which is an observation for which $\xi > 1$. The set of classification errors is represented by the sum of all the ξ_j. Hence, the two hyperplane finding constraints become as follows:

- For every j, $y_j(m \cdot x_j + b) \geq 1 - \xi_j$
- $1/2 \, \|m\|2 + \delta \Sigma_j \, \xi_j$ is minimal

3.8 Feature space and construction

Linear space, which is also known as vector space, is huge clusters containing objects, also called vectors, that are added together and multiplied by scalars. Now these vector spaces are connected with vectors called as the feature space vectors. These space features are associated with a new technique called as dimensionality reduction. The dimensionality reduction technique usage can be found in the areas of information theory and dimension reductions. The process denotes to the number of random variables used under consideration by getting the set of essential variables. The technique represents a lower dimension of the original dataset, containing as much of the information as possible in a simpler way for

Table 7.4 List of operators used in feature construction.

Operators	Symbols
Constructive	For equality checking $=$, $\neq$
Arithmetic	$+,-,\times,/$
Array	Max (S), min (S), average (S)
Sophisticated	Count (S,C) for counting the number of features found in the feature vector S, which satisfies some conditions on vector C

interpretation of the user. This is where the functions dissect into two parts, one we have already seen before, known as feature selection, and the other we are about to see is feature extraction.

The higher level of features that are acquired from the present state features, which are then added to the feature vector, is known as feature construction. Feature construction is the solicitation representing a collection of operators that are constructive to the existing set of features, which then results in creating new features.

The examples of such operators are included in Table 7.4 for reference. Until now, feature construction is evaluated as a potential tool for increasing accuracy and interpretation of structures mainly on high-dimension tasks. The major applications included in this are the studies for diseases and identifying emotions from speech patterns.

3.9 Query feature extraction

Feature extraction is the process that starts from the given set of initial standards of estimated data values and builds up the acquired features that are to be informative and nonredundant to enable the subsequent learning and generalization steps for a simpler user interpretation. This is also related to our previous factor, dimensionality reduction. If the algorithm of the given input data is found to be large for processing, and in case has any of the redundancies, it is then reduced into feature vectors. The feature selection process comes when going for the prediction of a particular subset of initial features. The features that are selected contain the pertinent information to bring out the desired outcome from the initial data for the user. Feature extraction is the key to efficacious and prominent factors for model constructions. For image processing, the algorithms are utilized to identify and separate the wanted features from any digitized images and video streams. The technical terms that fall under this process are curvature, image motion, and low-level and shape-based feature recognitions.

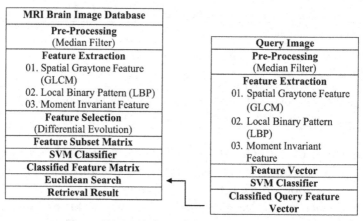

Figure 7.2 Work flow of the proposed system.

3.10 Euclidean search

The Euclidean search comes from the algorithm that is invented for computing procedural steps for calculating the predefined rules. The main idea is to denote that fractions can be reduced to their simpler forms and implementing division in modular arithmetic along with many other calculations; in other words, a method for finding the greatest common divisors among the many other features found. The main query is identified and processed according to the search and now is ready to display the result as shown in Fig. 7.2.

3.11 Retrieval

The required image result is finally displayed after the thorough process, from initiation until the last procedure, is completed.

4. Experimental results

A computer with an Intel core i5 processor has been used for conducting the experiments. The user-interface components with database of medical images serve as the frontier. MATLAB R2013a image-processing toolbox workspace was used as the feature database for storage and image processing work. Other MATLAB 8.1.0604 utilities were used for equations. Initially, the MATLAB 8.1.0604 database with 1500 medical images was used for testing the proposed CBMIR system. These images were acquired without any merging artifacts. No toolkit has been used and an easy understanding and representation is possible with a limited number of images. If a physician, when diagnosing a patient gets a new result, wishes to retrieve the previous one from the database visually similar images that have been already prediagnosed will be able to do

just that. The important part will be the experimental setup. The results taken are shown next, proving the effectiveness of the experimental setup.

We have clearly mentioned our results from Tables 7.5 through 7.10 along with Figs. 7.3 through 7.5 for better understanding.

Table 7.5 Retrieved esult of colored images.

Color-based feature extraction	Relevant image	Irrelevant image	Actual image	Time taken for retrieval in seconds
CCM	10	8	2	6
Histogram with feature extraction	9	6	3	5

Table 7.6 Calculation of retrieved performance of colored images.

Color-based feature extraction	Precision	Recall	Efficiency	Error rate
CCM	55	30	50	85
Histogram with feature extraction	68	40	65	20

Table 7.7 Retrieved result of texture-based retrieved images.

Texture-based feature extraction	Relevant image	Irrelevant image	Actual image	Time taken for retrieval in seconds
GLCM	12	6	3	4
LBP	8	10	4	5

Table 7.8 Calculation of retrieved performance of texture-based retrieved images.

Texture-based feature extraction	Precision	Recall	Efficiency	Error rate
GLCM	50	30	45	30
LBP	25	10	35	50

Table 7.9 Retrieved result of shape-based retrieved images.

Texture-based feature extraction	Relevant image	Irrelevant image	Actual image	Time taken for retrieval in seconds
CANNY EDGE with OTSU's method	10	7	4	6

Table 7.10 Calculation of the retrieved performance of shape-based retrieved images.

Texture-based feature extraction	Precision	Recall	Efficiency	Error rate
CANNY EDGE with OTSU's method	45	30	40	25

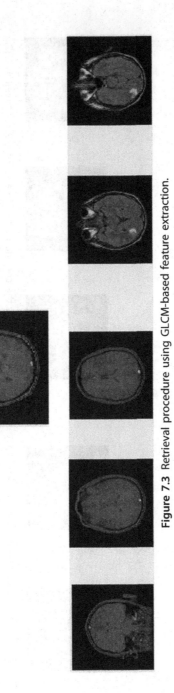

Figure 7.3 Retrieval procedure using GLCM-based feature extraction.

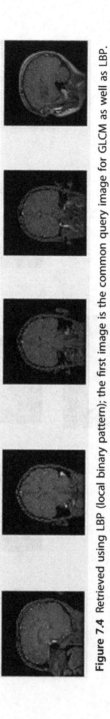

Figure 7.4 Retrieved using LBP (local binary pattern); the first image is the common query image for GLCM as well as LBP.

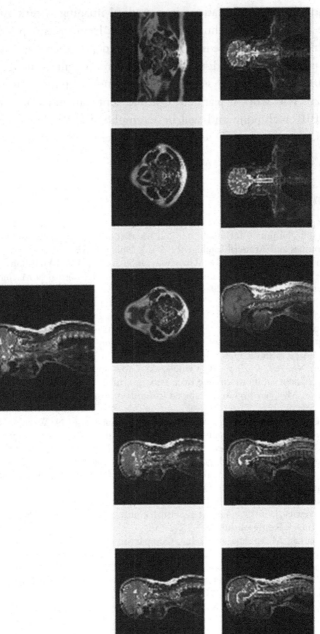

Figure 7.5 Retrieved using CANNY EDGE by OTSU's method with the query image being on top.

5. Conclusion

Even though the complications in a medical imaging system are reduced with the use of CBIR techniques, the disease level to its depth cannot be analyzed. If a particular case is to be studied in depth, then the segmentation helps in prediction of the disease level to its end. Digitized images produce background analysis for physicians to take the next step more clearly than to rationalize. This work is planned to implement semantic image retrieval— based CBIR technique and will be exemplified through the existing algorithms by combining 3D features to improve the performance measure of the system.

References

[1] V. Kapur, P.T. karule, M.M. Raghuwanshi, Content based image retrieval (CBIR) using soft computing technique, in: 2nd International Conference on Computational Techniques and Artificial Intelligence, 2013. Dubai (UAE).
[2] N. Srivastava, G.E. Hinton, A. Krizhevsky, I. Sutskever, R. Salakhutdinov, Dropout: a simple way to prevent neural networks from overfitting, Journal of Machine Learning Research 15 (1) (2014) 1929—1958.
[3] Q. Sun, Y. Yang, J. Sun, Z. Yang, J. Zhang, Using deep learning for content-based medical image retrieval, in: SPIE Medical Imaging, 2017.
[4] L. Tsochatzidis, K. Zagoris, N. Arikidis, A. Karahaliou, L. Costaridou, I. Pratikakis, Computer aided diagnosis of mammographic masses based on a supervised content-based image retrieval approach, Pattern Recognition 71 (2017) 106—117.
[5] H. Van Nguyen, K. Zhou, R. Vemulapalli, Cross-domain synthesis of medical images using efficient location-sensitive deep network, in: MICCAI, 2015.
[6] J. Eakins, M. Graham, Content-based Image Retrieval, University of Northumbria at Newcastle, 1992.
[7] I. El-Naqa, Y. Yang, N.P. Galatsanos, R.M. Nishikawa, M.N. Wernick, A similarity learning approach to content-based image retrieval: application to digital mammography, IEEE Transactions on Medical Imaging 23 (No. 10) (October 2004) 1233.
[8] C. Ramesh Babu Durai, A generic approach to content based image retrieval using DCT and classification techniques, International Journal on Computer Science and Engineering 02 (06) (2010) 2022—2024.
[9] G. Raghupathi, R.S. Anand, M. L Dewal, Color and texture features for content based image retrieval, in: Second International Conference on Multimedia and Content-Based Image Retrieval, July 21—23, 2010.
[10] L. Pinjarkar, M. Sharma, K. Mehta, Comparison and analysis of content based image retrieval systems based on relevance feedback, Journal of Emerging Trends in Computing and Information Sciences 3 (6) (July 2012).
[11] X. Wang, et al., An interactive system for computer-aided diagnosis of breast masses, Journal of Digital Imaging 25 (5) (2012) 570—579.
[12] C.-H. Wei, S.Y. Chen, X. Liu, Mammogram retrieval on similar mass lesions, Computer Methods and Programs in Biomedicine 106 (3) (2012) 234—248.
[13] M. Jiang, S. Zhang, H. Li, D.N. Metaxas, Computer-aided diagnosis of mammographic masses using scalable image retrieval, IEEE Transactions on Biomedical Engineering 62 (2) (2015) 783—792.

[14] S. Ayyachamy, V. Mannivannan, Content based medical image retrieval for histopathological, CT and MRI images, Applied Medical Informatics 33 (3) (2013) 33—44.

[15] https://www.oasis-brains.org/#about.

[16] T.M. Phuong, Z. Lin, R.B. Altman, Selection, in: Proceedings/IEEE Computational Systems Bioinformatics Conference, CSB. IEEE Computational Systems Bioinformatics Conference, 2005, pp. 301—309. PMID 16447987.

[17] N. Long, D. Gianola, K.A. Weigel, Dimension reduction and variable selection for genomic selection: application to predicting milk yield in Holsteins, Journal of Animal Breeding and Genetics 128 (4) (2011) 247—257, https://doi.org/10.1111/j.1439-0388.2011. 00917.x. PMID 21749471.

[18] Y. Zhang, Z. Dong, P. Phillips, S. Wang, Detection of subjects and brain regions related to Alzheimer's disease using 3D MRI scans based on eigen brain and machine learning, Frontiers in Computational Neuroscience 9 (2015) 66, https://doi.org/10.3389/fncom.2015.00066. PMC 4451357. PMID 26082713.

[19] G. Roffo, S. Melzi, M. Cristani, Infinite Feature Selection. 2015 IEEE International Conference on Computer Vision (ICCV), 2015-12-01, pp. 4202—4210, https://doi.org/10.1109/ICCV.2015.478. ISBN: 978-1-4673-8391-2.

[20] G. Roffo, S. Melzi, Features Selection via Eigenvector Centrality" (PDF), September 2016. NFmcp2016. Retrieved 12 November 2016.

[21] R.M. Haralick, K. Shanmugam, Its'hak Dinstein, Textural features for image classification, IEEE Transactions on Systems, Man and Cybernetics 3 (No. 6) (1973) 610—621.

[22] T. Ojala, M. Pietikainen, D. Harwood, A comparative study of texture measures with classification based on feature distributions, Pattern Recognition 29 (1) (1996) 51—59.

[23] C. Cortes, V. Vapnik, Support-vector networks, Machine Learning 20 (1995) 273—297.

[24] M. Agarwal, S. Amit, B. Lall, 3D local ternary co-occurrence patterns for natural, texture, face and bio medical image retrieval, Neurocomputing 313 (2018) 333—345.

[25] A. Qayyum, S.M. Anwar, M. Awais, M. Majid, Medical image retrieval using deep convolutional neural network, Neurocomputing 266 (2017) 8—20.

[26] Y. Wu, S. Wang, Q. Huang, Multi-modal semantic autoencoder for cross-modal retrieval, Neurocomputing 331 (2019) 165—175.

[27] X. Yang, N. Wang, B. Song, X. Gao, BoSR: a CNN-based aurora image retrieval method, Neural Networks 116 (2019) 188—197.

[28] Y. Gu, et al., Clustering-driven unsupervised deep hashing for image retrieval, Neurocomputing 368 (27) (2019) 114—123.

[29] M. Sotoodeh, M.R. Moosavi, R. Boostani, A novel adaptive LBP-based descriptor for color image retrieval, Expert Systems with Applications 127 (2019) 342—352.

[30] M.A. Khan, A.S. Jalal, A framework for suspect face retrieval using linguistic descriptions, Expert Systems with Applications 141 (2020) 1—11.

CHAPTER 8

Early detection of Parkinson's disease using data mining techniques from multimodal clinical data

Sneham Priya, R. Priyatharshini, Rudraraju Shruthi, V. Pooja, R. Sai Swarna
Easwari Engineering College, Chennai, India

Contents

1. Introduction

Incidence of Parkinson's disease (PD) will increase with age. An anticipated 4% of people are diagnosed with PD earlier than the age of 50, but the disease can be detected at an early stage. Hence mining disease patterns from early clinical data can play a valuable role in detection and diagnosis in advance. In healthcare research emblematic and computing methods can be

Advanced Machine Vision Paradigms for Medical Image Analysis
ISBN 978-0-12-819295-5
https://doi.org/10.1016/B978-0-12-819295-5.00008-1

combined with the knowledge of expert physicians for developing tools for improving healthcare. This disorder is a neurological ailment that reasons reminiscence loss and dementia. It is especially found in individuals over the age of 60, but can also result from concussions or traumatic brain injuries. Statistics mining is a computational manner to discover hidden patterns in datasets through building predictive or category fashions that may be learned from the past and carried out to future cases. With the tremendous quantum of clinical information to be available to hospitals, scientific facilities, and clinical research corporations, medication subsidized by means of information mining strategies can beautify the best of healthcare supplied and assist physicians in making informed decisions relating to affected person care.

Speech attributes are key to discovering the start of PD, with marked vocal hindrance distinguished in around 90% of all individuals who are in initial stages of their illness. There has been considerable enthusiasm in structuring PD-symptomatic and telemonitoring vocal attribute-based frameworks. Analysts discovered that demonstrative apparatuses—for example, natural and hereditary biomarkers as well as imaging strategies—show a high degree of precision in anticipating the onset of PD. As of now, there are more than eight applications in the market. Some are these are language instruction applications, while others track the progress of PD in patients with regard to tremor, equalization, and walk, utilizing delicate accelerometers (sensors). The main motivation of the proposed work is to diagnose PD at the earliest and commence treatment. We use two types of datasets, voice and spiral, which are analyzed and the results given in the following.

2. Review of literature

The literature reviewed reveals that numerous systems have been proposed for the diagnosis of PD. Study of speech impairment for 200 patients with PD is done to diagnose the overall severity in Ref. [1]. Tracking Parkinson's sickness symptom development regularly requires a patient's presence through a trained scientific team of workers, which is time consuming. I developed a remote application for Unified Parkinson's Disease Rating Scale (UPDRS) assessment with clinically useful accuracy [2] with the help of speech checks. Speech with signal processing algorithms was presented for extracting disease patterns of common PD development. Speech signal processing algorithms are developed for high-accuracy classification of PD [4]. Investigation of the Parkinson speech dataset with several types of sound recordings is done in Ref. [5]. Various classification methods are attempted for the spiral image data for diagnosing PD [5]. Despite the plethora of data mining approaches that detect PD, the literature survey highlights the need for a framework for early diagnosis of the disease from spiral datasets so as to facilitate immediate treatment planning.

In [6] the projected number of people with Parkinson disease in the most populous nations is discussed. A Literature Review of the Potential Clinical and Socioeconomic Impact of Targeting Unmet Needs in Parkinson's Disease is discussed in [12]. Parkinson's speech data set is analyzed with multiple types of sound recordings [5] for analyzing the speech patterns. Novel speech signal processing algorithms accurately classifying the Parkinson's disease is discussed in [4, 14]. Summary data mining techniques for detecting Parkinson disease is discussed in [7, 8]. The suitability of dysphonia measurements for telemonitoring of Parkinson's disease is discussed in [11]. A telemonitoring system to accurately monitor the Parkinson's disease progression from noninvasive speech tests is developed [12], A classifier framework for Parkinson's disease detection from various vocal tests and from Digitized spiral drawing is developed in [9, 10, 13, 19].

3. Materials and methods

Demands on the healthcare industry to maintain huge swathes of patient data, particularly particulars about clinical tests, imaging, recommendation and medication, have risen steadily, owing to a massive increase in the general population. The proposed predictive analytics framework utilizes vocal and spiral datasets to detect how severely PD has affected people. A model is developed using data mining techniques to detect PD early with a minimal error rate. PD voice and spiral image datasets from the UCI Machine Learning Repository are used as clinical data to mine disease patterns that help predict PD. The training datasets are used to develop the model that automatically diagnoses PD. Early detection of the disease results in an extended life span and improved lifestyle, helping patients lead peaceful lives.

For a cost-effective study of PD and a better comprehension of the disorder, standing prognostic examination methods are utilized. This study applies classification strategies like the decision tree, support vector machine (SVM), Naïve Bayes, random forest, and k-nearest neighbor (KNN) to analyze PD patients' records. The input datasets are grouped into convenient sizes and the classifiers tested against each, following which the one with the highest precision is selected. The random forest and KNN are preeminent classifier models in data mining and examination in the domain of design information frameworks. Initially, the voice dataset is processed using data mining techniques. Features are then extracted from the spiral image dataset and optimal attributes identified to predict PD. Finally an ensemble-based method is used to diagnose PD. The architecture of proposed disease diagnosis framework is shown in Fig. 8.1.

4. Voice dataset processing

The Parkinson's dataset contains speech samples of individuals with PD and healthy humans that contains constant vowels, phrases, small sentences, and numbers. To accumulate the speech samples, the mike changed into positioned at a distance of 10 cm from the sufferers. The voice dataset from the UCI device learning repository is used for our experimental look. The capabilities characterizing the voice dataset are given in Table 8.1. Pattern mining strategies, which include K-means clustering [15], SVMs [17], decision-tree category [16], random forest, and the KNN [18] are applied at the voice dataset to mine sickness styles, based totally on which sickness classification is finished and the overall performance of every method on the

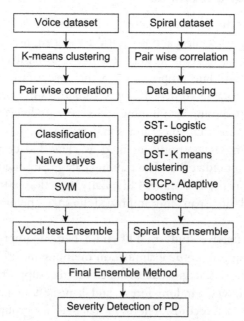

Figure 8.1 Workflow of proposed system.

Table 8.1 Results of ensemble-based classification.

Vocal test	Static spiral test	Dynamic spiral test	Final diagnosis
Abnormal	Abnormal	Abnormal	Extremely critical
Normal	Abnormal	Abnormal	Critical
Abnormal	Normal	Normal	Early stage (might have PD)
Normal	Normal	Normal	Normal

voice dataset in comparison. From each pattern collected, 26 linear and time-frequency capabilities are extracted. Further to the statistics gathered from the 40 human beings mentioned, a distinct dataset was created from different individuals with PD.

Features that characterize the disease patterns are extracted from the speech sample. Jitter is a frequency parameter used to measure the frequency of a speech sample. Pulse parameters such as number of pulses, number of periods, mean, and standard deviation of periods are used. Jimmer is used for measuring the amplitude of speech samples. Voicing parameters such as fraction of locally unvoiced frames, and number and degree of voice breaks are also extracted from speech samples. In addition, pitch and harmonicity parameters such as autocorrelation, noise-to-harmonic and harmonic-to-noise are also used for characterizing the patterns of diseased samples. A total of 26 samples are collected for the voice dataset. Sustained vowels such as "a", "o", "u"; numbers from 1 to 10, rhymed short sentences, and words in the Turkish language are used from samples [5].

4.1 Clustering voice dataset using K-means

It should be cited as: the distribution of voice data set data samples is shown in Fig. 8.2 which is clustered using K-means clustering approach. Clustering is a method that includes the grouping of fact points. K-means clustering set of rules is applied to organize the speech attributes of the voice dataset. It clusters records with similar traits. The set of rules randomly assigns each pattern in a dataset to a cluster, and reveals the centroid of every cluster. It circulates record points to the cluster whose centroid is closest and computes a brand new centroid for every cluster. These steps recur until the variation in intra-cluster similarity is minimal.

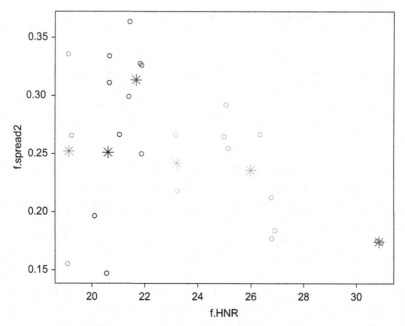

Figure 8.2 Distribution of voice dataset samples.

4.2 Voice dataset classification using decision tree

Classification is a machine learning technique used to categorize data into a given number of classes. It will predict the class labels or categories for the new data. A decision tree is a supervised machine learning technique that predicts the class label of data objects. A decision tree makes use of a structure to specify sequences of decisions and consequences. C4.5 decision tree algorithm is applied on the voice dataset to categorize the data samples for disease classification. The decision tree structure constructed for voice dataset is given in Fig. 8.3. The outcome of disease classification using the c4.5 decision tree classification is shown in Fig. 8.4.

4.3 Voice dataset classification using SVM

SVM is a supervised machine learning approach that is used for classification. In this technique, each statistics object is plotted as a point in an n-dimensional space with the value of each function being the cost of a selected coordinate. Hereafter, classification is finished by designing a hyperplane that differentiates between the two classes. In a two-dimensional area, the hyperplane is a line dividing a plane in two parts, with every

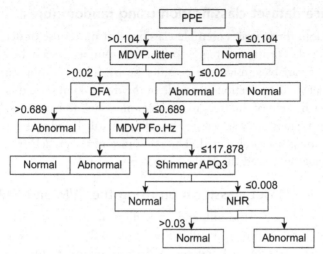

Figure 8.3 Decision Tree Model for Voice dataset.

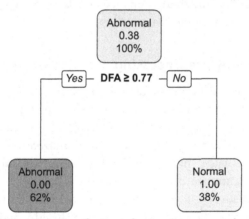

Figure 8.4 Classification of voice dataset samples.

class mendacity on both aspects. Through partitioning the available facts into distinct sets, we drastically lessen the variety of samples that can be used for getting to know the model. A system known as K-fold cross validation (CV) is implemented for comparing the final results of the set of rules where the training set is divided into k smaller sets. The performance of k-fold move-validation is the average of the values computed in the loop.

4.4 Voice dataset classification using random forest

The random forest is an ensemble classifier that makes use of decision tree models for classification or regression. Let the number of cases be N and the number of variables inside the classifier be M. The m input variables are used to decide the selection at a node of the tree, and m should be less than M. For each node of the tree, m variables on which to base the selection at that node are randomly selected. The split primarily based at the m variables in the training set is calculated. The random forest approach applied at the voice dataset executed the highest prediction accuracy.

4.5 Voice dataset classification using the SVM and KNN

SVM and KNN are the influential classification methods used in pattern recognition. KNN provisions all existing cases and classifies new cases based on a likeness measure. A data object is classified by using a majority vote for its neighbor classes. The object is assigned to the most familiar class among its KNN. The KNN method is applied on the voice dataset and it also produced the highest prediction accuracy.

5. Spiral dataset preprocessing

The spiral imaging data set includes 15 healthy people and 62 humans identified with PD (referred to as people-with-parkinson's (pwp)).Two kinds of handwriting is recorded for every subject, the static spiral test (sst) and dynamic spiral test (dst). The sst is often utilized for quantifiable examination of activities like motor functioning, assessing tremor, and detecting the occurrence of disease. The dst is analogous to the sst. The objective of this study is to evaluate the affected person's hand stability or hand tremor degree. The spiral test images of healthy and unhealthy patients are presented in Figs. 8.5 and 8.6. The spiral test image dataset holds information on samples of every test that every system user has ever taken. Features characterizing PD patterns are extracted from the spiral CT image dataset acquired from the UCI machine learning repository. Features such as position of the pen and screen, grip angle, pressure, and time are extracted for discriminating healthy and unhealthy samples.

The algorithm used for optimal feature extraction is the principal component analysis (PCA), a well-established mathematical method for reducing data dimensionality while retaining as many variations as possible. PCA achieves dimension reduction by making new, artificial variables

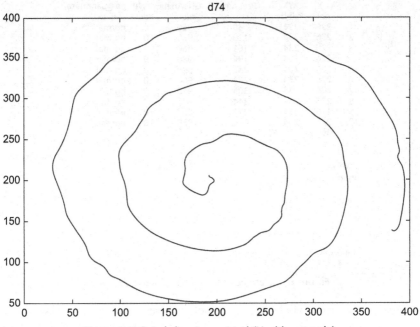

Figure 8.5 Spiral drawing-normal (Healthy sample).

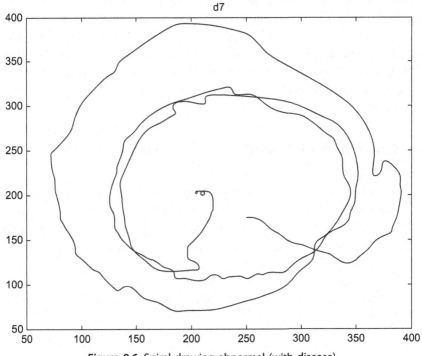

Figure 8.6 Spiral drawing abnormal (with disease).

```
   `\ `X`     Y      Pressure   GripAngle  PWP   par_parameters
    <dbl>   <dbl>     <dbl>       <dbl>    <dbl>    <fct>
 1   226    234        80         960       0     normal
 2   226    234       119         960       0     normal
 3   226    234       161         960       0     normal
 4   226    234       194         980       0     normal
 5   226    234       241         980       0     normal
 6   226    234       273         980       0     normal
 7   226    234       305         970       0     normal
 8   226    234       344         970       0     normal
 9   226    234       378         960       0     normal
10   226    234       403         960       0     normal
 # ... with 367 , 552 more rows

Levels:
abnormal normal


>
>pred1<-predict(model1, control_new)
>summary(pred1)
abnormal      normal
   24954       2648
```

Figure 8.7 Classification of spiral image data set.

referred to as principal elements. Pearson's correlation coefficient is applied on the dataset for identifying the extremely correlated attributes. It is observed from the experimental study that the attributes "z" and "stress" are highly correlated. As more facts become available, in the attribute "stress" the characteristic "z" was eliminated. Remaining attributes with no correlation, including "Subject", "Timestamp", and "TestID", had additionally been eliminated. The performance of various classifier models such as SVM, Naïve Bayes, random forest, and KNN is tested with the spiral imaging dataset. The dynamic test output of the spiral image dataset is shown in Fig. 8.7.

6. Ensemble-based prediction from voice and spiral dataset

The ensemble detects the severity of the patient's symptoms via integrating both the voice and spiral test modules. Ensemble-based prediction is used with the spiral imaging dataset where multiple learning algorithms are used to predict the single outcome based on majority of votes. The output of the ensemble is a single prediction that establishes whether the patient is at risk. The final diagnosis is decided through combining the predictions from vocal dataset and spiral ensemble, which have a diagnosis as given in Table 8.1.

7. Evaluation metrics

Measures to evaluate the accuracy of prediction such as sensitivity and specificity are used for predicting the outcome of the disease classification. Accuracy will give the ratio of correctly classified instances to the whole number of instances, as seen here:

$$\text{Accuracy} = \frac{TP + TN}{TP + TN + FP + FN} \tag{8.1}$$

where TP is the number of true positives, TN is the number of true negatives, FP is the number of false positives, and FN is the number of false negatives.

Sensitivity will give the ratio of true positive instances to the total actual positive instances as seen here:

$$\text{Sensitivity} = \frac{TP}{TP + FN} \tag{8.2}$$

Specificity is the ratio of true negative instances to the total actual negative instances as seen here:

$$\text{Specificity} = \frac{TN}{TN + FP} \tag{8.3}$$

8. Experimental results

The performance of the disease classification models was compared on the basis of accuracy, with the random forest and KNN algorithms outperforming the rest for both voice and spiral image dataset abnormalities, respectively, as shown in Tables 8.2 and 8.3. The performance of SVM and Naïve Bayes is compared and the performance analysis graph is shown in Fig. 8.8. It is observed that SVM gives better accuracy than the Naïve Bayes

Table 8.2 The Performance of the SVM and Naïve Bayes on the voice dataset.

Vocal test	Accuracy	Specificity	Sensitivity
Naïve Bayes	62.50%	85%	91.43%
SVM	95.83%	90%	100%
Random forest	100%	97.82%	97.83%
K-nearest neighbor	100%	96.83%	97.72%

Table 8.3 Performance of SVM on spiral image dataset.

Classifier	Accuracy	Specificity	Sensitivity
Static Spiral Test (SVM)	100%	85%	90.43%
Dynamic Spiral Test (SVM)	96.3%	90%	100%
Random forest	100%	99.65%	84.72%
K-nearest neighbor	100%	95.43%	96.97%

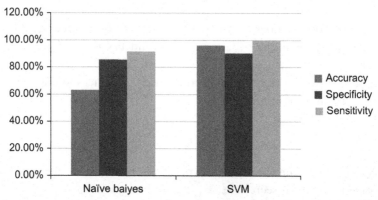

Figure 8.8 Performance comparison of SVM and Naive Bayes on voice and spiral image data set.

method. The performance comparison graph of random forest and KNN on vocal and spiral dataset is given in Figs. 8.9 and 8.10 respectively.

9. Conclusion

Early detection of PD is vital in terms of administering treatment and supporting patients for immediate treatment planning. Application of machine learning techniques on spiral and speech datasets helps in developing models for mining the disease patterns. Signs of PD differ from affected person to patient; such being the case, the use of multimodal data taking a look at facts concerning both voice and spiral drawings affords the simplest PD detection mechanism in patients having unusual symptoms. Due to a wide diversity of clinical data, medical diagnosis is challenging. To improve the accuracy of clinical decision support systems, multimodal clinical data is needed to accurately characterize the disease patterns, which really improves the reliability and robustness of prediction models.

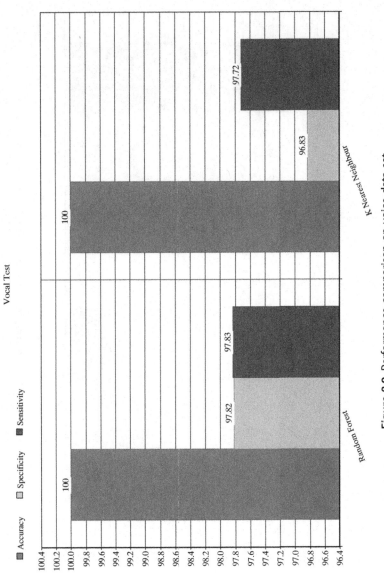

Figure 8.9 Performance comparison on voice data set.

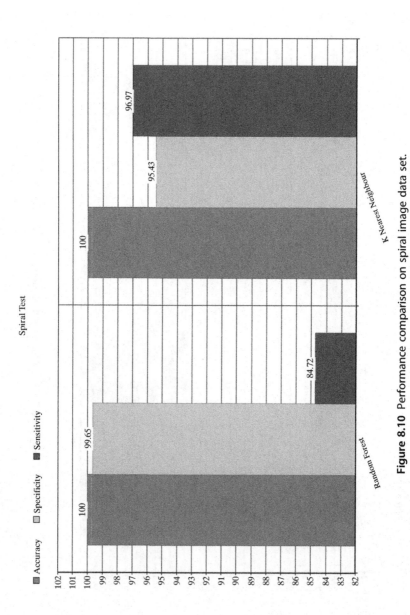

Figure 8.10 Performance comparison on spiral image data set.

References

[1] A.K. Ho, R. Iansek, C. Marigliani, J.L. Bradshaw, S. Gates, Speech impairment in a large sample of patients with Parkinson's disease, Behavioural Neurology 11 (3) (1999) 131—137.

[2] A. Radhakrishnan, K. Kalmadi, Big data medical engine in the cloud (BDMEiC): your new health doctor, Infosys Labs Briefings 11 (1) (2013) 41—47.

[3] A. Tsanas, M.A. Little, P.E. McSharry, L.O. Ramig, Accurate telemonitoring of Parkinson's disease progression by noninvasive speech tests, IEEE Transactions on Biomedical Engineering 57 (4) (2009) 884—893.

[4] A. Tsanas, M.A. Little, P.E. McSharry, J. Spielman, L.O. Ramig, Novel speech signal processing algorithms for high-accuracy classification of Parkinson's disease, IEEE Transactions on Biomedical Engineering 59 (5) (2012) 1264—1271.

[5] B.E. Sakar, M.E. Isenkul, C.O. Sakar, A. Sertbas, F. Gurgen, S. Delil, et al., Collection and analysis of a Parkinson speech dataset with multiple types of sound recordings, IEEE Journal of Biomedical and Health Informatics 17 (4) (2013) 828—834.

[6] E. Dorsey, R. Constantinescu, J.P. Thompson, K.M. Biglan, R.G. Holloway, K. Kieburtz, et al., Projected number of people with Parkinson disease in the most populous nations, 2005 through 2030, Neurology 68 (5) (2007) 384—386.

[7] G. Yadav, Y. Kumar, G. Sahoo, Predication of Parkinson's disease using data mining methods: a comparative analysis of tree, statistical and support vector machine classifiers, in: 2012 National Conference on Computing and Communication Systems, IEEE, 2012, pp. 1—8.

[8] Concepts and techniques, Concepts and Techniques D Mining - Jiawei Han and Micheline Kamber, 2001.

[9] M. Behroozi, A. Sami, A multiple-classifier framework for Parkinson's disease detection based on various vocal tests, International journal of telemedicine and applications 2016 (9) (2016). https://doi.org/10.1155/2016/6837498.

[10] M. San Luciano, C. Wang, R.A. Ortega, Q. Yu, S. Boschung, J. Soto-Valencia, et al., Digitized spiral drawing: a possible biomarker for early Parkinson's disease, PloS One 11 (10) (2016) e0162799.

[11] M. Little, P. McSharry, E. Hunter, J. Spielman, L. Ramig, Suitability of dysphonia measurements for telemonitoring of Parkinson's disease, Nature Precedings 56 (4) (2008) 1015. https://doi.org/10.1109/TBME.2008.2005954.

[12] M. Tinelli, P. Kanavos, F. Grimaccia, The value of early diagnosis and treatment in Parkinson's disease, A Literature Review of the Potential Clinical and Socioeconomic Impact of Targeting Unmet Needs in Parkinson's Disease (2016). London School of Economic and Political Science.

[13] M. Wang, B. Wang, J. Zou, M. Nakamura, A new quantitative evaluation method of spiral drawing for patients with Parkinson's disease based on a polar coordinate system with varying origin, Physica A: Statistical Mechanics and Its Applications 391 (18) (2012) 4377—4388.

[14] P.F. Guo, P. Bhattacharya, N. Kharma, Advances in detecting Parkinson's disease, in: International Conference on Medical Biometrics, Springer, Berlin, Heidelberg, June 2010, pp. 306—314.

[15] S. Lloyd, Least squares quantization in PCM, IEEE Transactions on Information Theory 28 (2) (1982) 129—137.

[16] S. Sharma, J. Agrawal, S. Sharma, Classification through machine learning technique: C4. 5 algorithm based on various entropies, International Journal of Computer Applications 82 (16) (2013).
[17] M. Awad, R. Khanna, Support vector machines for classification, in: Efficient Learning Machines, Apress, Berkeley, CA, 2015, pp. 39–66.
[18] J. Sun, W. Du, N. Shi, A survey of kNN algorithm 1 (2018) 1–10.
[19] M. Isenkul, B. Sakar, O. Kursun, Improved spiral test using digitized graphics tablet for monitoring Parkinson's disease, in: Proc. Of the Int'l Conf. on E-Health and Telemedicine, May 2014, pp. 171–175.

CHAPTER 9

Contrast improvement of medical images using advanced fuzzy logic-based technique

Dibya Jyoti Bora
SCS, The Assam Kaziranga University, Jorhat, Assam, India

Contents

1. Introduction

The quality of medical images plays a major role in the determination of final accuracy of any diagnosis process when it is carried out through an automatic or semiautomatic technique based on image processing algorithms. Noises always disturb in the region-based analysis of an image. Noises may occur due to different reasons. Sudden intensity variation is one of them, so noises should be removed or reduced to a satisfactory level before the next higher level analysis. Also, often it is found that during the

Advanced Machine Vision Paradigms for Medical Image Analysis
ISBN 978-0-12-819295-5
https://doi.org/10.1016/B978-0-12-819295-5.00009-3

acquisition process or due to some other reason the images suffer from low contrast problems. The boundaries surrounding the region of interests are often vague by nature. This is due to the involvement of a high level of fuzziness on the edges. It affects the whole analysis process, hence affects badly on the accuracy of the diagnosis process overall. The traditional techniques are not able deal with this problem and cannot reduce the fuzziness. So, it is utmost required that some advanced techniques should be included as a part of preprocessing process to reduce the fuzziness through the boundaries. Considering these problems, an effort has been made in this chapter to develop a common framework for the preprocessing of medical images. The main goal of the proposed framework is (1) noise removal and (2) contrast improvement through reduction of the degree of fuzziness in the boundaries of region of interests of such images. The noise removal part is the first phase of the proposed framework, where a median filter-based technique is used for the same. In the second phase, an integrated type 2 interval-based fuzzy set contrast limited adaptive histogram equalization (CLAHE) is used for contrast improvement. The outline of the remaining portion of the chapter is as follows: in the next section (Section 2), a literature review on the relevant research works is presented along with the motivation for the proposed work. This review of work in this section is very important as each paper considered is critically analyzed with a brief description of their proposed methodology. The flowchart of the proposed work and a brief discussion of the involved steps are included in Section 3. The next section is the methods-and-materials section where the different terminologies and methods involved in the proposed approach are thoroughly discussed. The experiment and results are discussed in Section 5. The conclusion and possible suggestions are drawn in Section 6. Finally, possible future works are noted in Section 7.

2. Review of the recent works and motivation toward the proposed work

Following are some noteworthy contributions in this domain.

Shi et al. [1] proposed a weighted median guided filtering method, which is applied for single-image rain removal. This technique has two main steps: first, the weighted median filter [2] filters the rainy image. The rain steaks are excluded, thereby retaining the most basic information of the original image. In the second step, the output image from the first step is used as a guide image and then convolution is performed with the original input. An edge-preserved rain-free image is produced as a result. In comparison to other state-of-the-art algorithms, this technique produces comparable results with low computation cost. The proposed median filter can be applied to medical images for the noise removal process as this is easy to implement and carries much less computational cost.

Kumar et al. [3] proposed an advanced technique based on median filter, which filters mammogram images and removes the impulse noise present there to a great extent. The steps involved in this proposed technique are as follows.

1. Input the mammogram image.
2. Initialize a 2 × 2 nonoverlapping window.
3. Check whether all the pixels are noisy or not.
    a. If not noisy:
        i.   Select a 2 × 2 window and detect the noise-free pixel in it.

        ii. From the noise-free pixels, find the median value.

        iii. The median value replaces the noisy pixel (of step ii).
    b. If noisy:
        i.   The median value replaces all the pixels.
4. Shift the window.
5. Output the processed image.

The authors tested the proposed technique with the MIAS database images collected from United Kingdom national breast screening program. For all possible range of noise density, this filter performs better than the others in comparison. The proposed filter also works at high noise density, which is verified through the mean square area (MSE) and peak signal-to-noise ratio (PSNR) values calculation and comparison.

Chanu et al. proposed a quaternion vector median filter (two stage) [4] to remove impulse noise from medical images. To signify the differences of two pixels, they used quaternion. After that pixel sorting is done, a rank is assigned based on the aggregated sum of pixel differences with other pixels inside the filtering window. For the detection of impulse noise, they target the central pixel. It is declared as corrupted when the rank becomes greater than a threshold value of rank, and the least difference between it and the other pixels in the four-edge direction inside the window is larger than a fixed threshold. The output of vector median filter is then placed in place of the noisy pixel. Again, in the case of color images, the chromaticity components and intensity are both used for the noise removal process. The experimental results claim the supremacy of this technique over other traditional techniques in comparison.

James et al. [5] used the variability changes of the images at local regions in the CT images to introduce a noise detection technique in the same. As the proposed technique is a local region-based technique, it has other applications like background detection and segmentation of images. Its simplicity is one of its advantages. Also, its applicability to multimodel images is one more advantage. But it needs to finds out the weights again when the imaging device is adjusted with progress in time. So it may be considered as one disadvantage of the proposed technique. Gaussian noise and speckle noise is introduced on some computed tomography (CT) scan images to verify the reliability of this proposed technique.

Two important hybrid median filters (hybrid min and hybrid max) introduced in Ref. [6] are described as follows.

1. Hybrid min filter

$$g(p) = \min \left\{ \left\{ median \begin{cases} f(p), p \in L_3(p) \\ f(p), p \in R_3(p) \end{cases} \\ f(p) \end{cases} \right.$$

From the equation it is very clear that the pixel value of a point p is replaced with the minimum of median pixel value of left neighbor, right neighbor, and p.

2. Hybrid max filter

$$g(p) = \max \left\{ \left\{ median \begin{cases} f(p), p \in L_3(p) \\ f(p), p \in R_3(p) \end{cases} \\ f(p) \end{cases} \right.$$

Here the pixel value of a point p is replaced by the maximum of median pixel value of left neighbors, right neighbors, and p.

Different statistical quantity measures apply the root MSE and PSNR for comparing the performance of the proposed technique with other existing techniques. From the experimental results, it is proved that the proposed hybrid techniques outperform the existing techniques. Time efficiency is one more advantage of the proposed technique.

An iterative relaxed median filter is introduced by Vijayarajan et al. [7]. The main aim of the proposed work is to improve PSNR of the filtered image and through the cluster error index. Validation of fuzzy C-means (FCM) clustering over median filtered MR images is conducted. The steps involved are briefly stated here:

1. Calculate PSNR between the original input image and input one.
2. The filtered image may be refiltered again.
3. Calculate PSNR of the new one obtained in step 2.
4. The following condition is checked:

$$\text{if } [\text{PSNR}(i) - \text{PSNR}(i-1)] < 0$$

$$\text{then stop and PSNR} = \text{PSNR}(i-1) \quad (a)$$

or

$$\text{if No. of iterations} = \text{Maximum no. of iterations}$$

$$\text{stop, return PSNR}(i) \quad (b)$$

5. Repeat steps 3 and 4 until the one of the conditions (a) or (b) is satisfied.

The proposed technique is found to perform better than the other filtering methods under consideration. Also, through different validity measures, efficiency of these median filtering techniques over FCM clustering is observed.

A directional weighted median filter is proposed by Nair et al. [8] with the main objective being the restoration of medical images that may have undergone corruption due to different high density impulse noises. An efficient directional weighted median filter is included in the proposed technique. Only the corrupted pixels in the image undergo the filtering process and the uncorrupted pixels are not changed. High edge preservation and computationally efficient are the advantages of the proposed technique as it is very important feature with respect to medical images.

The preceding are some selected works in the domain of median filter-based techniques for noise removal. Now, for the contrast improvement part, the following are some notable contributions that can be referenced for fuzzy logic-based contrast improvement techniques.

An intuitionistic fuzzy set-based technique is introduced by Chaira for medical image enhancement. The author used an alternative intuitionistic fuzzy generator for the same [9]. This generator contains a parameter, lambda. The intuitionistic fuzzy entropy is maximized to find the optimal value of lambda. After the contrast intensifier is applied to the intuitionistic fuzzy image an enhanced image results. The proposed technique succeeds to improve the contrast of vaguely illuminated structures in medical images.

It also helps to segment the abnormal lesions or extracts blood vessels fairly accurately. The author also proposed some advanced fuzzy logic-based techniques based on type-2 fuzzy logic from the one introduced in Ref. [10], which may be referred for the improvement of the quality of medical images. Here, a type-2 fuzzy logic-based technique using Hamacher T co norm as an aggregation operator is introduced. The required parameters for this co norm are calculated from the average of the image. The Hamacher T co norm used here are algebraic operators. No min or max terms are involved in these operators and they are computationally simple. The effectiveness of the proposed technique is found to be better than the other methods like nonfuzzy, fuzzy, and intuitionistic fuzzy in comparison.

Sheet et al. [11] introduced a brightness-preserving-dynamic-histogram-equalization technique where they mainly focus on improving the brightness, preserving contrast enhancement as well as reducing the computational complexity involved. The authors use fuzzy statistics for the demonstration and processing of the input images. And it helps to handle the vagueness of gray level values in an enhanced way. A better performance is observed for the same. A similar type of work may also be found in [13].

A nonsubsampled contourlet transform (NSCT)-based enhancement technique is introduced by Zhou et al. [12], which combines adaptive threshold with an improved fuzzy set. A fuzzy if–then rule is employed to separate the different regions. The proposed technique works in the following way: the input image is first decomposed into an NSCT domain. For that they use low-frequency subband and several high-frequency subbands. The coefficients of the low-frequency component are processed with a linear transformation. An adaptive threshold method is employed for the removal of high-frequency image noise. At last, the global contrast is enhanced through the improved fuzzy set and the Laplace operator enhances the details of the medical images. The Laplacian filter is an isotropic filter with the power to enhance image details. The authors prove through experimental analysis that the proposed method is better than the existing methods with respect to better quality enhancement result.

A type-2 fuzzy set with the integration of an unsharp masking-based technique is proposed in Ref. [14]. The proposed technique successfully improved the quality of poor contrast medical images. Also, one more efficient approach for color image enhancement is introduced in Ref. [15]. This technique introduce an improved median filter, Improved_Median(),AA_CLAHE() — an efficient CLAHE. The combination of the two makes this approach capable of dealing with the contrast improvement task of poor quality noisy images. This technique can also be adopted for medical images. Both of these techniques focus on selection of suitable color spaces if the contrast improvement is done for color images.

From the previously reviewed techniques, it is clear that noise removal is the first mandatory part of an efficient contrast improvement process, since if noises exist in the input medical image, then merely applying a contrast improvement technique will just deteriorate the quality of the image since there is a high probability that it will amplify the noises also. And, for contrast improvement, a fuzzy set technique is highly recommended for medical images since these images are highly vague in nature. The hard techniques fail to successfully remove this level of fuzziness to a satisfactory level (found through experiments in many relevant cases).

This motivates us to develop a contrast improvement approach, which will be a two-phased approach where in the first phase, noises present will be removed.

The main objective why a median filter-based technique is employed for the noise removal process is because of the edge-preserving nature of the same while dealing with the corrupted pixels. In a critical image analysis process, like the one in the case of medical imaging, edges should not be disturbed as it signifies the region of interest exactly where the analysis and hence the diagnosis process is carried out. Otherwise, it may impose a certain level of inaccuracy to the final result of the analysis process.

The second phase is the fuzzy set-based contrast improvement part.

3. Steps involved in the proposed approach

The proposed approach consists of the following steps:

1 The original medical image is sent as input.
2 Color conversion from RGB to HSV
3 V-channel extraction
4 Process the V-channel with Improved_Median Filter(); say the output channel is V'.
5 **T2F_Clahe()**
   a. The channel V' is sent as input to type-2 interval type fuzzy set-based method, type2fuzzy(); say the output is V''.

b. Postprocessing of the V'' for contrast management with improved CLAHE; say, it outputs V'''.

6 Replace the old V-channel with V'''.

7 HSV to RGB conversion takes place and the improved enhanced version of the input color medical image is obtained as output.

The methods and different terminologies that are part of the proposed technique are discussed in detail in Section 4.

4. Methods and materials

This section is divided into different subsections where the terminologies and methods that are the part of the proposed approach are discussed thoroughly.

4.1 Medical imaging

Nowadays, medical imaging has become an emerging area where new research ideas and technologies are evolving from different parts of the globe every day. The goal of medical imaging is to diagnose and treat patients in an accurate way and restrain from any harmful side effects. In fact it helps to understand the inside of the body without the need for any critical invasive process like surgery [16]. Different types of imaging technology are used in medical imaging to acquire an image of an internal part of the human body. Some popular ones among them are ultrasound, CT, X-ray, and magnetic resonance imaging (MRI).

Some high-frequency sound waves are transmitted in ultrasound from the probe to the body via the conducting gel, which then bounce back after hitting the different structures within the body. This creates an image that will be used for diagnosis. As ionizing radiation is not used, it is considered safer and the most preferred choice for pregnancy. There is a slightly different type of ultrasound technique named Doppler, which allows the blood flow through arteries and veins. On the other hand, although X-rays are extensively used and very popular because it is low cost, faster, and comparatively simple for the patient to undergo, a few risks are involved in this case as the radiation used here may cause radiation-induced cancer or in a pregnant patient it may even cause a disturbance in the growth of an embryo or fetus. CT is a form of X-ray that uses the latter one to produce cross-sectional images of the body [16]. It offers a greater lucidity than conventional X-rays. Also, it may prevent the need for exploratory surgery in many cases. MRI uses a strong magnetic field and radio waves to generate images of the body. It can create the view inside a joint or ligament to be seen. In MRI, ionizing radiation is not used, so can less risk is involved. Still, it is not recommended during the first stage diagnosis. Generally, cost involved is also high in this case. Hematoxylin and eosin (HE) stain is also becoming popular in medical diagnosis. Details on HE stain imaging can be found in Refs. [17,18].

Although these techniques are considered advanced in the area of medical imaging, they are prone to some errors or inaccurate results [9,10,12]. The reason may be presence of noise or poor contrast due to high level of vagueness through the regions of interest. So there arises the need of some preprocessing techniques based on different image processing algorithms.

4.2 Noise and its types

Noise can be defined as unwanted information that is generally acquired during image acquisition or other processes like coding and transmission. Various unwanted effects that may affect the accuracy of the diagnosis process are produced by noise [19]. The influence of noise is generally increased due to low light conditions and limited exposure types [20]. It leads to degradation of specimens as noise often creates artifacts in the images leading to false diagnosis.

If $I(x, y)'$ is the medical image after the acquisition process, then

$$I(x, y)' = H(x, y) + I(x, y)$$

where $H(x,y)$ denotes the function of image noise and $I(x,y)$ is the original image.

So, before processing these images, it is suggested to take some measure for noise removal. Also, as there are different types of noises, having an idea about them will help to design a noise removal technique specific to the current type present in the input medical image. Following are the major types of noises generally found in medical images.

1. Gaussian Noise

This type of noise is also known as electronic noise. It generally arises in amplifiers or detectors and is caused by natural sources like the discrete nature of radiations of warm objects [19]. This type of noise disturbs the gray values of the images. This can be easily visible from the following equation:

$$P(g) = \sqrt{\frac{1}{2\pi\sigma^2}} e^{-\frac{(g-\mu)^2}{2\sigma^2}}$$

Here g indicates the gray value, σ indicates standard deviation, and μ stands for mean.

2. White Noise

In case of white noise, noise power spectrum is constant and is equivalent to power spectral density function. For this type of noise, the spectrum (noise) is constant and proportional to power spectral density function. Also, correlation is not possible in white noises as here every pixel value is different from your neighbors.

3. Salt-and-Pepper Noise

This type of noise comes under impulse noise. Salt noise is introduced by adding random bright (i.e., pixel value 255) all over the image, while pepper noise is introduced by adding random dark pixels (i.e., pixel value 0) all over the image. This type of noise is introduced by the addition of both random bright and dark pixels. The image with salt-and-pepper noise generally has bright pixels in a dark region but dark pixels in a bright region. As a result, black-and-white dots appear in the image. This noise creates dead pixels, bit errors during transmission, analog-to-digital converter error, and so on. Median filters may be used to deal with this type of noise.

4. Speckle Noise

This is a kind of granular noise that may exist in an image inherently. It degrades the quality of an image. In general ultrasound images are more often poorly affected because of inherent speckle noises, so speckle noise reduction is a mandatory preprocessing step before the analysis of such ultrasound images. It is found that monogenic wavelet transform may be used for the speckle reduction process [21].

5. Poisson Noise

This is also known as shot noise or quantum noise. The statistical nature of different electromagnetic waves such as X-rays, gamma rays, and so on makes the appearance of this noise to be visible. Bilateral filter-based techniques may be used for removal of this type of noise.

These are the noises from which medical images suffer a lot, thereby lowering the quality of the images. It is suggested that some measure should be taken for the noise removal process. Here, an improved median filter-based technique is introduced for the same.

4.3 Improved mean value-based median filter, Improved_Median()

A nonlinear filter that is mostly used as a preprocessing step in the medical image analysis process is the median filter, and it fuels the enhancement of the results of some later stages like edge detection or segmentation. This type of filter has an advantage that it has the ability of removing noises while preserving the edge details. But the capability of the median filter to remove noise is totally dependent on the median value selected [15]. For example, when, in the selected window, the maximum number of pixels is noise, there is a high probability that the median value may be an impulse itself. In such a situation, mean value works better than median. So, using this fact, an improvement can be made to the traditional median filter [15]. To detect whether a pixel value is noise or not, the following criteria are used. In the current window, if the median value is equal to either the maximum value or minimum value, then its status is assigned as an impulse. The proposed median filter consists of the following steps.

A 3×3 window W_{xy} is considered the current window for the targeted pixel P_{xy}. Let P_{min}, P_{max}, and P_{med} be the minimum, maximum, and median gray values in W_{xy}, respectively.

Algorithm, **Improved_Median()**:

if $P_{med} == P_{min}$ or $P_{med} == P_{max}$

$$\text{then } P_{med} \leftarrow \left(\frac{P_{i-1} + P_{i+1}}{2} \right),$$

(*here* i represents the *i*th location in the sorted pixel values and $P_i = P_{med}$)

$P_{xy} \leftarrow p_{med}$

else $P_{xy} \leftarrow P_{med}$

Fig. 9.1 shows the result of applying the above Improved_Median() on an HE stain image. The salt-and-pepper noise of density 0.02 is added to the image.

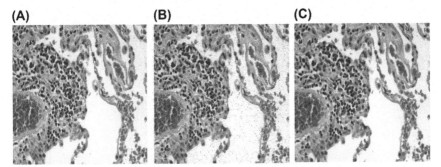

(A)   **(B)**   **(C)**

Figure 9.1 (A) HE stain image; (B) noisy version; (C) output from the improved_median(). (From Enwikipediaorg, H\u0026E Stain, 2019, [online] Available at: https://en.wikipedia.org/wiki/H%26E_stain, Accessed 4 Jun. 2019)

4.4 HSV color space

In color image processing, an abstract mathematical model known as color space is used to characterize the colors in terms of intensity values. This color space uses a three-dimensional coordinate system. For different types of applications, a number of different color spaces exists. Although, RGB is the default color space, in this work HSV color space is used since it has a devoted channel (V-channel) for the intensity measurement [26]. Details on this color space along with its efficiency comparison with other available color spaces like LAB is presented in Ref. [22] (also see Fig. 9.2).

4.5 Type-2 fuzzy set

The fuzzy-set concept was introduced by Zadeh in 1965 [23]. Generally, fuzzy-set-based techniques are used for dealing with vagueness in various problems like segmentation, quality improvement, and so on [24]. But the type-1 fuzzy set does not include any procedure to measure the uncertainty that may present in the membership function. So, in 1975, Zadeh introduced the concept of the type-2 fuzzy set [25], which is an extension of the type-1 fuzzy set. The main objective of the type-2 fuzzy set is to deal with the fuzziness involved in the primary membership function of the type-1 fuzzy set. Fig. 9.3 introduced by Mendel [26] more clearly depicts the relation between the type-1 fuzzy set and type-2 fuzzy set.

A type-2 fuzzy set can be described mathematically as

$$A_{TYPEII} = \left\{ x, \widehat{\mu}_A(x, \mu) \middle| \forall x \in X, \forall u \in J_x \subseteq [0,1] \right\} \qquad (9.1)$$

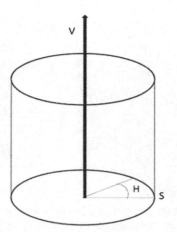

Figure 9.2 Hue, saturation, and value.

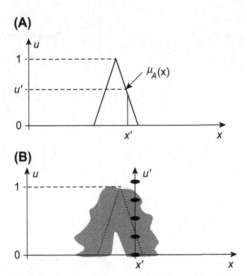

Figure 9.3 (A) A typical type-1 membership function, (B) blurriness generates the type-2 membership function.

where $\widehat{\mu}_A(x, \mu)$ represents the Type II membership function, and the primary membership function is represented by J_x.

The upper and lower limits are

$$\mu^{upper} = [J_x]^\alpha$$
$$\mu^{lower} = [J_x]^{1/\alpha}$$

(9.2)

where $0 < \alpha \leq 1$.

The diagram in Fig. 9.4 shows the relation of upper and lower bounds in a type-2 fuzzy set with respect to a type-1 fuzzy set.

Footprint of uncertainty is used to express the vagueness that may be involved in the primary membership of a type-2 fuzzy set. Consider the following equation (J_x is the primary membership function):

$$FOU(A_{TYPEII}) = \bigcup_{x \in X} J_x$$

(9.3)

A type-2 fuzzy set-based enhancement technique is used in our proposed approach. Through experiments it is found that it has a comparatively higher capability of dealing with the fuzziness involved in medical images like HE stain images.

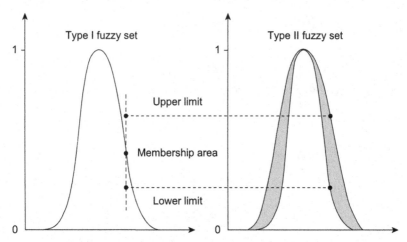

Figure 9.4 Diagram representing upper and lower limit defining membership area with respect to type-1 and type-2 fuzzy set. (From T. Chaira, February. Contrast enhancement of medical images using type II fuzzy set, In: 2013 National Conference on Communications (NCC), 2013, IEEE, 1—5)

4.6 Type-2 (V-channel)

In Ref. [14], a type-2 fuzzy set-based technique is proposed. Here type-2 (V-channel) is presented, which is an advanced version of the same. After conversion to HSV from RGB color space, value channel is extracted and filtered with improved mean value based median filter, Improved_Median(). Then this filtered value channel, say V-channel (of size M × N), is fuzzified by using J_x (primary membership function):

$$J_x = \frac{V - V_{\min}}{V_{\max} - V_{\min}} \tag{9.4}$$

where V has the intensity values of the range 0—L-1, $V_{\min}$ is the minimum V value, and $V_{\max}$ is the maximum V value.

The upper and lower bounds are calculated with Eq. (9.2) (Section 4.5). Trial-and-error strategy is used to find a suitable value of α. The logic behind this new type-2 fuzzy set-based contrast enhancement policy is that a darker region should turn into a brighter one in the enhanced version, and to implement this fact, a comparatively greater value of μ^{upper} for the dark portion should be assigned, and in that way, comparatively higher gray values will be assigned for them. The following membership is designed by considering this fact:

$$\widehat{\mu}_A = k \cdot \left(\frac{\mu_{low} \cdot \lambda + \mu_{high} \cdot (1 - \lambda)}{1 - (1 - \lambda) \cdot \mu_{low} \cdot \mu_{high}} \right) \tag{9.5}$$

The following equation is used to calculate λ:

$$\lambda = \frac{V_{mean}}{L} \tag{9.6}$$

where V_{mean} is the mean gray value and L indicates the number of gray levels in the image.

In Eq. (9.5), by manipulating k ($k > 0$, the contrast enhancement factor), the contrast can be changed from low to high. k has been assigned the value 1 for the current proposed work.

4.7 Adaptive ameliorated CLAHE, AA_CLAHE()

Histogram equalization is a popular contrast management technique frequently adopted for medical image enhancement. But here the whole improvement process is reliant on the probability density function (PDF). So the presence of a high peak totally worsens the cumulative density function calculation because it is directly dependent on PDF values. This affects the homogenous regions by pushing an overamplification of noises. If the PDF value is restrained, then the contrast enhancement can be limited, which in turn will solve the overenhancement problem of histogram equalization. Overenhancement implies appearance of darker regions in the enhanced image. From this, the concept of CLAHE arises. Adaptive ameliorated CLAHE, AA_CLAHE (), is an advanced version of CLAHE introduced in Ref. [15]. Beginning with a 3 × 3 window, this technique tries to find a proper window size by iteratively calculating the entropy of the contrast-enhanced image at every observation. Then this value is compared with the same obtained in the last iteration.

Here two cases will arise:

Case 1: If in the current iteration the entropy value becomes greater, the size of the window is increased by two and processes CLAHE for that window.

Otherwise, go to Case 2.

Case 2: The algorithm will stop its iteration, and the enhanced image obtained at the last stage will be output as the resultant image.

The maximum window size is 128, hence, at the maximum condition, from the input image, only two tiles can be formed. To obtain the final contrast improved image, an interpolation technique known as bicubic interpolation is applied. The steps involved are [15]:

Algorithm: **AA_CLAHE():**

Input: Value channel

Output: Enhanced value channel

Step 1. Consider an N × N window and assign N = 3 (Initialization).

Step 2. For every tile of the image, the histogram is created and then analyzed.

Step 3. BSB_T() is employed for the clipping and redistribution of the clipped part.

Step 4. The next stage involves the process of bicubic interpolation. This results in the final contrast-enhanced image.

Step 5. Entropy, E_i is calculated and Eq. (9.7) is used:

$$E = - sum(p. * \log_2(p)) \tag{9.7}$$

where p is the histogram count.

Step 6. Do $N \leftarrow N + 2$

Step 7. Steps 2–5 will be repeated with the new window size, and the entropy E_{i+1} of the contrast-enhanced image will be evaluated for the current step.

Step 8. Stop if $E_{i+1} < E_i$ else repeat until $N <= 128$.

Step 9. An enhanced image with the largest E value will be the one with better quality and hence output the same.

The algorithm **BSB_T()** proved to be an efficient one regarding clipping and redistribution of the clipped pixels. The illustration of the steps involved in this technique can be found in Ref. [22] (also see Fig. 9.5).

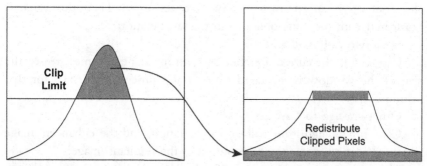

Figure 9.5 Clip limit and redistribution of clipped pixels. (From T. Chaira, February. Contrast enhancement of medical images using type II fuzzy set, In: 2013 National Conference on Communications (NCC), 2013, IEEE, 1–5.)

The bicubic interpolation algorithm can produce a clear picture quality while preserving the image details in an improved way than a bilinear one [15]. This is the reason why bicubic interpolation is used to produce the final contrast-enhanced version of the input image by merging the contrast-limited histogram equalized tiles of the original medical image.

5. Experiment and result discussion

The experimental results are demonstrated in this section. As the proposed technique is specifically designed for medical color image enhancement, HE stain images are targeted in this paper. For gray images the implementation part is simpler that the color ones. The test images are collected from Refs. [27,28]. The comparative analysis of the results is done with the same obtained with traditional algorithm histogram equalization, CLAHE, and one recent technique from Bora [17]. As our proposed technique has Improved_Median() as the first step for noise removal, in all the mentioned techniques for comparison, median filter is used as the first step for the noise removal process. Both the subjective and objective evaluations are adopted here. But, in our case, the human visual perception will be the reliable one to detect the quality of image enhancement. Hence, visual perceptions of six subject experts are collected with respect to the enhancement result. For the objective evaluation, we have selected PSNR and entropy.

The results for four HE stain images are shown in Figs. 9.6—9.9.

From these images it is very clear that the HE stain images are fuzzy in nature in the sense that the boundaries surrounding the region of interests are vague in nature. Again, when salt-and-pepper noise (of density 0.2) has been added, it becomes more difficult to analyze them. So, if noise affects a medical image like a HE stain image it will increase the chance of inaccurate diagnosis result. Hence, it is indeed a mandatory step to include a preprocessing technique to deal with this problem: first a suitable technique to remove noise and then a contrast enhancement technique for quality improvement. The four different techniques used for performing the preprocessing are histogram equalization, CLAHE, Bora's method [17], and the proposed advanced fuzzy logic-based technique. From the results it is seen that median filter with histogram equalization is not able to perform good preprocessing. Some dark region appears, making the HE stain image difficult to be processed for the next step. Although CLAHE succeeds in producing a better result in comparison to histogram equalization, vagueness still appears around the cell and nuclei of the HE stain images. Bora's

(A)   (B)

(C)   (D)

(E)   (F)

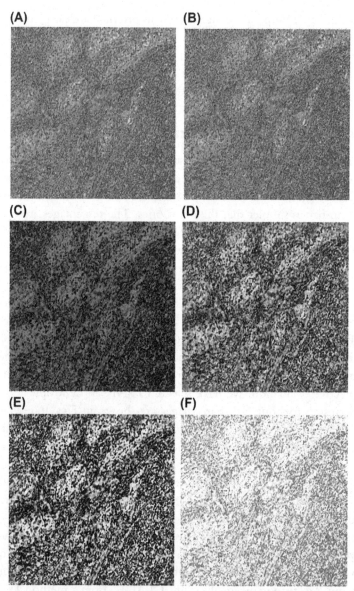

Figure 9.6 (A) Original image; (B) noisy version after adding salt-and-pepper noise of density 0.2; (C) histogram equalization-based preprocessing; (D) CLAHE-based preprocessing; (E) preprocessing using Bora's method [15]; (F) the proposed technique.

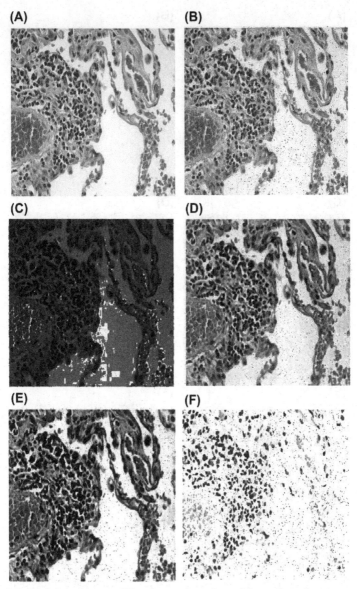

Figure 9.7 (A) Original image; (B) noisy version after adding salt-and-pepper noise of density 0.2; (C) histogram equalization-based preprocessing; (D) CLAHE-based pre-processing; (E) preprocessing using Bora's method [15]; (F) the proposed technique.

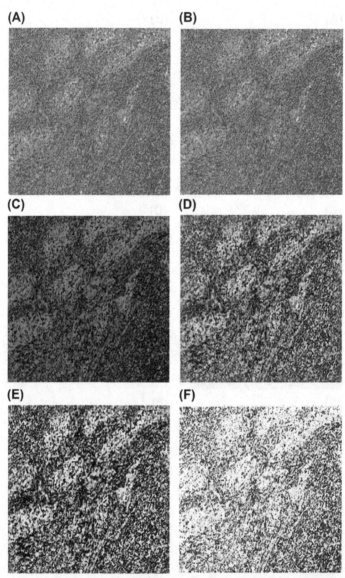

Figure 9.8 (A) Original image; (B) noisy version after adding salt-and-pepper noise of density 0.2; (C) histogram equalization-based preprocessing; (D) CLAHE-based preprocessing; (E) preprocessing using Bora's method [15]; (F) the proposed technique.

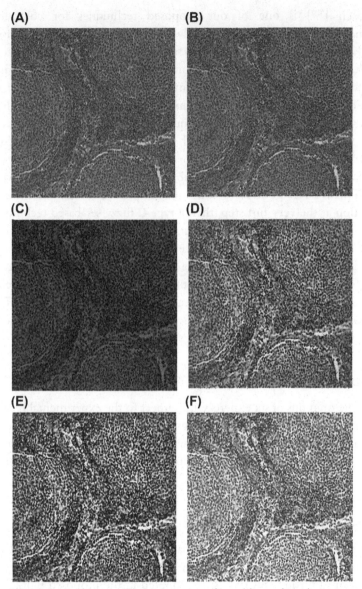

Figure 9.9 (A) Original image; (B) noisy version after adding salt-and-pepper noise of density 0.2; (C) histogram equalization-based preprocessing; (D) CLAHE-based preprocessing; (E) preprocessing using Bora's method [15]; (F) the proposed technique.

approach [17] is one of our proposed techniques for color image enhancement. This comprises an advanced median filter and ameliorated CLAHE. Results produced by this approach are better than histogram equalization and CLAHE. One reason is that the median filter used here is able to detect noises and thereby remove noises more efficiently than the traditional median filter. And the ameliorated CLAHE included here is adaptive by nature. So, overall the quality of results is improved. But the degree of fuzziness still high, which is clearly visible from the resultant images (the (E) subfigure of Figs. 9.6—9.9). An advanced fuzzy logic-based technique should be used to deal with this level of fuzziness. Our proposed technique is a very good integration of an improved median filter (for noise reduction at the very first step, then a type-2 fuzzy set-based technique for reducing the fuzziness level, and last, an ameliorated CLAHE for overall contrast improvement). The improvement of the quality of the input HE stain images are very clearly visible in the results (the (F) subfigure of Figs. 9.6—9.9). Vagueness throughout the cell and nuclei are reduced to a satisfactory level and along with the contrast is improved without affecting the color of the images. The proposed approach successfully produces superior results than the other methods in comparison.

6. Subjective evaluations

Here the opinions of six experts with respect to the experimental results are considered. The experts give their views on the results based on the level by which fuzziness is decreased, and how much the original color information is reinstated on the original HE stain medical images. Table 9.1 presents their report.

7. Objective evaluation

Although subjective evaluation is what exactly matters in the field of image analysis, for mathematical verification of results, we are relying on objective evaluation. Entropy and PSNR are adopted in the proposed work for the same. Eq. (9.8) is used to calculate entropy:

$$E = - sum(p\log_2(p)) \tag{9.8}$$

Table 9.1 Subjective evaluation.

Expert	Is fuzziness level decreased to an accepted level?	Is image quality improved after enhancement, yes or no?	The quality improvement rating (range 1−10;1 implies the lowest and 10 implies the highest rating)
1	Yes	Yes	7
2	Yes	Yes	7
3	Yes	Yes	8
4	Yes	Yes	9
5	Yes	Yes	9
6	Yes	Yes	8
Average	*Yes*	*Yes*	*8*

The proposed approach succeeds in producing an average value of 8, which implies from the subjective evaluation point of view that the proposed approach succeeds in producing an efficient enhancement on the input noisy HE stain image.

where p is the histogram count.

The PSNR of an image is given by

$$\text{PSNR} = 10 \log_{10} \left(\frac{MAXi^2}{MSE} \right) \quad (9.9)$$

Here MAX_i for the image is the maximum pixel value possible and MSE is the mean squared error. Eq. (9.10) is used to calculate its value:

$$\text{MSE} = \sum_{y=1}^{M} \sum_{x=1}^{N} [I(x, y) - I'(x, y)]^2 \quad (9.10)$$

where M, N represents the dimensions of $I(x,y)$, the original image, $I'(x,y)$ is the improved one.

A higher value of PSNR is expected for a better quality of enhancement as it implies a better suppression of noise.

From Tables 9.1 and Table 9.2, and Fig. 9.10, we have seen that for the proposed approach, the entropy and PSNR values with respect to each image and also for overall average are comparatively higher than the same of other methods. This also proves the supremacy of the proposed technique in color medical image contrast improvement.

Table 9.2 Objective evaluation.

Image no.	Objective evaluation	Histogram equalization	CLAHE	Bora [15]	Proposed approach
Image 1	Entropy	4.2681	4.3412	4.7775	4.7819
	PSNR	20.0411	20.0432	20.0432	20.0442
Image 2	Entropy	5.2651	5.4397	4.7816	6.9670
	PSNR	19.8144	23.4183	23.4191	23.4619
Image 3	Entropy	5.2655	5.4228	5.4328	5.4819
	PSNR	19.8164	23.4117	23.4431	24.0108
Image 4	Entropy	4.3227	4.4841	4.4844	5.1017
	PSNR	18.0351	18.2103	18.2215	19.7295
Average	Entropy	4.78035	4.92195	4.869075	*5.583125*
	PSNR	19.42675	21.270875	21.281725	*21.8116*

Table 9.3 Time-based evaluations.

Techniques	Average time taken (in seconds)
Histogram equalization	0.982814
CLAHE	1.837591
Bora [15]	5.182051
Proposed technique	7.894219

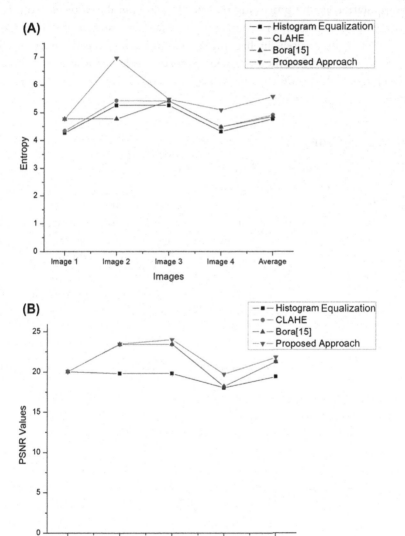

Figure 9.10 (A) Comparison of entropy values; (B) comparison of PSNR values.

8. Time comparison

Table 9.3 shows the average time taken by the respective algorithms. The time is the average execution time taken by the methods for all the images.

The time consumed by the proposed approach is higher than the other methods in comparison (from Table 9.3 and Fig. 9.11). The reason behind this is very obvious as the proposed technique involves a very high level of computation in the processing of type-2 fuzzy membership function. But, in medical image analysis, accurate result is what we seek, so it may result in the cost of moderately high complexity. And as per the accuracy is concerned, the results of the proposed approach are better in quality than the other methods in comparison, which will automatically guarantee an accurate medical diagnosis.

9. Conclusion

Currently, computer-based medical image analysis plays a very important role in the critical disease diagnosis process. Image processing algorithms are used for the same. Generally these medical images are carrying a high level of fuzziness around the region of interests, which creates difficulty for the hard image processing algorithms to process them, thus hampering the accuracy of the diagnosis process. Hence the fuzziness of the images should be removed or reduced to a satisfactory level first during the preprocessing process. Also, medical images usually seem to be suffering from noise that arises during the acquisition process. So, noise removal should also be done

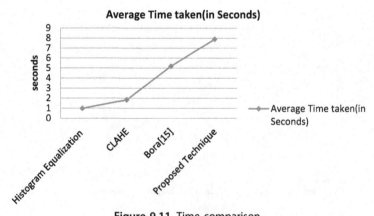

Figure 9.11 Time comparison.

before the enhancement process; otherwise noisy pixels may also be amplified with other pixels. Currently we have different medical imaging technologies that make medical images also available in color, like HE stain images for example. We need a preprocessing technique that would be applicable to color medical images also; then that technique will easily adoptable for gray or black-and-white medical images. When color is concerned, color spaces play a very important role in color-based computations. So, considering all of these facts and problems, an advanced fuzzy logic-based technique is carefully designed for contrast improvement of medical images. The proposed approach is a suitable combination of an improved median filter, a type-2 fuzzy set-based technique and ameliorated CLAHE. Together these techniques successfully deal with the problem of noise removal, reducing the fuzziness level, and overall contrast improvement.

In the near future, the proposed approach will be integrated with an FCM-based segmentation technique for better accuracy and the focus will be on HE stain segmentation since the HE stain images prove to be the gold standard in the medical diagnosis process because of its distinct cell and nuclei analysis.

References

[1] Z. Shi, Y. Li, C. Zhang, M. Zhao, Y. Feng, B. Jiang, Weighted median guided filtering method for single image rain removal, EURASIP Journal on Image and Video Processing 2018 (1) (2018) 35.

[2] Q. Zhang, L. Xu, J. Jia, in: Proceedings of the IEEE Conference on Computer Vision and Pattern Recognition: June 24-27, 2014; Ohio, USA. 100+ Times Faster Weighted Median Filter (WMF), IEEEUSA, 2014, pp. 2830−2837.

[3] P. Kumar, M. Chandra, S. Kumar, Trimmed median filter for removal of noise from medical image, in: Proceeding of the Second International Conference on Microelectronics, Computing & Communication Systems (MCCS 2017), Springer, Singapore, 2019, pp. 201−209.

[4] P.R. Chanu, K.M. Singh, Impulse noise removal from medical images by two stage quaternion vector median filter, Journal of Medical Systems 42 (10) (2018) 197.

[5] A.P. James, A.P. Kavitha, Mean-variance blind noise estimation for CT images, in: Advances in Signal Processing and Intelligent Recognition Systems, Springer, Cham, 2014, pp. 235−243.

[6] D. Bharathi, S.M. Govindan, A new hybrid approach for denoising medical images, in: Advances in Computing and Information Technology, Springer, Berlin, Heidelberg, 2013, pp. 905−914.

[7] R. Vijayarajan, S. Muttan, Iterative relaxed median filter for impulse noise removal and validation of FCM clustering using cluster error index in median filtered MR images, in: International Conference on Computing and Communication Systems, Springer, Berlin, Heidelberg, 2011, December, pp. 792–801.

[8] M.S. Nair, J. Reji, An efficient directional weighted median switching filter for impulse noise removal in medical images, in: International Conference on Advances in Computing and Communications, Springer, Berlin, Heidelberg, 2011, July, pp. 276–288.

[9] T. Chaira, Enhancement of medical images in an Atanassov's't intuitionistic fuzzy domain using an alternative intuitionistic fuzzy generator with application to image segmentation, Journal of Intelligent and Fuzzy Systems 27 (3) (2014) 1347–1359.

[10] T. Chaira, February. Contrast enhancement of medical images using type II fuzzy set, in: 2013 National Conference on Communications (NCC), IEEE, 2013, pp. 1–5.

[11] D. Sheet, H. Garud, A. Suveer, M. Mahadevappa, J. Chatterjee, Brightness preserving dynamic fuzzy histogram equalization, IEEE Transactions on Consumer Electronics 56 (4) (2010) 2475–2480.

[12] F. Zhou, Z. Jia, J. Yang, N. Kasabov, Method of improved fuzzy contrast combined adaptive threshold in NSCT for medical image enhancement, BioMed Research International 2017 (2017) 1–10.

[13] B. Subramani, M. Veluchamy, MRI brain image enhancement using brightness preserving adaptive fuzzy histogram equalization, International Journal of Imaging Systems and Technology 28 (3) (2018) 217–222.

[14] D.J. Bora, An ideal approach for medical color image enhancement, in: Advanced Computational and Communication Paradigms, Springer, Singapore, 2018, pp. 351–361.

[15] D.J. Bora, An efficient innovative approach towards color image enhancement, International Journal of Information Retrieval Research 8 (1) (2018) 20–37.

[16] Open Medscience, Medical imaging modalities - medical radiation | open medscience [online] Available at: https://openmedscience.com/medical-imaging/, 2019. Accessed 2 Jun. 2019.

[17] Enwikipediaorg, H\u0026E Stain, 2019 [online] Available at: https://en.wikipedia.org/wiki/H%26E_stain. Accessed 4 Jun. 2019.

[18] D.J. Bora, HE stain image segmentation using an innovative type-2 fuzzy set-based approach, in: Histopathological Image Analysis in Medical Decision Making, IGI Global, 2019, pp. 276–299.

[19] A.K. Boyat, B.K. Joshi, A Review Paper: Noise Models in Digital Image Processing, 2015 arXiv preprint arXiv:1505.03489.

[20] B. Goyal, A. Dogra, S. Agrawal, B.S. Sohi, Noise issues prevailing in various types of medical images, Biomedical and Pharmacology Journal 11 (3) (2018).

[21] S. Gai, B. Zhang, C. Yang, L. Yu, Speckle noise reduction in medical ultrasound image using monogenic wavelet and Laplace mixture distribution, Digital Signal Processing 72 (January 1, 2018) 192–207.

[22] D.J. Bora, Importance of Image Enhancement Techniques in Color Image Segmentation: A Comprehensive and Comparative Study, August 9, 2017 arXiv preprint arXiv:1708.05081.

[23] L. Zadeh, Fuzzy sets, Information and Control 8 (3) (1965) 338–353.

[24] D.J. Bora, Performance comparison of K-means algorithm and FCM algorithm with respect to color image segmentation, International Journal of Emerging Technology and Advanced Engineering 7 (8) (August 2017) 460–470.

[25] L.A. Zadeh, The concept of a linguistic variable and its application to approximate reasoningâ€"I, Information Sciences 8 (3) (1975) 199–249.

[26] J. Mendel, R. John, Type-2 fuzzy sets made simple, IEEE Transactions on Fuzzy Systems 10 (2002) 117–127, https://doi.org/10.1109/91.995115.

[27] L. Shamir, N. Orlov, D.M. Eckley, T.J. Macura, I.G. Goldberg, IICBU 2008: a proposed benchmark suite for biological image analysis, Medical and Biological Engineering and Computing 46 (9) (2008) 943–947.

[28] HE stain, https://en.wikipedia.org/wiki/H\%26E_stain.

CHAPTER 10

Bone age assessment using metric learning on small dataset of hand radiographs

Shipra Madan, Tapan Kumar Gandhi, Santanu Chaudhury
Department of Electrical Engineering, Indian Institute of Technology, Delhi, New Delhi, India

Contents

1. Introduction

Skeletal growth progresses with change in shape and size of the bones of the skeleton with age. Discordance in the bone age and chronological age further directs diagnostic evaluation of growth-related, endocrine, or metabolic disorders. Although bone age assessment remains the routine radiological procedure performed in pediatrics, the paradigm has not changed significantly since the work from Greulich and Pyle [1] or Tanner-Whitehouse [2] in which an atlas of radiographs of representative ages is used to compare the child's radiograph to determine the bone age, whereas the Tanner-Whitehouse method uses a scoring system by examining 20 specific bones to calculate bone age. Both techniques require a considerable

Advanced Machine Vision Paradigms for Medical Image Analysis
ISBN 978-0-12-819295-5
https://doi.org/10.1016/B978-0-12-819295-5.00010-X

259

amount of time and a significant amount of radiologist expertise, which further leads to intra- and interobserver variability resulting in contradictory line of action when bone age and chronological age discrepancies are encountered. This kind of diagnosis is highly subjective and qualitative due to sole human observation basis

Therefore, there's a compelling need to develop a computer-aided model for bone age prediction in order to quickly bring the cases of bone age discrepancies for the correct line of treatment. Deep learning approaches have attracted a lot of attention in the medical domain lately. However, these techniques rely heavily on a large amount of data to perform effectively, which is usually not the case in the medical image analysis domain. Our framework uses ideas from metric learning and learns new concepts from little data.

In this work, the sections are organized as follows. The importance and motivation behind this work is detailed in Section 2. Section 3 introduces the related fundamental work carried out in the past to deal with the problem of bone age assessment. The proposed methodology based on metric learning paradigm along with dataset and architecture is presented in Section 4. The hyperparameters used during training of the proposed model and its resultant visualization embeddings are presented in Section 5. Sections 6 and 7 cover the discussion and conclusion of the chapter.

2. Motivation

There is heterogenous group of disorders characterized by defective bones called skeletal dysplasias or osteochondrodysplasias. These disorders are very rare in individuals, but the collective incidence is high, suggesting that they constitute an important health problem.

Bone age classification can provide a very comprehensive assessment of biological and structural maturity of immature patients from their hand radiographs. Critical clues in the pattern of abnormalities present in the bones, particularly of the hand, can help in early detection of growth and endocrine disorders of children at risk.

These disorders are generally present in childhood and come to light due to disproportionate short stature. As radiographs available for children are very few, there is a need to build an automated approach that can work on small datasets. All existing methodologies for bone age assessment leverage deep learning networks on large datasets, whereas our proposed framework uses metric learning that trains on less data and yields ceiling level performance in classification accuracy.

3. Related work

Deep learning has been widely used in various medical decisions because of its superiority in learning from the embedded features present in the data for better classification. Convolutional neural networks have demonstrated significant performance improvement in biomedicine, for example, in diabetic retinopathy [3] and lung diseases using lung CT scans [4], compared to other machine-learning models.

Recently several deep learning architectures were proposed for bone age assessment. Chen et al. [5] used VGGNet as the baseline model and augmented the images with random flips, rotations, and cropping. Further they used GoogleNet for its fewer parameters and augmented the loss function with L2 loss.

Hyunkwang et al. [6] proposed a fully automated deep model to segment the hand bones and then standardized the input by normalizing and resizing as a preprocessing step. Pretrained models like VGG16 and GoogleNet were used for classification. Spaminato et al. [7] also used pretrained models like OverFeat, GoogleNet, and OxfordNet and their custom model BoNet that get trained from scratch.

Vladmir et al. [8] first preprocessed the radiographs by segmenting the hand radiographs, followed by contrast normalization and key points detection to register the images. Finally, they have adopted VGG style convolutional neural network (CNN) as regression and classification models. All these techniques mentioned have used standard deep learning models either by using pretrained networks or training from scratch on large datasets, and these approaches also use an additional preprocessing step of segmentation of hand images.

Few-shot learning methodologies [9,10] have been successfully used in varied image classification problems on natural images. Some of the key contributions leveraging few-shot-learning methodology are semantic segmentation [11], object detection [12], image segmentation [13], and image translation [14].

However, few-shot learning has not received much attention from the research fraternity in the domain of medical image analysis. Nevertheless, the key idea had been there from the early 2000. Fei-Fei et al. [15] developed a variational Bayesian model where previously learned classes were used to predict new unseen classes. Puch et al. [16] proposed a triplet-loss-based Siamese network for brain imaging modality recognition.

A hierarchical hidden Markov model using a Bayesian inference procedure to recognize new words by unknown speakers has been illustrated by Lake et al. [17]. Wu and Denis have addressed one-shot learning in the context of path planning algorithms for robotic actuation. Wei-Hung et al. [18] proposed deep Siamese convolutional neural networks for content-based medical image retrieval using a diabetic retinopathy fundus image dataset to help clinicians make decisions by retrieving similar cases and images from electronic medical image databases.

Mijung et al. [19] used the concept of one-shot learning for early diagnosis of glaucoma using high-resolution fundus images.

In this work, we have proposed an end-to-end framework for bone-age assessment in a classification setup without any kind of region of interest extraction and with limited training samples as input data.

4. Methodology

4.1 Data

For our study, we have used the dataset released by the Radiological Society of North America, consisting of 12,611 radiographs. Example images representing the dataset are shown in Fig. 10.1.

The dataset came with a csv file consisting of gender information and age in months for all the subjects of the dataset except the test set. It has been mentioned in the literature that gender and other racial features influence skeletal development, however we have not used this information in our approach, thereby keeping the focus intact on metric learning. We have used data from four classes—5, 8, 11, and 14 years—with 150 images per class for our experimental study. In various experiments, 50%–70% of the images from the dataset form the training part, and the rest forms the

1 years 2 years 3 years 4 years 5 years 6 years 7 years 8 years 9 years

10 years 11 years 12 years 13 years 14 years 15 years 16 years 17 years 18 years

Figure 10.1 Sample input images.

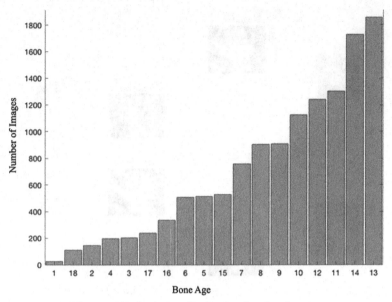

Figure 10.2 Bone-age distribution for the dataset.

validation set. Example images representing the dataset distribution are shown in Fig. 10.2.

4.2 Architecture

Metric learning works on the principle to capture the similarity among samples while using an optimal distance metric like Euclidean distance for learning tasks. As far as the research conducted in this area of metric learning is concerned, Siamese networks [20] and triplet networks [21] have been studied.

To apply the triplet loss, a pair of images are compared. The encodings should be similar for the pair belonging to the same bone age class whereas the encodings are quite different when the pair of images is from different bone age classes.

In triplet loss, one image referred to as an the anchor is chosen, and then the distance between the anchor and the positive image(i.e., the image from the same bone age class) is calculated. The underlying objective of learning is to reduce this distance to minimum. With the anchor, when paired with the negative example (i.e., the image from different bone age class), the distances are much further apart. This gives the name triplet loss as three images (anchor, positive, and negative image) are compared in terms

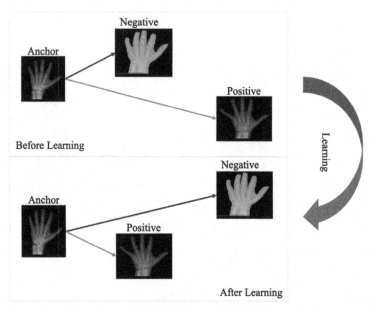

Figure 10.3 Before (top) and after (bottom) minimizing triplet loss function.

of some distance all the time. Fig. 10.3 shows the triplet loss and the role of margin diagrammatically.

Triplet net is a type of algorithm devised to learn embedding $f(x)$ from an image x onto a feature space R^d. Hence, the squared distance between the images of the same class is small compared to the squared distance between a pair of images belonging to different classes.

To measure the similarity between sample pictures, input images need to be transformed into a smaller representation, say a single vector. This representation is usually called an embedding and the embeddings exhibit the property that the two similar images produce embeddings such that the mathematical distance between them is small. Similarly, two very different images produce embeddings with large mathematical distance between them. The embedding is further L2 normalized, so that each embedding is forced to stay on the d-dimensional hyperspace.

$$\| f(x) \|_2 = 1 \tag{10.1}$$

Samples generated, called triplets (x, x^+, x^-), to be fed to the triplet net are referred to as anchor, positive, and negative. The anchor and the positive belong to the same class, while the negative sample belongs to a different class. For the selected set of input triplet images (x, x^+, x^-),

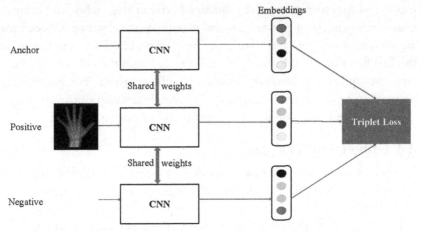

Figure 10.4 Image classification pipeline using triplet network.

similarity function is given as $s(x, x')$, which satisfies $s(x, x^+) > s(x, x^-)$, and the distance function learned satisfies the condition $d(x, s(x, x^+) < d(x, s(x, x^-)$.

For our experiments, which is a case of multiclass image classification, the distance function is defined as:

$$d(x, x') = ||f(x) - f(x')||_1 \qquad (10.2)$$

where $f(x)$ is implemented with a convolutional neural network. The embedding size used for our experimental setting is 128. Although trying 256 might increase the performance, considering memory constraint, 128 is the ideal choice for our case.

Triplet selection is a crucial step for effective learning of the similarity network, where the network should clearly learn to differentiate between samples of different categories. A good mix of easy, hard, and semi-hard triplets is generally used for optimized learning of the network. Fig. 10.4 shows the network mechanism with triplet loss on anchor, positive, and negative sample from one of the chosen triplets.

4.3 Loss function

Loss function used in triplet networks is called triplet loss and is defined as:

$$L = \max(d(x, x^+) - d(x, x^-) + m, 0) \qquad (10.3)$$

where m is the margin that pushes the negative samples away from the anchor and brings positive samples closer to the anchor. In other words, triplet loss tries to minimize the distance between the anchor and positive image belonging to the same class and maximizes the distance between the anchor and a negative image of a different class [22]. Therefore, by using this loss function we calculate the gradients and with the help of the gradients, we update the weights and biases of the network. For training the network, we take an anchor image and randomly sample positive and negative images and compute its loss function and update its gradients.

4.4 Embedding function

In order to compare similarity between two images, the first step is to transform the input picture into a smaller representation, say a single vector. This representation of the image in a single vector is usually called an embedding. For high performing network, these embeddings should have the following properties:

- Two similar images, anchor and positive, create embedding, so that distance between them is small
- Two different images, anchor and negative, create embedding, so that distance between them is large
- These embeddings are L2-normalized.

To achieve these properties, we train a specialized neural network with the input images that produces embeddings with these properties. Fig. 10.5 shows the neural network used in this study.

Embedding dimensionality is the key factor to ensure high accuracy and performance of the network. In the FaceNET paper [21], the authors chose 128 dimensional float vectors to represent face characteristics. Increasing the dimensionality improved performance slightly but not much, and hence

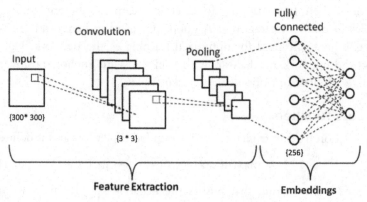

Figure 10.5 Embedding CNN architecture.

they have considered the size 128 to ensure good computational trade-off in performance.

For this experiment, the embedding function used is a stack of three convolutional layers with 3*3 filter size and max pooling layers to reduce the input size. Finally, a flattened 256-dimensional feature vector is generated, keeping the memory constraints in view, with a dropout of 0.5 and with L2 regularization. As mentioned, we have used 128 as the embedding dimension for this present scenario.

5. Results

5.1 Training details and hyperparameters

The hyperparameters used for our experimental setting based on available memory resources and constraints for optimized network performance are listed below:

- Embedding size: 128
- Batch size: 32 triplets comprising of 16 hard and 16 random samples from 100 triplets
- Optimizer: ADAM
- Learning rate: 1e3
- Margin: 0.2

We trained the model for 80,000 epochs on GPU node with NVIDIA V100 graphic card and used the trained model to see the class separation learned by the model by plotting the class sample embedding before and after training scenarios. Higher resource specification can enable bigger batch size of triplets to be loaded and that might give better performance.

5.2 Visualizing embeddings

Performance evaluation is an indispensable parameter before any machine learning model is deployed. However, it is more important to know the learning ability of the model in addition to the performance aspect. This is necessary so as to ensure that the model has not learned something really unimportant and irrelevant. The most sophisticated and logical way of approaching this problem is from a data visualization perspective.

By visualizing how the model clusters the data, we can get an idea of what the model has actually learned to classify similar and dissimilar data points. This is crucial in order to understand why a model makes certain predictions. An embedding is essentially a low-dimensional space onto which a high-dimensional vector can be mapped. During translation, an

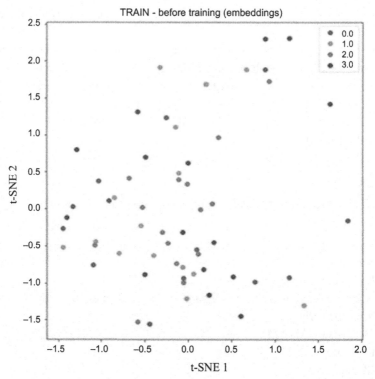

Figure 10.6 Visualizing X-ray images from different classes using t-SNE (before training).

embedding preserves the semantic relationship of the inputs by placing similar inputs close together and thereby pushing the dissimilar data points further in the embedding space. Visualizing data in one or two dimensions is easy, but it's not clear how to visualize embeddings that are 8-dimensional or 32-dimensional in nature. t-SNE is a dimensionality reduction algorithm often used for visualization. It learns a mapping from a set of high-dimensional vectors, to a space with a smaller number of dimensions (usually 2), which is hopefully a good representation of the high-dimensional space. Fig. 10.6 shows the embeddings generated by our model before learning and Fig. 10.7 shows the embeddings generated by our model once the model is learned.

6. Discussion

With emergence and widespread use of multimodality imaging in clinical setups, image recognition and analysis have become vital to understand

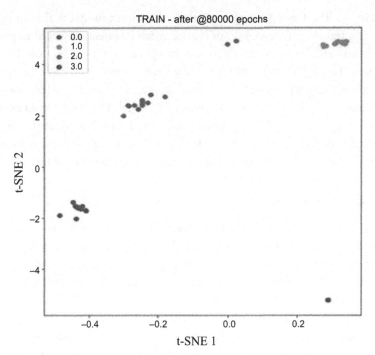

Figure 10.7 Visualizing X-ray images from different classes using t-SNE (after training).

complex diseases in a better way. Important biomarkers captured from rare diseases are an aid in understanding the disease, however the availability of these images is scarce. This scenario of limited medical data makes techniques like metric learning much more important and are capable of giving more accurate performance compared to conventional CNN models.

In this study we presented evidence that triplet networks are a valid solution for image classification in few-shot learning cases. The proposed framework used 10 times less data (i.e., 1200 images only as compared to the data size of 12,000 images used by regular CNNs) to perform optimally in a regression setting.

Moreover, all the studies carried out in the past [6—8], looked at bone age assessment as a regression problem, thereby reporting the predicted bone age deviation in months. We have targeted it as a classification problem, however, and succeeded in separating the classes to a large extent as shown in the embeddings. The mean absolute error reported in all the cases in regression setting is in the range of 5—8 months, thereby introducing an intrinsic error in bone age estimation.

One of the key advantages of using the triplet model is that once the model is trained for a given set of classes, it can be effectively used to predict other unseen classes of different age categories unlike the typical CNN models. This process of retraining is a very resource-intensive and time-consuming activity. In all CNN models, every new class added requires thousands of new images for retraining the model. However, in a real-time scenario it is not realistic to acquire such a high number of labeled images from the medical centers. Hence few-shot learning models that work on smaller data sets have better potential for research on similar problems.

7. Conclusion

In this chapter we have presented a model for performing multiclass classification to predict bone age by learning latent representation of images using an end-to-end structure, thereby using a triplet of images. Our approach demonstrated the effectiveness of metric learning with customized embedding function and efficient mining of triplets on small-sized dataset by yielding promising results. Our results clearly indicated that this approach's performance is comparable to the state-of-the-art single CNN architectures, which practically require enormous data, which in turn requires expert intervention in terms of time and effort that is usually not the case in the medical domain. Future investigation will focus on segmenting out the region of interest so that the machine won't learn undesired features from the input images. In addition, standardizing the input images in terms of contrast, experimenting with different embedding architectures, and evaluating our model on different types of disease dataset will be our future course of actions. In order to better understand the feature embeddings generated from the images, visualization-based networks can be explored as opposed to conventional black-box type of neural nets. It would be an added bonus to see if the features learned by our model match up to the regions seen by radiologists while performing bone age assessment manually.

References

[1] W.W. Greulich, S.I. Pyle, Radiographic Atlas of Skeletal Development of the Hand and Wrist, Stanford University Press, 1959.
[2] R.M. Malina, G.P. Beunen, Assessment of skeletal maturity and Prediction of adult height (TW3 method), American Journal of Human Biology 14 (2002) 788–789.
[3] S. Dutta, B.C. S Manideep, M. Basha, et al., Classification of diabetic retinopathy images by using deep learning models, International Journal of Grid and Distributed Computing 11 (1) (2018) 89–106.

[4] M. Anthimopoulos, S. Christodoulidis, L. Ebner, et al., Lung pattern classification for interstitial lung diseases using a deep convolutional neural network, IEEE Transactions on Medical Imaging 35 (5) (2016) 1207−1216.

[5] M. Chen, Automated Bone Age Classification with Deep Neural Networks, 2016.

[6] L. Hyunkwang, T. Shahein, S. Giordano, et al., Fully automated deep learning system for bone age assessment, Journal of Digital Imaging 30 (2017) 427−441.

[7] C. Spampinato, S. Palazzo, D. Giordano, et al., Deep learning for automated skeletal bone age assessment in X-Ray images, Medical Image Analysis 36 (2017) 41−51.

[8] V. Iglovikov, A. Rakhlin, A. Kalinin, A. Shvets, Pediatric Bone Age Assessment Using Deep Convolutional Neural Networks, 2018 arXiv:1712.05053.

[9] O. Vinyals, C. Blundell, T. Lillicrap, D. Wierstra, et al., Matching networks for one shot learning, in: Neural Information Processing Systems, NIPS), 2016.

[10] J. Snell, K. Swersky, R. Zemel, Prototypical networks for few-shot learning, in: NIPS, 2017, pp. 4077−4087.

[11] C. Zhang, G. Lin, F. Liu, R. Yao, C. Shen, Canet: class-agnostic segmentation networks with iterative refinement and attentive few-shot learning, in: CVPR, 2019.

[12] Y. Wang, Q. Yao, Few-shot Learning: A Survey, 2019 arXiv:1904.05046.

[13] N. Dong, E. Xing, Few-shot semantic segmentation with prototype learning, BMVC 3 (2018), p. 4.

[14] M.Y. Liu, X. Huang, A. Mallya, T. Karras, T. Aila, J. Lehtinen, J. Kautz, Few-shot unsupervised image-to-image translation, in: ICCV, 2019.

[15] L. Fei Fei, R. Fergus, P. Perona, A bayesian approach to unsupervised one-shot learning of object categories, IEEE Ninth International Conference on Computer Vision 2 (2003) 1134−1141.

[16] S. Puch, I. Sanchez, M. Rowe, Few-shot learning with deep triplet networks for brain imaging modality recognition, in: Domain Adaptation and Representation Transfer and Medical Image Learning with Less Labels and Imperfect Data, Springer, 2019.

[17] B.M. Lake, C.Y. Lee, J. R Glass, J.B. Tenenbaum, One Shot Learning of Generative Speech Concepts, Cognitive Science Society, 2014.

[18] Y.A. Chung, W.H. Weng, Learning Deep Representations of Medical Images Using Siamese CNNs with Application to Content Based Image Retrieval, 2017 arXiv:1711.08490vol. 2.

[19] M. Kim, J. Zuallaert, W.D. Neve, Few-shot learning using a small-sized dataset of high-resolution FUNDUS images for glaucoma diagnosis, in: Proceedings of the 2nd International Workshop on Multimedia for Personal Health and Health Care, 2017, pp. 89−92.

[20] G. Koch, R. Zemel, R. Salakhutdinov, Siamese neural networks for one-shot image recognition, in: ICML Deep Learning Workshop, 2015.

[21] F. Schroff, D. Kalenichenko, J. Philbin, FaceNet: A Unified Embedding for Face Recognition and Clustering, 2015, pp. 815−823, arXiv:1503.03832vol. 3.

[22] S. Liu, Y. Song, M. Zhang, et al., An Identity authentication method combining liveness detection and face recognition, Sensors 19 (21) (2019) 4733.

CHAPTER 11

Conclusion and future research directions

Sandip Dey[1], Debanjan Konar[2], Sourav De[3], Siddhartha Bhattacharyya[4]

[1]Sukanta Mahavidyalaya, Department of Computer Science, Dhupguri, Jalpaiguri, West Bengal, India; [2]Sikkim Manipal Institute of Technology, Department of Computer Science and Engineering, Sikkim Manipal University, Majitar, Sikkim, India; [3]Cooch Behar Government Engineering College, Department of Computer Science and Engineering, Cooch Behar, West Bengal, India; [4]Christ University, Department of Computer Science and Engineering, Bangalore, Karnataka, India

Contents

1. Concluding remarks

The field of medical imaging and processing has made giant strides in recent years thanks to ever-evolving intelligent tools and techniques to assist in yielding robust and fail-safe solutions to the challenges involved [1–4]. Medical imaging modalities such as positron emission tomography, magnetic resonance imaging (MRI), computed tomography (CT), and ultrasound, apart from revealing features of internal organs, also call for fruitful early detection of diseases and their diagnosis. Therefore, the proper analysis of medical image data is an essential requirement in many medical diagnosis experiments. The most difficult proposition in these analysis techniques stems from the enormity and variety of data under consideration. In addition, the medical image data are not always properly discernible, which leads to an additional challenging dimension. The contributory chapters in this book aim to report some of findings and solutions to the challenges and issues encountered in medical image analysis. The chapters try to augment the knowledge base in terms of envisaging several different novel computationally intelligent methods for addressing the challenges.

Advanced Machine Vision Paradigms for Medical Image Analysis
ISBN 978-0-12-819295-5
https://doi.org/10.1016/B978-0-12-819295-5.00011-1

Computational intelligence has been at the helm of affairs as far as rendering effective and fail-safe solutions to most engineering and technological problems. Computer-aided diagnosis (CAD) has been empowered with intelligent tools for the successful diagnosis of various life risk diseases [5]. Early diagnosis of prenatal coronary heart disease (CHD) is a fundamental requirement to achieve a significant reduction in infant mortality rates. The scarcity of adequate literature on this indicates that a computerized solution for prenatal CHD screening is a major research topic in the computer vision community. A CAD system to characterize asymmetric appearance—oriented prenatal CHD fully from fetal heart images is thus an immediate requirement. Such a system will be capable of providing an appropriate diagnostic decision about prenatal CHD in advance. This system may also find use in providing diagnostic decision support through distributed computing in different places of a medical facility. Different types of CHDs may also be integrated into a single CAD system.

Morphological extreme learning machines [6] use neural networks with hidden layers of random weights, with nodes based on nonlinear morphological operators of dilation and erosion. Morphological extreme learning machines are competitive neural network architectures in relation to usual kernel approaches and activation functions. Such machines may be used to support medical imaging diagnosis by detecting and classifying breast lesions in mammogram images. Obvious advantages offered by these machines include lower time complexity and easy implementation. Four-dimensional (4D) medical imaging analysis [7,8] is a field in its infancy that needs to be explored more. 4D medical imaging is manifested in different imaging modalities such as 4D CT, 4D ultrasound scan, and 4D flow MRI, to name a few. 4D CT is highly suitable for radiation oncology, which is affected by motion artifacts. Similarly, 4D ultrasound is helpful in fetal studies. 4D flow MRI is useful in accurately treating cardiac problems. However, the need for huge storage space limits the use of 4D modalities. Moreover, the analysis of such huge data also calls for time-intensive algorithms.

Medical image fusion [9] is an active procedure that is useful for the diagnosis and medical assessment of disease stages, and treatment evaluations in neurocysticercosis, neoplastic disease, and Alzheimer's and astrocytoma diseases. Fusion algorithms assist radiologists in accurate representation, better perception, and an accurate description of lesions and disease acquired in the brains of patients with neurocysticercosis, neoplastic,

Alzheimer's, and astrocytoma disease. Multimodal medical image fusion combines all relevant and unique data from multiple input images into a single composite image that facilitates more accurate diagnosis and better outcomes. Hybrid fusion algorithms may be useful when it comes to analyzing these multimodal medical image data.

Given the high dimensional feature space associated with different binary descriptors [10,11] often used in medical image analysis, optimal feature characterization is a major challenges faced by medical diagnosticians. Metaheuristic algorithms are therefore used to address this problem owing to their efficiency in exploring and exploiting the high-dimensional search space of binary descriptors.

Although complications in medical imaging systems are reduced with the use of content-based image retrieval techniques [12], the disease cannot be analyzed to its level of depth. If a particular case is to be studied in depth, semantic image segmentation helps to predict the disease level to its end. Properly segmented images produce a background analysis for physicians to take the next step more clearly instead of rationalizing the samples. It is a common saying that prevention is better than cure. Hence, early detection of any disease is always a much-sought affair when it comes to medical image analysis and understanding, and Parkinson's disease is no exception in this regard. Early detection of Parkinson's disease [13,14] is vital in terms of administering treatment and supporting patients for immediate treatment planning. Application of machine learning techniques on spiral drawing and speech data sets helps develop models to mine the disease patterns. Signs of Parkinson's sickness differ among persons; thus, the use of multimodal data considers both voice and spiral drawings. Faithful processing of multimodal clinical data is the foremost requirement to improve the accuracy of clinical decision support systems. This also helps to characterize disease patterns accurately, which improves the reliability and robustness of prediction models.

Of late, computer-based medical image analysis has had an important role in the critical disease diagnosis process. Image processing algorithms are used for this. Generally, these medical images have a high level of fuzziness around the regions of interest, which creates difficulty for hard image processing algorithms to process them. This hampers the accuracy of the diagnosis process. Hence, the fuzziness of the images should first be removed or reduced to a satisfactory level during preprocessing process [15,16]. Also, medical images usually seem to suffer from noise that arises during the acquisition process. Therefore, noise removal should be done before enhancement; otherwise, noisy pixels may become amplified with other image pixels. In addition, different medical imaging technologies such as hematoxylin—eosin stain images make medical images available in color. Hence, a preprocessing technique should work well with both color and gray or black-and-white medical images. Considering all of these issues, an advanced fuzzy logic—based technique should be carefully designed for the contrast improvement of medical images.

2. Future avenues

With the constant efforts of scientists and researchers, advanced machine intelligence algorithms and techniques are envisaged to take care of existing challenges encountered in medical imaging. Hybrid algorithms involving fuzzy and rough sets are being evolved to handle uncertainty prevalent in medical image information. Also, novel and efficient metaheuristic algorithms are being invented to yield optimized results and outcome. With the advent of quantum-inspired metaheuristic algorithms, scientists are confident they can achieve robust and fail-safe solutions to the constant challenges and issues associated with processing medical images.

References

[1] J. Duncan, Medical image analysis: progress over two decades and the challenges ahead, IEFE Transactions on Pattern Analysis and Machine Intelligence 22 (1) (2000) 85—106.
[2] J. Hoffman, S. Kaplan, The incidence of congenital heart disease, Journal of the American College of Cardiology 39 (12) (2002) 1890—1900.
[3] A.A. Goshtasby, 2-D and 3-D Image Registration: For Medical, Remote Sensing, and Industrial Applications, Wiley Press, 2005.
[4] S.C. Shapiro, Encyclopedia of Artificial Intelligence, John Wiley & Sons, New York, NY, United States, 1992.
[5] R. Kapoor, S. Gupta, Prevalence of congenital heart disease, Indian Pediatrics 45 (4) (2008) 309.
[6] G.Z.H.D.X. Huang, R. Zhang, Extreme learning machine for regression and multiclass classification, IEEE Transactions on Systems, Man, and Cybernetics, Part B (Cybernetics) 42 (2) (2012) 513—529.
[7] P.X. Shajan, N.J.R. Muniraj, J.T. Abraham, 3d/4d image registration and fusion techniques: a survey, International Journal of Computer Science and Information Technologies 3 (4) (2012) 4829—4839.
[8] G. Li, D. Citrin, K. Camphausen, B. Mueller, C. Burman, B. Mychalczak, R.W. Miller, Y. Song, Advances in 4d medical imaging and 4d radiation therapy, Technology in Cancer Research and Treatment 7 (1) (2008) 67—81.
[9] A.A. James, B.V. Dasarathy, Medical image fusion: a survey of the state of the art (Elsevier), Information Fusion 19 (2014) 4—19.

[10] I. Cruz-Aceves, S. Ivvan-Valdez, A novel evolutionary morphological descriptor for the segmentation of coronary arteries, in: IEEE Latin American Conference on Computational Intelligence (LA-CCI), IEEE, 2018, 2014.

[11] I.C.S.F. Cruz-Aceves, M. Hernandez-Gonzalez, A new binary descriptor for the automatic detection of coronary arteries in xray angiograms, in: 14th International Symposium on Medical Information Processing and Analysis vol. 10975, SPIE, 2018.

[12] V.K.P.T. Kapur, M.M. Raghuwanshi, Content based image retrieval (CBIR) using soft computing technique, in: 2nd International Conference on Computational Techniques and Artificial Intelligence, 2013.

[13] A. Tsanas, M.A. Little, P.E. Mcsharry, L.O. Ramig, Accurate telemonitoring of Parkinson's disease progression by noninvasive speech tests, IEEE Transactions on Biomedical Engineering 57 (4) (2009) 884−893.

[14] A. Tsanas, M.A. Little, P.E. Mcsharry, L.O. Ramig, Novel speech signal processing algorithms for high-accuracy classification of Parkinson's disease, IEEE Transactions on Biomedical Engineering 59 (5) (2012) 1264−1271.

[15] F. Zhou, J. Zhenhong, J. Yang, N. Kasabov, Method of improved fuzzy contrast combined adaptive threshold in NSCT for medical image enhancement, BioMed Research International 10 (2017) 1−10.

[16] B. Subramani, M. Veluchamy, MRI brain image enhancement using brightness preserving adaptive fuzzy histogram equalization, International Journal of Imaging Systems and Technology (2018) 217−222.

Index

Note: 'Page numbers followed by "*f*" indicate figures and "*t*" indicate tables and "*b*" indicate boxes.'

Printed in the United States
By Bookmasters